AF505823

Wordsworth and the Passions of Critical Poetics

Wordsworth and the Passions of Critical Poetics

Stuart Allen

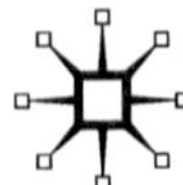

First published 2010 by
PALGRAVE MACMILLAN

Palgrave Macmillan in the UK is an imprint of Macmillan Publishers Limited, registered in England, company number 785998, of Houndmills, Basingstoke, Hampshire RG21 6XS.

Palgrave Macmillan in the US is a division of St Martin's Press LLC, 175 Fifth Avenue, New York, NY 10010.

Palgrave Macmillan is the global academic imprint of the above companies and has companies and representatives throughout the world.

Palgrave® and Macmillan® are registered trademarks in the United States, the United Kingdom, Europe and other countries.

ISBN 978–0–230–24817–5   hardback

This book is printed on paper suitable for recycling and made from fully managed and sustained forest sources. Logging, pulping and manufacturing processes are expected to conform to the environmental regulations of the country of origin.

A catalogue record for this book is available from the British Library.

Library of Congress Cataloging-in-Publication Data

Allen, Stuart James, 1971–
    Wordsworth and the passions of critical poetics / Stuart Allen.
        p. cm.
    ISBN 978–0–230–24817–5 (alk. paper)
    1. Wordsworth, William, 1770–1850—Criticism and interpretation.
        2. Wordsworth, William, 1770–1850—Aesthetics.   3. Emotions
        in literature.   4. Poetry—Psychological aspects.   5. Affect
        (Psychology)   I. Title.
    PR5892.E5A55 2010
    821'.7—dc22

                                                                    2010009403

10   9   8   7   6   5   4   3   2   1
19 18 17 16 15 14 13 12 11 10

Printed and bound in Great Britain by
CPI Antony Rowe, Chippenham and Eastbourne

For Jackie, John and Katy Allen

Contents

Acknowledgements

I thank the Department of English at Bridgewater State College and the staff of the Clement C. Maxwell Library. I am profoundly grateful to Jon Mee for his brilliant and generous supervision of my D.Phil. I would also like to thank the following: Andrew Chapman, John Chesley, Andrew Dixon, Robert Flanagan, Stefanie Gehrig Clark, James Hampshire, Daniel Holmes, John Hooker, Sean Janson, Simon Jarvis, Sara Jansson, Thomas Kiely, Paula Masters, Reuben Pasquini, Marvyn Petrucci, Jon Roberts, Anthony Shuttleworth and Joanne Tong.

At Palgrave Macmillan, Paula Kennedy, Benjamin Doyle, Ann Marangos and the anonymous reader have been wonderful.

Finally, I would like to express my immense gratitude to Eugenia Williamson.

Part of Chapter 4 was published as 'Wordsworth and the Thought of Affection', *European Romantic Review* 16.4 (2005) (co-authored with Jonathan Roberts): 455–70; part of Chapter 4 was published as 'Wordsworth's Ear and the Politics of Aesthetic Autonomy', *Romanticism* 9.1 (2003): 37–54 (Edinburgh University Press, www.euppublishing. com); part of Chapter 6 was published as 'Metropolitan Wordsworth: Allegory as Affirmation and Critique in *The Prelude*', *Romanticism on the Net* 40 (2005): 30 paragraphs, http://www.erudit.org/revue/ron/2005/v/ n40/012461ar.html.

List of Abbreviations

Edmund Burke, *An Appeal from the New to the Old Whigs* (London 1791). — OW

——, *A Philosophical Enquiry into the Origin of our Ideas of the Sublime and Beautiful*, ed. J. T. Boulton (London: Routledge 1958). — PE

——, *The Writings and Speeches of Edmund Burke*, VIII: *The French Revolution*, eds. L. G. Mitchell and William B. Todd (Oxford: Clarendon Press 1989). — R

Anthony Ashley Cooper, Third Earl of Shaftesbury, *Characteristicks of Men, Manners, Opinions, Times*, 2 vols, ed. Philip Ayres (Oxford: Clarendon Press 1999). — C

Alexander Gerard, *An Essay on Taste. To which is now added Part Fourth, Of the Standard of Taste; With Observations Concerning the Imitative Nature of Poetry* (London and Edinburgh: Cadell 1780). — ET

William Wordsworth, *Prose Works of William Wordsworth*, eds W. J. B. Owen and J. W. Smyser, 3 vols (Oxford: Clarendon Press 1974). — PrW

——, *The Letters of William and Dorothy Wordsworth*, ed. Ernest De Selincourt, 2nd edn, vol. 1, *The Early Years 1787–1805*, ed. Revd Chester L. Shaver (Oxford: Clarendon Press 1977–88). — EY

Introduction: Poetry, Feeling and Criticism

In the 1802 Preface's celebrated definition of poetry, Wordsworth places revolutionary emphasis on the relationship between verse and feeling. 'I have said,' he writes, 'that poetry is the spontaneous overflow of powerful feelings: it takes its origin from emotion recollected in tranquillity' (*PrW*, 1. 148). He goes on to insist that no matter how distressing its content, a poem is read with pleasure because rhyme and meter are associated with delight. Rhyme and meter temper

> the painful feeling always found intermingled with powerful descriptions of the deeper passions. This effect is always produced in pathetic and impassioned poetry; while, in lighter compositions, the ease and gracefulness with which the Poet manages his numbers are themselves confessedly a principal source of the gratification of the Reader (*PrW*, 1. 150).

Contained in this short passage are two ideas that were discussed relentlessly by eighteenth-century Whig aestheticians: the centrality of affect to human being, and the need to regulate said affect. Filleting the Preface for its intellectual debts to philosophers who ascribed at least as much importance to the affections as to reason, however, misses the fact that Wordsworth asserts much more than the presence of disciplined feeling in poetry or his art's disciplinary function. He proposes that poetry *is* feeling, that the arrangement of language as verse itself produces pleasure, and that metered pleasure makes it possible for the reader to field a whole slew of emotions otherwise difficult to bear.[1] This book addresses the questions that arise once Wordsworth's claims about poetic feeling are taken seriously. What happens to the theories of affect debated in the prose writings of Whig aestheticians when they enter Wordsworth's lyric and narrative poetry? What difference does it make to say that a poem *is* feeling rather than simply the vehicle of a feeling that 'belongs' to author or reader? What are the political implications of poetry that enables readers to experience a range of feelings perhaps otherwise inaccessible? The short answer is that Wordsworth derives from Whig aesthetics the notion that feeling has a critical, or cognitive, component – that it can make judgements, particularly on social, political and philosophical matters. The more complicated answer is that during the years around his 'Great Decade' (roughly 1797–1807) Wordsworth transforms his poetry into a dialectical and materialist art that, through a 'specialist' sensitivity to quality of feeling, is uniquely positioned to critique public and private life.

In the last decade, a number of book-length studies have called for scholarship that resists emptying art into history, ideology or gender, and that instead engages with the *literary* nature of the object of criticism more fully.[2] In many ways, they grapple with the same distortions – usually arising from the *exchange* of poetry for other discourses – that I identify below in work on Wordsworth. A fertile, yet still under-represented, resource for developing an alternative to prevailing modes of literary explication can be found in the work of Georg Lukács, Theodor Adorno and J.H. Prynne.[3] Theorising literary mimesis as more than the mechanical reflection of a non-poetic content, these writers think aesthetic feeling.[4] What follows, then, draws on these thinkers in order to articulate the transformations of Whig feeling that occur in 'The world is too much with us', a poem itself about exchange. What emerges is a highly political (yet neither simply radical nor Whig) Wordsworthian thought that is entirely inseparable from the complex texture of the poem's affects; or, to put it the other way around, a poetic feeling that is critical in origin and extension.

A critique of modern Man's consumption of the natural world, 'The world is too much with us' has been read as an example of the 'aestheticisation' (a word used pejoratively, of course, to mean 'objectification') of nature. Feeling impoverished by the want of connection with nature, and in order to poetically close the gap between Man and world, Wordsworth re-imagines nature in his own image. For some commentators, the poem unwittingly turns nature into something that can be consumed by the poet. Having 'saved' nature from industry and commerce, Wordsworth renders it raw material for art. Blind to its own 'ideology', Wordsworthian lyric essentially repeats the crime it condemns.[5]

While brilliantly half right, what this reading fails to mention is that as a poem about alienation 'The world is too much with us' contemplates with great intensity a 'new' and unusually modern kind of affect – one largely untouched, and never named, in Whig aesthetics. Indeed, the most striking things about it are Wordsworth's affective originality and the poem's own obstacles to the smooth workings of the process of conversion and consumption it contains. A highly self-conscious meditation on poetic feeling, 'The world is too much with us' is only too aware – and *critically* so – of its affects.

Wordsworth states that 'Getting and spending, we lay waste our powers: / Little we see in nature that is ours / We have given our hearts away, a sordid boon!'[6] These lines acknowledge that domination of nature amounts to the denial and sacrifice of human nature, that 'For this, for everything, we are out of tune' (8). Following this admission, Wordsworth's 'aestheticisation' of nature is not as straightforward, in the poem's own terms, as it initially appears. In order to receive the gift of fullness from nature, he has to construct it all over again as an object. The estrangement he feels at the beginning of the poem, it seems, might very well turn out to be a function of the 'objectification' that he initiates in order to return the 'second nature' of civilisation to something more like first nature. 'The world is too much with us' mimics the repeating cycle of alienation that the contradictory process displayed in the poem causes. Rather than an alchemy of one thing into another, the poem *stages* reason's demented activity. Through mimesis, the poem seeks not just to think alienation in the abstract, but to achieve an experiential understanding of it. The sensual form of the poem becomes its knowledge, and is not false consciousness or an empty exercise.[7]

Wordsworth does not even try to reconcile Man and nature. If he attempted to solve their conflict aesthetically, the poem would be fair game for accusations that lyric betrays the thing it represents. Wishing to experience a specific moment of alienation in order to truly know it, Wordsworth's call for reconciliation also confesses that the cure reason offers is poisoned. This is not a resigned admission that reason is useless or too sick to help. 'The world is too much with us' does not support an irrationalist or nihilist philosophy. Binding reason to mimesis, the poem thinks reason's false consciousness at the same time that it resists the temptation to find harmony in abstraction. Generalisations about alienation would erase the mimetic moment of a cognition, and thus unthinkingly replicate the socially fated antagonism of mind and matter, civilisation and nature, the poem deplores.

If 'The world is too much with us' is a critique of the damage human reason does to itself with instrumental rationality, the poem also insists on the somatic aspect of subjectivity. Line 6 depicts the winds 'howling at all hours', nature in a state of torment:

> This Sea that bares her bosom the Moon;
> The wind that will be howling at all hours,
> And are up-gathered now like sleeping flowers;
> For this, for everything, we are out of tune (5–8).

The mellifluous and regular rhythm enables the poet to feel nature's anxiety without suffering sympathetic devastation. A Whiggish strategy of regulation is present in these lines, not because Wordsworth regards powerful emotions as ungentlemanly or subversive, but because he is trying to dwell with potentially dangerous passions in order to investigate them.[8]

At the heart of the poem, immediately following the 'aestheticisation' of nature at the beginning, a scar appears. The exclamation at line 4 ('A sordid boon!') is echoed in line 9, as the verse responds to its aesthetic-redemptive strategy: 'It moves us not. – Great God! I'd rather be / A Pagan suckled in a creed outworn' (9–10). These lines are not words of compassion for nature or sorrow about Man's alienation from it. Rather, they convey Wordsworth's loss of faith in poetry's ability to engage with the world through mimesis – that is, non-instrumentally. Only a fully Whig Wordsworth would have to regulate the 'enthusiasm' of nature, or his response to it, for fear that emotional transports come without a 'return ticket back to a coherent subjectivity'.[9] In these lines, poetry has failed to properly comprehend nature's unhappiness and has no need to defensively regulate passion. The poet's lack of an 'enthusiasm' of sorrow about his sense of alienation is the fundamental problem. We have given our hearts away and poetry cannot restore us.

Georg Lukács argues that lyric poetry desires to escape the asphyxiation of second nature (man-made civilisation that has come to appear natural) and return to (first) nature through a 'protean mythology of substantial subjectivity' – a subjectivity that, mythically free from the limitations of material existence, resides in 'the purest interiority of the soul'.[10] But the lyric subject, protesting against second nature and straining to lift 'itself above the obscurely-determined multiplicity of things', only *appears* to harmonise with first nature.[11] Although the almost primeval wail of the poet seems to be akin to mute first nature, lyric in fact eschews the natural world. Lukács observes, however, that the lyric subject acknowledges its betrayal of nature through the expression of guilt. The dash at line 9 of 'The world is too much with us' intrudes at the centre of the poem, as if interrupting the speaker's own poetical pseudo-disturbance – and the exclamation mark reminds the reader of the earlier, genuinely exasperated cry.[12] The lyric voice here confesses that its eloquence is artificial and false. Halfway through 'The world is too much with us', then, Wordsworth draws attention to the 'protean' lyric subject's domination of nature by aesthetic means. What was once dull alienation develops now into guilty discomfort about his ersatz concern for the agitation of the sea and winds. Henceforth, the poem attempts to properly mimic alienation – mimic the withering of feeling – and becomes a critical commentary on the 'aestheticisation' of nature that it still strives to perform.

'The world is too much with us' witnesses, at once calm and emotional, to its transformation of nature into poetic fodder, thus honouring as best it can the very thing it sells out. Wordsworth does not transcend second nature. The emphatic and exclamatory language intimates Wordsworth's anxiety about his complicity with second nature, but it is also a sign of poetry's 'failure'. The poem can only defy second nature in the instant it reproduces it. Mimetically intimate with its material, the artwork understands its role in the emergency. Lukács helps us to read mimesis in 'The world is too much with us' with an eye to the affects, such as guilt and melancholy, located in the poetic subject (or poetic subjectivity) with which it flouts the ideology of second nature.

J. H. Prynne combines Lukács' theory of emphatic, lyrical language with something closer to the received wisdom on Wordsworth. He argues that the emphatic language of lyric is a mark of both (Lukácsian) angst and (Wordsworthian) 'jubilation interfused'.[13] This language recognises that there is a rift between first and second nature, and it quotes 'recursively the power of poetic speech itself, calling it in evidence to locate a dialectical convergence of outward and inner sense'.[14] Moments of lyricism register alienation and then mobilise the resources of poetry to broker a reconciliation between Man and nature. Prynne argues, after Lukács, that poetry reveals the traces of Man's first nature that inwardly persist and long to live with, rather than dominate, nature. Wordsworth's awkward cry in 'The world is too much with us' can be seen as both a Lukácsian admission of art's guilty entwinement with the processes of alienation *and* a sign that 'poetic subjectivity' still hopes to think without domination. This is not quite jubilation, perhaps, but Prynne is more eager than Lukács to keep open the possibility of a future modelled on a difference from the present rather than repetition of the past.

Fixing on linguistic register, Lukács and Prynne both note that the expressiveness of lyrical language indicates an affective subjectivity that exists exclusively in a poem, albeit one inevitably also compromised by second nature. What neither of them remarks upon, however, is the element of the ridiculous, or juvenile, that sometimes arises in lyric poetry. Like so much of Wordsworth's writing, 'The world is too much with us' is an emotionally eccentric work. There is something comical about the tonal shift that occurs between the relatively conventional Whig critique of commerce to imagery of 'This Sea that bares her bosom to the moon; / The winds that will be howling at all hours' (5–6), to Wordsworth's wish to 'Have sight of Proteus rising from the sea; / Or hear old Triton blow his wreathèd horn (13–14).[15] Although the poet's 'Great God!' is hardly playful, the poem certainly verges on kitsch, if defined as a ('outworn' poetic) convention of beauty (or, in this case, sublimity) that is mistaken for something 'authentic'. It is impossible, though, to be certain whether the poem truly believes in the classical world it evokes, or whether it deliberately deploys such imagery as kitsch. The poem hangs between the two options, and thereby appeals to a classical (as mediated by Milton and Spenser) mythology it wants to believe in but cannot.[16] As a consequence of this 'indeterminacy', the poem's rejection of commerce also seems close to a dismissal of the idea of poetry as a solution.

It is unnecessary to conclude, however, that 'The world is too much with us' declares poetry at best useless and at worst wicked. Because poetry captures every minute fluctuation of affect and thought – through linguistic mimesis – something resembling true (as opposed to false) consciousness surfaces, even if in the diminished form of consciousness of error. Ultimately, the poetic presence of collaboration, despair and kitsch signify that hope still remains.[17] If this conclusion is in danger of reducing the sonnet to a motto, in the light of the word 'suckled' these last lines might be viewed not as kitsch but as 'infantile'. Alienation activates a regressive wish to live in the infant's storybook world of gods, titans and heroes. Yet, because there is nothing remotely adult about identificatory reason's domination of nature, even this reading can be stood precisely on its head. According to Adorno, as the rational 'refuge of mimetic comportment' opposed to this destructive kind of reason, 'Art brings to light what is infantile in the ideal of being grown up'.[18] Only from within the rule of an irrational domination that masquerades as rational does the poem's dissent look like naivety or childishness.[19] This may be why Wordsworth thinks of the restoration of experience (or, the escape from alienation) in terms of archaic myth, the pre-historic (10). From the alienated, over-rationalised standpoint of the present, nature can *only* be thought of as matter to dominate, a terrifying threat or a dream of mindless bliss. Its meaning thoroughly over-determined by society, nature has been effectively eliminated or 'denatured'.[20] In the end, myth is as close as Wordsworth dares get to nature without running the perceived risk of surrendering what is left of his subjectivity to 'thinglike irrationality'.[21]

'The world is too much with us' attempts to live playfully, perhaps even slightly hysterically, alongside what remains of nature, having previously subsisted in anguish with an administered nature regarded as ruined, dangerous or alien. Wordsworth's visionary and hyperbolic 'aestheticisation' of nature is the poem's feeling thought, its attempt to feel and think the mediation of spirit and matter that instrumental reason forgets or suppresses. The poem attends patiently to both its alienation and its unfulfilled longing for plenitude – indeed, it affirms the interdependence of the two states. To transform alienation into plenitude (or vice versa) would be idealism, when the 'purpose' of the poem is to criticise (ideological) polarities that facilitate the conversion of one thing into another – such polarities including the separation of the mental from the material and Man from nature.[22] With feeling, the poem contests ideology, cognisant that the goal of ideology-critique – the complete abolition of error and establishment of absolute truth – is itself a destructive ideological fantasy.

It is inevitable that I am getting ahead of myself, perhaps, because of lyric's unwillingness to be bound by convention.[23] Poems like 'The world is too much with us' have a long gestation in Wordsworth's authorship and do not appear suddenly out of nowhere. This book as a whole, then, provides an historical ground for Wordsworth's innovations in poetic thought and feeling. It is through close engagement with Whig aesthetics at particular moments of his development that Wordsworth discovers ways to turn pleasurable and painful affects into material, and by poetically bringing spirit and matter into dialectical relation thereby reveal their critical force. The remainder of this introduction appraises the most important recent historical and political readings of Wordsworth.

II

Several studies have detailed the links between Wordsworth, Whig aesthetics and Sensibility. Chris Jones' *Radical Sensibility* cites the Whig philosopher Lord Anthony Ashley Cooper, the Third Earl of Shaftesbury, as a major influence on Wordsworth. Jones argues that the poet exploits both the radical and conservative wings of eighteenth-century thinking about affect. Although the portrayal of feeling in the poetry and fiction of Sensibility often disclosed the conservative assumptions of an individual author, the literature also 'echoed the efforts of philosophers such as Shaftesbury and Hume to describe the workings of the social passions in their efforts to empower natural feeling as the basis of progressive civil society'.[24] Sensibility even provoked conflicting interpretations later on among anti-Jacobins who, for the most part, condemned its 'cult' of high emotion as dangerously destabilising. Edmund Burke famously 'wept' in order to display his humanity and thereby justify his defence of tradition.[25] According to Jones, Wordsworth recognised the variance intrinsic to the discourse of Sensibility, as well as its usefulness for thinking about politics and human experience, and ultimately subscribed to 'a far more extended idea of Sensibility than any other author' of the time.[26]

Jones' work is a fine example of what can be accomplished when literature is taken to be in thoughtful dialogue with the history of ideas to which it belongs rather than a largely passive imprint of period ideologies. Yet despite highlighting the poet's complex relationship to Sensibility, Jones' model only grants Wordsworth the ability to feel and think in ways that Sensibility – in both its radical and conservative manifestations – allows. Wordsworth is, finally, an amalgam of eighteenth-century ideas about affect, and anything unusual or 'original' in the poetry is referred back to the intellectual background for explanation. Jones gives little weight to whether feeling takes the form of poetry, fiction, memoir or philosophy, and is brief on Wordsworth's own thoughts about the changes that occur to the affects valued by Whig philosophy when accommodated by his poetry.[27] I argue, by contrast, that both Wordsworth's theoretical writing on prosody and his poetic practice are highly self-conscious about the implications of any aesthetic reformulation of Whig philosophical themes.

The key study of Wordsworth's Burkeanism remains James Chandler's *Wordsworth's Second Nature*. Chandler's research places Wordsworth squarely in a Whig context, with Burke as his foremost guide.[28] Chandler makes a concerted effort to explore the ways in which the ideas Wordsworth inherits are altered in the poetry, and his analysis of the 'spots of time' goes beyond mere delineation of parallels between Wordsworth and Burke. For Chandler, the 'spots' represent 'the triumph not only of mental discipline, but also of discipline-as-tradition, a discipline grounded on what Burke calls prejudice'.[29] The continuity of self that the 'spots' imply corresponds to Burke's valorisation of tradition and its power to direct (or 'prejudice') interpretation of both the past and present. Chandler's understanding of Wordsworth's poetic adoption of Burke proceeds from this initial point. The real achievement of the 'spots' is that the 'realm of *immediate sensation* drops away, and the poet is left in the presence only of images depicted on his brain and the obscure feelings that represent the emotions that were initially responsible for those images'.[30] Chandler simultaneously loosens Burke's grip on Wordsworth and upholds the bond between the two writers. Reassessing, and effectively demoting, the role of affect – the foundation of Burke's philosophy of sentiment, habit and custom – Chandler filters Wordsworth's Burkeanism through Paul de Man's theory of linguistic indeterminacy. The 'spots of time' become hermeneutic scenarios in which language-feelings in the present derive their meaning from their similarity to language-feelings connected with a past event, which itself is only of significance because of the pressure applied by the present occasion. Past and present are inextricably entwined in the poet's mental representations, with the result that the identity of one instant is at once produced and unravelled by its dependence on another comparable moment.[31] Nevertheless, in his endeavour to accommodate Wordsworth to Burke and de Man, Chandler, like Jones, tends to sideline the precise nature of the link between poetry and feeling.

With its concentration on affect, scholarship concerned with the relationship between genre and gender offers an intriguing attempt to marry historicism and formalism. Adela Pinch notes that 'contemporary criticism still seems afraid of seeing Romanticism as being in any way about emotion – as if to do so would involve believing that poetry really *was* the spontaneous overflow of powerful feeling'.[32] Mistaking disenchantment for sophistication, Romantic Studies has suppressed one of the defining features of its object – affect. Jones and Chandler could be viewed as party to this 'intellectualisation' of Romanticism.[33] As Pinch shows, though, it is difficult to address feeling head on. If affect is often buried beneath intellectual history, another fate sometimes awaits Wordsworthian feeling in recent feminist writing. Suggesting that critics might attain authenticity by facing up to the subject from which they appear to have shrunk in fear, from the outset Pinch indentures affect to politics.[34] The matter of poetic emotion seems less compelling than Wordsworth's 'relations both to sentimental poets and the sentimental figures of female suffering he frequently borrows in his early work'.[35] Pinch's real goal is to expose Wordsworth's use, and domination, of women – the poet's 'conversion of an intertextual relationship into an interpersonal one' and *vice versa*.[36] For the most part, she views feeling in terms of power.[37]

Pinch's writing on images of suffering women in 'On seeing Miss Helen Maria Williams weep at a tale of distress' and 'Goody Blake and Harry Gill' is exemplary ideology-critique. She uncovers voyeurism, heterosexism and anxieties about women in Wordsworth, and concludes that the poet calculates that risking the 'masochistic introjection of a woman's suffering' will be 'productive of a [male] lyric voice'.[38] Notwithstanding her discovery of strange patterns of misogyny in Wordsworth's poetry, Pinch's lexicon reveals problems with methodology. She assumes an 'economic' model of affect – that is, she couches her enquiry in a jargon of the ownership and exchange of feelings in order to evaluate who stands to profit from their circulation.[39] This approach is immensely fruitful, as it uncovers a system of affective accountancy motivating Romantic poetry. One of the arguments of the present book, nonetheless, is that by exchanging poetry with another discourse (including economics), criticism fails to properly discuss poetry itself and ignores a crucial tenet of Wordsworthian poetics – the notion that poetry *is* feeling and not simply a container for feelings that find their way in from 'outside'. Whether Wordsworth is right about poetry and feeling is open to dispute. But disregarding his theory amounts to the rejection of an aspect of his work that might protest the asymmetry of exchange to which feminist and 'materialist' writers object.[40] Fixating on exchange, much contemporary criticism repeats the process it opposes. Another chief concern of this study, as a consequence, is the extent to which Wordsworth's art is autonomous – or deliberately resistant to exchange – and the significance of any autonomy attained.

III

For most commentators, 'materialist criticism' means emphasising the 'non-poetic' stuff upon which poetry is said to be predicated: in the case of Jones and Chandler, eighteenth-century politics and aesthetics; for Pinch, Sensibility's assumptions about gender; for G. Garbrielle Starr, the conventions of the eighteenth-century novel.[41] Such approaches move to abstract a content from poetry that can then be submitted to a critical approach. Starr herself sources the abstraction of much criticism, including that which calls itself 'materialist', to the neo-Platonist line of aesthetics that begins with Shaftesbury, 'where, as Adorno puts it, aesthetic taste becomes autonomous by being separated from "cuisine and pornography"'.[42] She poses a question fundamental to this book: 'what does aesthetic enquiry provide that ethical, political, historical, or hermeneutic enquiries do not?'[43] She even compiles a long list of the distinguished theorists she believes have 'betrayed' the aesthetic to some degree: 'Given the examples of Shaftesbury, Hutcheson, Smith, Scarry, Eagleton, De Man, or Derrida, it might appear that thinking the aesthetic all but requires its immediate translation into something else, whether it's ethics, ideology, or politics'.[44] Work that sinks art into its others, according to Starr, diverges from the goals of materialist criticism correctly defined. But in her critique of the 'false' materialism of those writers who do 'something more like substitution than analysis', she concludes with statements as vague as 'Human beings have problems with the unique'.[45] Starr thus shows the difficulty faced by criticism that tries to inoculate itself against the siren song of 'metaphysics'. After all, one does not outwit substitution and abstraction simply by appealing to the 'real', matter or the unique. As Simon Jarvis points out, the idea that something exists entirely independent from abstraction is idolatry.[46]

Unlike Starr, I do not hold the Whig line that begins with Shaftesbury, passes through, for example, Hume, Gerard and Kames, and culminates in Burke, to be the root of modern criticism's inability to look directly at art without converting it into another discourse. On the contrary, I contend that this tradition gives the relationship between the material and the abstract its most thorough treatment in the eighteenth century, a fact often forgotten in genealogies of the aesthetic that focus on Continental philosophy.[47] What makes Whig aesthetics so extraordinary is that, regardless of its lack of a theory of aesthetic autonomy – because aestheticians were primarily interested in the affective dimension of subjectivity rather than the interpretation of artworks – types of affect that surpass its remit regularly appear in the texts. Critics have observed as such, but I advance the debate by arguing that Wordsworth is unusually responsive to these scattered moments. In his poetry, the vast architecture of Whig aesthetics is brought to bear on ideas about the character and function of art, and the possibility or desirability of the artwork's autonomy. Without nursing a secret 'metaphysics' of feeling, Wordsworth makes affect an object of enquiry in its own right because he wishes to meditate upon affect *before* it is recruited into discourses of subjectivity, taste or class. To inspect Wordsworth's relationship to Whig aesthetics is not to construct another history of ideas for a poet already burdened by an embarrassment of critical contexts. Concurring with Alan Bewell's description of Wordsworth's greatest poetry as a 'struggle with a discursive paradigm',[48] I ask how Whig philosophy aids a poet who is fascinated with 'emotion-in-itself' and the idea that poetry is feeling. Reflecting on why Wordsworth finds Whig philosophy so amenable, and what elements of this thought enter his increasingly autonomous poetic practice, I present eighteenth-century aesthetics as less 'gentlemanly' than often believed and Wordsworth as more 'materialist'.[49]

The first two chapters examine the influence of eighteenth-century Whig aesthetics on Wordsworth. Chapter 1 establishes the extent of Wordsworth's Shaftesbureanism. Paul Hamilton has argued that recent readings of Shaftesbury's theory of polite conversation explore either 'exclusiveness and the counter-public spheres which were strategically ignored as part of its cultural project' or 'the genie let out of the bottle: the emancipatory dynamic in conversation that exceeds any polite self-regulation'.[50] I certainly stress those aspects of Shaftesbury that are insufficiently accommodated in his writing, and follow Jones' contention that Shaftesbury's generally conservative thought contains a progressive strand that attracts Wordsworth.[51] However, I also propose that the poet's own peculiar interest in feeling leads him to distil from the aesthetician the notion that affect can *analyse* social life. The model of affective critique that Wordsworth develops ultimately equates fully to neither Whig nor republican ideology.

Later in the eighteenth century, thinkers like Hume and Gerard conclude that the discipline of Whig aesthetics requires specialists in taste – critics. Edmund Burke goes to some lengths to balance this new promotion of specialists with Shaftesbury's reservations about expertise and praise for the disinterested gentleman. Chapter 2 argues that Wordsworth exploits the considerable strains in Whig thought that Burke's *A Philosophical Enquiry into the Origin of our Ideas of the Sublime and Beautiful* attempts to negotiate. *The Borderers, Letter to the Bishop of Llandaff* and *The Convention of Cintra* use the Irishman's rejection of abstraction and the individual, and praise of feeling and tradition, to extend Wordsworth's 'affective' analysis of contemporary society and politics. Indeed, after Burke, Wordsworth begins to identify the Poet as uniquely positioned to nurture affect's critical component.

Against republican rationalism, Burke asserts in the *Enquiry* and *Reflections on the Revolution in France* that language – poetic language, in particular – is an archive of the affective associations that underpin tradition and national cohesion. However, he also inadvertently reveals that the mimetic and positional aspects of language are entwined. Burke hopes that poetry will ground his traditionalism, but Chapter 3 proposes that he reveals poetry in the act of fabricating feelings that it claims to discover. Having derived from competing strands of Whig aesthetics the idea that the Poet can be at once 'aristocratic' and bourgeois, ordinary and radically individual, Wordsworth investigates the antagonism between mimetic and positional language disclosed by Burke. With reference to Coleridge's objections to the Preface in *Biographia Literaria*, I argue that Wordsworth believes poetry's exceptional facility with mimetic and positional language, as well as its constitutively metrical form, gives it superior access to the 'truth-content' of feeling. Not only is the Poet perfectly situated to think feeling, for Wordsworth it is solely *in* poetry that affect is truly critical.

As language proves an unreliable custodian of affect, Burke relocates the foundations of tradition to the affection people have for the land (home and nation). While Wordsworth's views on the relationship between locale and feeling often appear Burkean, he breaks with Burke and figures poetry itself as a relatively autonomous *place* of feeling. In Chapter 4, I demonstrate that Wordsworth resists Burke's conscription of land to (abstract) ideological ends, and instead imagines his poetry as the only arena in which thinking remains true to its material objects. Bringing intellect and the senses into dialectical relationship through repeated attention to looking and listening, parts of *Lyrical Ballads* and *The Prelude* negate political abstraction in favour of – or perhaps more accurately, in a promise to – the specific and often fleeting.

A dialectical poetics that negates political dogma, Wordsworth's art tends to be reactive, and subsequently lacks an identity of own. In his prose fragment 'The Sublime and the Beautiful', however, Wordsworth moves beyond the structural negativity of dialectics and conceives a positive – that is, 'primary' – poetics.[52] Chapter 5 argues that, synthesising Burkean sensationist traditionalism with Kantian subject-centred anti-materialism, Wordsworth posits thought as fundamentally embodied. Whereas the sublime and beautiful enable Burke to shape his fantasy of the Revolution, in *The Prelude* Wordsworth uses the same categories to penetrate Paris. Tarrying with it in verse, the poem is more than a reading of the Revolution: it becomes instead a parallel event-in-itself. With the 'spots of time', Wordsworth leaves his critique of Burkean tradition behind and presents *The Prelude* as an alternative – and fully embodied – tradition in its own right. Deeply attuned to the dependence of content on form, Wordsworth's art is experimental and, by definition, oriented towards the future.

In establishing poetry as a relatively autonomous counter tradition, Wordsworth discovers that he has separated his art from the society it would address. From as early as the 'Lucy poems', his work is suffused with a melancholy sense of impotence and isolation. The final chapter explores Wordsworth's attempts to rejoin the world by destroying poetry. Nevertheless, he ultimately seeks a poetic solution to the problem, and in doing so he creates a dialectical mode of allegory. In Book 7 of *The Prelude*, Wordsworth makes formal contact with London in order to experience, understand and measure his work's proximity to, and distance from, the city. Dialectical allegory thus enables him to also imagine a happy sociability that, although absent in real life, remains possible. Embodying political hope in the form of *The Prelude*, moreover, Wordsworth avoids empty utopianism. In the London Books of *The Prelude*, he engages with public and political life without reverting to abstraction or attempting to legislate for anyone other than himself.

1
Shaftesbury, Wordsworth and Affective Critique

This chapter examines the extent of Shaftesbury's influence on Wordsworth, with particular reference to the poet's concurrence with the philosopher's view that feeling must be regulated through self-division and polite sociability. A number of commentators have emphasised Wordsworth's acceptance of Shaftesbury's Whig civic humanist strictures against strong feeling. Jon Mee, for instance, has persuasively argued that while Wordsworth agrees with Shaftesbury's insistence on the regulation of the passions, the poet admits enthusiasm into his work in order to discipline it and thereby exhibit his command over emotion. The 'combustible matter [of feeling] . . . seems to remain in excess of its disciplinary plot': in short, enthusiasm fuels Wordsworth's Shaftesburean poetics.[1]

Mee complicates Chris Jones' already very sophisticated contention that the poet makes the philosopher available to 1790s radicals. However, I depart from both of these powerful versions of intellectual history by proposing that, rather than adapt Shaftesbury, Wordsworth begins to reconfigure 'Whiggism' for political, philosophical and poetic ends that its aestheticians would hardly recognise. Focussing on the numerous places in *Characteristicks of Men, Manners, Opinions, Times* where the otherwise smooth operation of Shaftesbury's ideology becomes troubled, I argue that Wordsworth exploits such 'interruptions' in order to advance his enquiry into affect.

The 'inconsistencies' of *Characteristicks* leave later Whig thinkers like Edmund Burke with more than a complex legacy to assimilate (a subject taken up in much of the next chapter). By approving certain kinds of affect, Shaftesbury goes far beyond his own understanding of their usefulness in the ideological task of moderating vulgar feeling for the sake of maintaining privilege. I suggest that Wordsworth recognises the implications of Shaftesbury's remarkably independent-minded aesthetics, and gradually develops it into a theory of affective critique – a dialectical theory of affect, in essence – that differs from the 'radical' Shaftesbureanism described by Jones. Wordsworth generalises the restricted critical component of Shaftesburean affect into a general mode of feeling thought. The Earl might politely chafe against the limits of Whig civic humanism, but Wordsworth translates this strand of eighteenth-century British aesthetics into a theory of critical affect that is nowhere on the line from Whig to republican upon which he is commonly located.[2]

I

According to Ashfield and de Bolla, the eighteenth century is marked by the gradual loosening of

> the old certainties, those which grounded and provided guarantees for the subject in a predominantly religious culture. It is this change from an epistemology based in theological belief and debate to one in which man must find from within himself the grounds of knowledge, which above all others distinguishes the enlightenment as the single most important moment in the history of the concept of the aesthetic.[3]

The enlightenment subject can no longer rely on theological absolutes to find a place in the world. Instead, he must situate himself by attending to his felt experience. Aesthetics in the period is 'about how we are formed as subjects, and how *as subjects* we go about making sense of our experience'.[4]

The central concerns of Wordsworth's 1800 Preface to *Lyrical Ballads* descend from this emphasis on feeling in eighteenth-century aesthetics. Key statements in the Preface correlate poetry with affect. Wordsworth writes that *Lyrical Ballads* was

> published, as an experiment which, I hoped, might be of some use to ascertain, how far, by fitting to metrical arrangement a selection of the real language of men in a state of vivid sensation, that sort of pleasure and that quantity of pleasure may be imparted, which a Poet may rationally endeavour to impart (*PrW* 1. 118).

While declaring a commitment to originality and the experimental, Wordsworth presents his poetry as fundamentally a matter of feelings.

Indeed, despite the almost scientific tone and rationalist idiom, he emphasises sensation and pleasure. The most famous section of the Preface, in fact, reinforces the high status accorded to affect:

> I have said that poetry is the spontaneous overflow of powerful feelings: it takes its origin from emotion recollected in tranquillity: the emotion is contemplated till by a species of reaction the tranquillity gradually disappears, and an emotion, similar to that which was before the subject of contemplation, is gradually produced, and does itself actually exist in the mind. In this mood, successful composition generally begins . . . (*PrW* 1. 148).

Although the first passage posits sensation as the cause and effect of poetry, whereas the second is essentially a description of the act of writing, in both excerpts affect is foremost. The idea of 'emotion recollected in tranquillity' is not simply the slogan of an emergent Romanticism, then, but is also evidence of Wordsworth's interest in the same family of concerns to which eighteenth-century aesthetics devotes itself (*PrW* 1. 148).

Duncan Wu notes that Wordsworth had probably read Shaftesbury by 1785.[5] However, it is more likely that Wordsworth initially came into contact with the philosopher second hand through his reading of Thomson's *The Seasons* (1730) and, more decisively, Akenside's *The Pleasures of the Imagination* (1744).[6] Both Thomson and Akenside belong to what Michael Meehan calls '"the school of Shaftesbury"', and allusions to these writers can be found in Wordsworth's earliest known poem, the 1785 *Lines Written as a School Exercise*.[7] Coleridge's 1795 *Moral and Political Lecture* and letters from around this period confirm the importance of Akenside in Wordsworth's circle.[8] Writing to John Thewall in 1796, Coleridge expresses admiration for 'the *head* and fancy of Akenside'.[9] As Kelvin Everest states, Coleridge's attempts in the 'Conversation Poems' (1795–8) 'to formulate the significance of his experience of nature, are not far from Akenside'.[10] The poet-collaborators inevitably would have discussed Akenside and his Shaftesbureanism.

According to Julie Ellison, in Shaftesbury's 'quasi-pastoral *Moralists*, rhapsodies to nature and unabashed excesses of fancy are challenged, but nonetheless allowed, in the sequestered retreats of gentlemen'.[11] Wordsworth's poetics of 'emotion recollected in tranquillity' continue this train of Shaftesbury's thought. Indeed, Shaftesbury almost looks like the 'nature poet' Wordsworth is often taken to be, particularly when he asks the reader 'to remember how he has many times address'd the Woods and Rocks in audible articulate Sounds, and seemingly expostulated with himself' (*C* 1. 95).[12] A vital dimension of poetry, for Wordsworth, is exactly that it contemplates past emotion by re-presenting it, separating the subject from his emotion, through the act of solitary composition in a pastoral setting.[13]

With their turn to feeling, eighteenth-century aestheticians were not simply attempting to substitute a redundant theological worldview with one founded on the senses. Their writing was, in fact, inseparable from the great political and economic changes that occurred in the second half of the seventeenth century, and which mark the next hundred years as the beginning of modernity. English society (*British* society after the 1707 Act of Union) underwent a remarkable change between the Restoration in 1660 and the end of the Seven Years' war in 1763. In effect, Britain transformed its agricultural and mercantile base into an industrial and global capitalist economy.

The ascendancy of the market, and its accompanying disregard for all other values, threatened to produce an ideological void. The Whigs, however, presented the Glorious Revolution of 1688 as the triumph of Liberty over that 'Tyranny which, though it strangled the Romans, had been averted as a threat in Britain's case by the Settlement'.[14] This historical comparison with Rome, and suggestion that the British sub-jugation of the King to Parliament had improved on the ancient model, created the ideal climate for civic humanism to flourish, a cultural for-mation rooted in republican political theory.

Borrowing from the political discourses of republican Rome, Renaissance Italy and the English Civil War, the civic humanists 'defined liberty in terms of the virtuous participation of the citizen-like subjects in their government'.[15] But the virtuous citizen was not just anyone. As John Barrell has shown, 'The art of government was . . . to be entrusted to those who could claim the public virtue of disinterested-ness . . . and their task was to *regulate and subdue that variety of contrary passions and interests.*'[16] To qualify as virtuous and disinterested a man was required to be 'of independent means, for the best guarantee of political independence is economic independence' and the freedom from specialisation it brings.[17] The virtuous citizen, in practice, was the Whig landowner whose inherited wealth liberated him from the seductive caprice of the market and put him above 'considerations of ambition, possession, consumption, and desire'.[18] The civic humanists recognised that while commerce made society possible, the maelstrom of competing interests unleashed might also wreck it. Thus, they accepted the necessity of commerce on the proviso that those abstracted from private interest manage political life.

For the civic humanists, the disinterested Whig landowner, 'the All-Comprehending Gentleman, both consummate social Actor and removed Observer', was the defender of *sociability* – the companionable adhesive uniting individuals beyond their private interests.[19] J. G. A. Pocock observes that the question of sociability was linked in the period with the notion of politeness: 'To most Whig defenders of civilisation, the rise of commerce and the rise of polite culture went together, under the name of "the progress of the arts".'[20] Debate – perhaps the greatest expression of liberty – was nowhere more evident than in a lively culture of art, science and criticism. Indeed, Michael Meehan suggests that the '"progress" poem', so common in the eighteenth-century and arguably most fully realised in *The Prelude*, should be read not only as a panegyric to liberty indicative of the period's dedication to the idea, but also as the incubator of 'greater demand for liberty'.[21] The discourse of civic humanism, then, is a core impulse behind Wordsworth's writing, and is especially apparent in his hope to be a universal and disinterested 'man speaking to men' (*PrW* 1. 138).[22] Nonetheless, it is important to note, as Meehan suggests, that although Wordsworth's long poem begins as a servant to the ideology of liberty, the demand for greater liberty made with every imaginative realisation of its hopes disentangles it from any straightforward obedience to a civic humanist programme. The poem is not limited to a mimesis of liberty, but produces ideas of freedom that exceed its Whig conception.

For Terry Eagleton, the discourse of aesthetics is an attempt by the new social and political order to portray itself as natural by taking 'root in the sensuous immediacies of empirical life'.[23] If the affections and appetites of the subject, even the most intimate, are shown to coincide with the structure of society, a social cohesion can be effected that is 'more deeply felt than any mere rational totality'.[24] Yet aesthetics in the period has to work hard to present itself as natural and true. Conscripted by ideology, it is by definition marked by contradiction. Neither disinterested theory, nor the innocent substitution of one world picture for another, nor merely a form of self-conscious ideological mystification, eighteenth-century aesthetics, as exemplified by the 'moral sense' philosopher, the Third Earl of Shaftesbury, exhibits all the uneasy antagonisms of its project and age.

Philip Ayres points out that Shaftesbury's work had a pronounced influence on European letters in the period. In particular, the German writers 'Lessing, Schiller, Goethe, Kant, Weiland, and Herder . . . [saw him] as the equal of Spinoza and Leibniz' (*C* 1. 28). However, it is Shaftesbury's 'undeniably major contribution' to the genesis of the 'Man of Feeling' in Britain, most famously presented in Laurence Sterne's novels, that is of greatest significance (*C* 1. 27). Expounded, disputed and developed in the writings of his disciple Francis Hutcheson, Shaftesbury's thinking was behind the direction taken by British aesthetics in the eighteenth century, and was further promulgated in the verse of James Thomson and Mark Akenside, two of Wordsworth and Coleridge's chief eighteenth-century precursors. But by the time Wordsworth writes the Preface, the potential of affect to disorientate rather than stabilise – and its capacity to even question and criticise – is increasingly apparent. Eighteenth-century aesthetics does not just give the subject a compass with which to locate himself: it also discovers aspects of experience that are at odds with its predominantly conservative agenda.

II

Many commentators agree that Shaftesbury is no defender of bourgeois principles. Disdainful of capitalism's soulless grasping, and wary of the excesses of wealth and its partner vice, his work is addressed to his own peer-group, and is not a middle-class manifesto for the 'democratisation of taste'.[25] Nevertheless, the very fact that Shaftesbury's writing was enlisted in the support of incompatible ideologies suggests that the affective aesthetics of the eighteenth century is not simply the handmaiden of a unified and dominant ideology, but is inhabited by a multiplicity of discursive energies.

Lawrence Klein argues that Shaftesbury saw that 'while the Church and the Court had traditionally dominated English culture to its detriment, post-1688 England and post-1707 Britain had the opportunity to create a new public and gentlemanly culture'.[26] His commitment to the aesthetics of affect, and the politics of affection, enabled Shaftesbury 'to attack the Tory loyalty to Church and Court in the name of a new Whiggish culture'.[27] By opposing the Church's influence on polity, and consequently its ability to enforce doctrine, Shaftesbury aligned himself with a Whig latitudinarianism profoundly distrustful of clerics. In his anti-Toryism, Shaftesbury remained supportive of the elite, and believed the decline of Church and Court would create the conditions for the aristocracy's resurgence. Shaftesbury wished to assert the gentleman against the churchman, preferring the influence of the privileged few to that of religious institutions or courtly opinion.

Although Shaftesbury considered atheism morally unthreatening, his attack on the Church was not an attack on religion itself. What he feared was that worship, when motivated by flawed theology, caused more harm than good. Such anti-intellectualism, as will be seen in the next chapter, is an important feature of Edmund Burke's thought and a reason for *The Prelude*'s rejection of Godwin in preference for autobiography.[28] Shaftesbury agreed that religion was founded on the affections, but also believed that elements of the Church – the High Church wing, to be precise – practiced with anti-social zeal, or *enthusiasm*. For Shaftesbury, religion that extended the bonds of affection from the self to society and beyond could be applauded; but he was outspoken in opposition to styles of worship that he felt undermined companionable human relations.

The starting point for Shaftesbury's most systematic work, *An Inquiry Concerning Virtue* (1699), is the tenet, foundational to the eighteenth-century's culture of Sensibility, that subjects have an innate faculty of judgement, analogous to the immediacy of the senses. It is necessary to quote Shaftesbury at some length in order to establish the character of his moral sense philosophy:

> THE MIND, which as Spectator or Auditor of *other Minds*, cannot be without its *Eye* and *Ear*; so as to discern Proportion, distinguish Sound, and scan each Sentiment or Thought which comes before it. It can let nothing escape its Censure. It feels the Soft, and Harsh, the Agreeable, and Disagreeable, in the Affections; and finds a *Foul* and *Fair*, a *Harmonious*, and a *Dissonant*, as really and truly here, as any musical Numbers, or in the outward Forms and Representations of sensible Things. Nor can it with-hold its *Admiration* and *Extasy*, its *Aversion* and *Scorn*, any more in what relates to one than to the other of these Subjects (*C* 1. 203).

The substance of Shaftesbury's position is that moral judgements, predicated on a 'natural' predilection for virtue, are as instinctive and irrefutable as pleasure. He argues that

> as in the *sensible* kind of Objects, the Species or Images of Bodys, Colours, and Sounds, are perpetually moving before our Eyes, and acting on our Senses, even when we sleep; so in the *moral* and *intellectual* kind, the Forms and Images of Things are no less active and incumbent on the Mind . . . (*C* 1. 203).

There is no qualitative difference between the mind's treatment of *intellectual* and *sensible* objects.[29] The mind responds to ideas in the same way that the senses respond to stimuli: 'the Heart cannot possibly remain neutral' and will make its judgement known (*C* 1. 203). Thus, whether it be concerned with sensible or intellectual objects, 'there arises a new Trial or Exercise of the Heart: which must either rightly and soundly affect what is just and right, and disaffect what is contrary; or corruptly affect what is ill, and disaffect what is worthy and good' (*C* 1. 204). The mind is joined to the heart in shared purpose, and experiences right and wrong instantaneously.

It is clear from this model that Shaftesbury has both naturalised and universalised moral discernment. By conflating moral judgement with physiological sensation, he can announce that the 'sense of Right and Wrong . . . [is] as natural to us as *natural Affection*': it is a faculty possessed by all Mankind, and harmonises with what might be called the 'order of the universe' (*C* 1. 210). Furthermore, the insistence that an individual's natural affections enable him to 'feel relation to whatever . . . [is] outside the self' allows Shaftesbury to metonymically connect parts with wholes in a significant way.[30] An individual's affections, shared by other individuals, encourage an extension of relationships towards 'families, tribes, polities, and ultimately to the species'.[31]

Chris Jones argues that in *An Evening Walk* (1794) the 'expansion of the affections is presented in a thoroughly Shaftesburyan way'.[32] Wordsworth writes:

> A Mind, that in a calm angelic mood
> Of happy wisdom, mediating good,
> Beholds, of all from her high powers required,
> Much done, and much designed, and more desired;
> Harmonious thoughts, a soul by Truth refined,
> Entire affection for all human kind;
> A heart that vibrates evermore, awake
> To feeling for all forms that Life can take,
> That wider still its sympathy extends,
> And sees not any line where being ends;
> Sees sense, through Nature's rudest forms betrayed,
> Tremble obscure in fountain, rock, and shade;
> And while a secret power whose forms endears
> Their social accents never vainly hears.[33]

Peace that originates in God moves outward from the individual to encompass nature and, finally, society. Jones identifies *The Moralists* as the origin of the phrase 'Entire affection', albeit with the caveat that Shaftesbury 'is perhaps only an ultimate source.'[34] Indeed, it will be seen later in this study how the civic humanist idea that affection is fundamentally sociable, and therefore the glue of society, is taken up in Edmund Burke's similarly metonymic vision of the nation.

For Shaftesbury, affective sociability does not stop at connecting the individual with the species: it makes it possible for people to understand their place in Creation. Thus, the individual is always oriented towards something greater than himself, and a 'moral sense' that is underwritten by God is established. Shaftesbury draws the conclusion that the subject's innate moral sense corresponds to the existence of a God who is '*just* and *good*' (C 1. 213). Possessing 'by nature a faculty whereby . . . [he is] able to distinguish and prefer what is right', the subject is fundamentally in step with God's will.[35] This notion of harmony forms the heart of Shaftesbury's thinking:

> Virtue, for Shaftesbury, consists in the well-balanced personality which reflects inwardly the harmony and order of the outside world. The virtuous character is the one in which all the elements are in accord with each other.[36]

In political terms, the virtuous man's obligation to remain in accord with the system means that he must accept his status as a social being and not succumb to the aggressive individualism encouraged by the period's burgeoning economics of self-interest.

It is essential to emphasise once again that, although Shaftesbury writes of a shared human nature, his thought is not democratic in intent.[37] He objects to the new middle class and its commercial, individualist ethos because he fears the chaos that would ensue should everyone pursue private interests or pleasures. Like many other writers at the time, he worries that 'vast wealth naturally produces Avarice, Luxury, or Effeminacy' – the 'natures' threatening to hierarchy and the social unity it supposedly ensures.[38] There was a widespread anxiety in the eighteenth century that Britain's economic success produced a subject who was

> on the whole a feminised, even effeminate being, still wrestling with his own passions and exteriors and with interior and exterior forces let loose by his fantasies and appetites, and symbolised by such archetypically female goddesses of disorder as Fortune, Luxury, and most recently Credit herself.[39]

At the same time, the benefits to the nation of increased employment and wealth were seen by many (notably Bernard Mandeville in *The Fable of the Bees* [1714–24]) to counterbalance the dangers represented by luxury. The self-interest generated by commerce was even thought to create a social and economic fabric so complex and entwined that political concord would follow. Indeed, Barrell suggests that

> The perception that in a complex society, the possibility of a comprehensive understanding has disappeared, is perhaps the crucial issue between Burke and Paine, as Burke argues that no one man is in a position to grasp, by speculation, the proper order of government and the function of established institutions, and so to demand that they be changed.[40]

Much of Burke's *Reflections on the Revolution in France*, in fact, is concerned with attacking the French for their failure to maintain the delicate balance between the stability of traditional institutions and the fluidity of commerce. Holding that reason corrupts and perverts everything under its sway, he regards the Revolution as inaugurating a dictatorship of dangerous fantasy and speculation.[41]

Shaftesbury does not encourage a liberation of the senses but, rather, moderation in all things. In order to live in harmony with Creation, the subject must 'have true *Resignation*, or Submission to the Rule and Order of THE DEITY' (*C* 1. 217). The great reward for this submission will be '*eternal Living, in a State of highest Pleasure and Enjoyment*'; and so, whilst in the world, the subject must curtail his desires and avoid anything that might tempt him away, through self-indulgence, from the 'common' good (*C* 1. 217). Sensibility's promotion of affective experience opens up the possibility of libertinism, the subject's recourse to 'the violence of Rage, Lust, or any other counter-working Passion' (*C* 1. 218). Sensibility might promise harmony, but it also creates the conditions for its disintegration. In order to neutralise the danger inherent in affective experience, therefore, it is necessary to tie virtue to '*true Interest*, and *Self-Enjoyment*' (*C* 1. 221). Shaftesbury attempts this, quite predictably, and late enough in his argument to almost suggest his recourse to a Hobbesian predication of the commonwealth on its submission to a sovereign power, through a theological argument. Happiness is greatest when achieved through virtue; and 'the Perfection and Height of VIRTUE must be owing to *the Belief of a God*' (*C* 1. 226). In this way, Shaftesbury argues, self-interest and public interest are conjoined. The organicism of *An Inquiry* is then reaffirmed through the suggestion that

> this Affection of a Creature towards the good of the Species or common Nature, is as *proper* and *natural* to him, as to any Organ, Part or

Member of an Animal-Body, or mere Vegetable, to work in its own
Course, and regular way of Growth (*C* 1. 227).

The cost of failure to comply with the natural order is likewise couched
in organic terms – a language that Burke employs in *Reflections* and
Wordsworth in *The Convention of Cintra*.

Any great passion – any *enthusiasm* – has a detrimental effect on both
the individual and society. Shaftesbury concedes that it may be 'harsh to
call that *unnatural* and *vicious*, which is only an Extreme of some natural
and kind Affection', but he is adamant that such affections are undesirable (*C* 1. 232). Even a subject's self-neglect, perhaps the consequence
of zealousness in the public interest, is deemed unhealthy as it disrupts
intercourse between an individual and society. Without such harmony
the subject will be unhappy. There is an almost puritanical edge to
Shaftesbury's warnings against pleasure, which he associates with 'the
enormous Growth of Luxury in Capital Citys' (*C* 1. 254). This motif of
the city corrupted by luxury recurs, of course, in a famous passage in the
Preface to *Lyrical Ballads* discussed in more detail below (*PrW* 1. 128).

Too much pleasure not only disrupts the moral order of the universe,
but eventually undermines the subject's ability to experience any pleasure and happiness at all. 'Idleness, Supineness, and Inactivity' cause
degeneration, which eventually manifests itself in quite spectacular
cases of 'Phrenzy, and Distraction' that rob the subject of individuality (*C* 1. 254; 1. 255). As the pleasure-seeker becomes more embroiled
in immoderation and vice, so his pleasure centres lose sensitivity. He
exhibits a lack of social feeling yet, like a drug addict, vainly craves
greater and greater stimulation: 'the *Appetite* of this kind is *false* and
unnatural; as is that of a Thirst arising from a Fever, or contracted by
habitual Debauch' (*C* 1. 261). Satisfaction declines as it becomes insa-
tiable, and the keenness of sensation is dulled. The subject is reduced,
through the disproportionate love of pleasure, to 'perpetual Disgust,
and Feverishness of Desire' – a condition near to madness (*C* 1. 252).

As already noted, this stance against over-stimulation continues in
Burke and Wordsworth.[42] Indeed, elements of the linguistic politics of
the Preface to *Lyrical Ballads* assume the Whig critique of luxury. Having
defended his choice of rustic language as a superior medium, imprinted
with 'the beautiful and permanent forms of nature', Wordsworth scrutinises the language of contemporary poets (*PrW* 1. 124). These writers

think that they are conferring honour upon themselves and their
art in proportion as they separate themselves from the sympathies

> of men, and indulge in arbitrary and capricious habits of expression
> in order to furnish food for fickle tastes and fickle appetites of their
> own creation (*PrW* 1. 124).

Modern poetry is distorted by affectation, 'false refinement . . . [and]
arbitrary innovation' – an artificial veneer similar in kind to the superficial, 'gross and violent stimulants' available in the city (*PrW* 1. 124;
1. 128). Wordsworth opposes to this ornamental literature the poetry
of the natural and spontaneous, of the 'great and universal passions
of men' (*PrW* 1. 144). According to Jerome McGann, however, his real
quarry is an aspect of eighteenth-century aesthetics that is given dangerous license by certain poets, most notably the Della Cruscans. In a
crowded literary marketplace, the Della Cruscans' sensual verse is competition for *Lyrical Ballads*. But the author of the Preface has objections
that go far beyond literary rivalry. McGann writes that 'Wordsworth and
Coleridge have embarked on a quest for permanence . . . [whereas] the
Della Cruscans court passion and intensity, but in doing so they leave
no doubt that these are splendid and wonderful *im*permanences.'[43]
Anxieties about the corruptibility of the body and its appetites in
eighteenth-century aesthetics drive Wordsworth's critique of the culture
represented by the Della Cruscans as shallow. Nevertheless, he is also
aware that eighteenth-century poetic traditions feed into the poetry
of the 1790s – including his own – and simply wishes to warn that
those traditions are 'not always correctly received or used'.[44] Despite
Wordsworth's interest in the poetics of spontaneity, he is wary of a sensualism that, he is convinced, borders on narcosis.

In his unpublished 1793 *Letter to the Bishop of Llandaff*, Wordsworth
vigorously expresses his fears of sensualist anarchy. He submits that 'the
extremes of poverty and riches have a necessary tendency to corrupt the
human heart', and that the wealth the nobility gains from legislated
social inequality is squandered through society's acceptance of vice
that 'binds down whole ranks of men to idleness' (*PrW* 1. 43; 1. 45).
From this theme of corruption among the upper orders, Wordsworth
quickly turns to the damage caused by promiscuity among the lower
orders. Too much feeling (or too narrow a range of feeling, perhaps), he
fears, quickly escalates into luxury and vice – disasters wherever they
occur. While decadence sometimes ruins members of the middle and
upper classes, among the poor such vice is often catastrophic: the 'promiscuous intercourse to which [they] . . . are compelled by the instincts
of nature' leads to the birth of children 'they are unable to support'

(*PrW* 1. 43). Wordsworth may have a republican sympathy for the underprivileged, but his sometimes paternalistic analysis of their plight owes much to Shaftesbury and the civic humanists.

III

An influential aesthetician, Shaftesbury was also a philosopher of great range. Although he pitted philosophy against the stranglehold of the Church, he found contemporary thought morally slight. What Shaftesbury sought was a combination of the insights of Descartes, Hobbes, Locke, and their successors, which put human understanding on a scientific basis, with a Socratic notion of philosophy as self-knowledge, self-discipline and wisdom. In other words, he wanted to make philosophy available for the civic humanist sensibility by re-orientating it from epistemology to ethics, from the academy to the world. In *The Moralists, a Philosophical Rhapsody* (1709), for example, he laments that 'We have immur'd her [philosophy] (poor Lady!) in Colleges and Cells' (*C* 2. 4). He therefore tempers affection with a thought directed towards sociable ends – ethics.

Affect might bring the individual into affectionate conformity with society and Creation, but if it becomes detached from sociability it can lead to terrible excess. For Shaftesbury, virtue cannot be considered solely an innate disposition, but must be nurtured by training and practice; and a central part of the *regulation* of affect is through the exercise of reason. It is important to be aware of one's place in a universe ordered by God, as it encourages the realisation, discussed in *A Letter Concerning Enthusiasm* (1708), that to 'wish against the Being of a God . . . is wishing against the Publick, and even against one's private Good too, if rightly understood' (*C* 1. 23). The relation between the parts of society and the whole ensure that an individual's good tallies with the good of all, and vice versa.

Wordsworth's proximity to Shaftesbury is at its greatest when the idea of regulation arises. The 1800 Preface's interest in habit coincides with the following sentiments from Akenside's notes to *The Pleasures of the Imagination* (1744):

It is here said [in the poem], that in consequence of the love of novelty, objects which at first were highly delightful to the mind, lose that effect by repeated attention to them. But the instance of *habit* is opposed to this observation; for *there*, objects at first distasteful are in time rendered entirely agreeable by repeated attention.[45]

The regularity of habit enables one to assimilate and preserve new objects. Indeed, in *The Prelude*, Wordsworth claims that habit deepened and matured his childish enthusiasm, his 'fits of vulgar joy' (1. 610):

> By the impressive discipline of fear,
> By pleasure, and repeated happiness,
> So frequently repeated, and by force
> Of obscure feelings representative
> Of joys that were forgotten, these same scenes,
> So beauteous and majestic in themselves,
> Though yet the day was distant, did at length
> Become habitually dear; and all
> Their hues and forms were by invisible links
> Allied to the affections (1. 632–41).

However, it is by envisaging imagination in terms of Shaftesburean regulation that Akenside most startlingly anticipates Wordsworth:

> So the glad impulse of congenial powers,
> Or of sweet sound, or fair proportion's form,
> The grace of motion, or the bloom of light,
> Thrills through Imagination's tender frame,
> From nerve to nerve: all naked and alive
> They catch the spreading rays: till now the soul
> At length discloses every tuneful spring,
> To that harmonious movement from without
> Responsive. Then the expressive strain
> Diffuses its enchantment: fancy dreams
> Of sacred fountains and Elysian groves,
> And vales of bliss: the intellectual power
> Bends from his awful throne a wondering ear,
> And smiles: the passions, gently sooth'd away,
> Sink to divine repose, and love and joy
> Alone are waking; love and joy, serene
> As airs that fan the summer.[46]

Wordsworth later refines Akenside's Shaftesburean formulation of imagination into the most quoted phrase of the Preface – that poetry is 'emotion recollected in tranquillity' (*PrW* 1. 148). The expressive 'shock' of imagination is dampened by the intellect, the agitation of the passions ameliorated. Indeed, Akenside offers a version of the mind's ability to subsume the visual under the visionary that Wordsworth later makes his own:

> Thus at length
> Endow'd with all that nature can bestow,
> The child of Fancy oft in silence bends
> O'er these mixt treasures of his pregnant breast,
> With conscious pride. From them he oft resolves
> To frame he knows not what excelling things;
> And win he knows not what sublime reward
> Of praise and wonder. By degrees, the mind
> Feels her young nerves dilate: the plastic powers
> Labour for action: blind emotions heave
> His bosom; and with loveliest frenzy caught,
> From earth to heaven he rolls his daring eye,
> From heaven to earth (3. 373–85).

Akenside here occupies a space somewhere between Shaftesbury's '"frothy" rhapsodies' of frenzied enthusiasm and Wordsworth's visionary imagination that animates the natural world into a 'new quickening'.[47] These similarities testify to Wordsworth's close reading of Akenside, abetted no doubt by Coleridge, and suggest that Shaftesbury is present in Wordsworth's most significant work.

Yet Shaftesbury's influence on the Preface is even more direct than these comparisons with Akenside might imply. The philosopher fears enthusiasm as the cause of a disharmony at odds with the 'natural' order. Excitement or zealousness mounts to an extremity that poses a threat to the balance of social relations. In *A Letter Concerning Enthusiasm*, however, Shaftesbury does not attempt to eradicate all manifestations of passion. He accepts that powerful emotions will out:

> There are certain Humours in Mankind, which of necessity must have vent. The Human Mind and Body are of both of 'em naturally subject to Commotions: and as there are strange Ferments in the Blood, which in many Bodys occasion an extraordinary discharge; so in Reason, too there are heterogenous Particles which must be thrown off by Fermentation (*C* 1. 12).[48]

He acknowledges the fact of enthusiasm, in both body and mind, the latter being of the most concern to him, and elaborates a technique for the regulation of strong feeling.[49]

Shaftesbury understands that enthusiasm robs the subject of his true interests and effectively denies him self-mastery. In solution to this problem, he recommends that the individual 'retire into some thick Wood, or rather take the Point of some high Hill' and have exorcising counsel with himself (*C* 1. 88). By this method, 'how thorowly he carries on the Business of *Self-Dissection*. By virtue of this SOLILOQUY he becomes two distinct *Persons*. He is Pupil and Preceptor. He teaches, and he learns' (*C* 1. 87). The self is 'form'd and disciplin'd . . . [by] being a strong *Self-Examiner*, and *thorow-pac'd Dialogist*, in this solitary way' (*C* 1. 92), and so remains true to itself and society:

> As cruel a Court as *the Inquisition* appears; there must, it seems, be full as formidable a one, erected in our-selves; if we wou'd pretend to that Uniformity of Opinion which is necessary to hold us to *one Will*, and preserve us in the same Mind, from one day to the next (*C* 1. 100).

If we are knowable to ourselves, we are knowable to others, and can occupy our assigned place in society: 'By examining the various Turns, Inflexions, Declensions, and inward Revolutions of *the Passions*, I must undoubtedly come the better to understand a human Breast, and judg the better both of others and *my-self*' (*C* 1. 153).

Continuing this line in *Soliloquy: or Advice to an Author* (1710), Shaftesbury writes that 'whatever may be the proper Effect or Operation of Religion, 'tis the known Province of Philosophy to teach us *our-selves*, keep us the *self-same* Persons, and so regulate our governing Fancys, Passions, and Humours' (*C* 1. 148). He goes on to recommend 'that celebrated Delphick Inscription, *Recognise your-self*: which was as much as to say, *Divide your-self, or Be Two*' (*C* 1. 93). Reason encourages the subject to reflect upon himself and so keep affection in check. Virtue is achieved by affection, but only when supervised by reason.

This aspect of Shaftesbury clearly impinges upon Wordsworth. In *The Prelude*, he describes the discovery of a consciousness-heightening self-division in Shaftesburean terms:

> . . . so wide appears
> The vacancy between me and those days,
> Which yet have such self-presence in my mind
> That, sometimes, when I think of them, I seem
> Two consciousnesses, conscious of myself
> And of some other Being (2. 28–33).

By stressing the roles of time and memory, Wordsworth supplements Shaftesbury's notion of rational self-division. Indeed, in the 'Bless'd the infant Babe' episode, reason is regarded as almost a function of (feeling's) temporality:

> Thus, day by day,
> Subjected to the discipline of love,
> His organs and recipient faculties
> Are quicken'd, are more vigorous, his mind spreads,
> Tenacious of the forms which it receives (2. 252–6).

This description of how the affectionate mind matures and 'spreads' represents a substantial modification of *An Evening Walk*'s more conventionally Whig narrative. In Shaftesbury, however, self-regulation is never far from the regulation of society through a culture of taste, or in this case, *judgement*.

IV

While the philosophical temperament is essential to Shaftesbury's aesthetics, the subject-centred nature of rational reflection cannot be allowed to become another form of anti-social behaviour. As described above, Shaftesbury socialises, thereby regulating, the experience of philosophical contemplation by dividing the individual into two parts capable of dialogue. In *The Moralists*, for instance, he uses Platonic dialogue to both structure his thinking and enact the content of his thought. Thus, society and conversation become arenas for the regulating duties of philosophy, and Shaftesbury's aesthetics of affection, by their very nature reaching out to the social, take on the appearance of a code of manners. As he writes in *Miscellaneous Reflections on the Preceding Treatises, and Other Critical Subjects* (1711), through the mutual society of head and heart, 'the respective Conduct and distinct Manners of each Party are regulated' (*C* 2. 206). Further regulation occurs, according to *Sensus Communis: an Essay on the Freedom of Wit and Humour* (1709), with interaction between similar individuals: 'We polish one another, and rub off our Corners and rough Sides by a sort of *amicable Collision*' (*C* 1. 39). The 'polite' regulation of one's own affections produces a society in which ''Tis the height of Sociableness to be thus friendly and communicative' (*C* 1. 52). Politeness increases politeness.[50]

As early as *Salisbury Plain* (1794), in his depiction of the night meeting between the traveller and the wandering woman, Wordsworth places a Shaftesburean emphasis on the regulatory value of sociability. The lonely traveller is tormented by nightmares induced by thunder, lightning and a 'watery storm / No moon to open the black clouds and stream'.[51] However, 'He half forgot the terrors of the night' (402), having listened to the woman's tale of distress and striven 'with counsel sweet her soul to chear' (403). It appears in the poem that by morning, as a result of this 'politeness', nature has been transformed into a 'pleasant scene' of 'groves and lawns and meads of green' where 'the merry milkmaid strays' (407; 409; 414). Wordsworth's focus is on two destitute characters, including a woman, and he ultimately expounds a radical politics of rational dissent, yet the form of this crucial incident is Shaftesburean.[52] Conversation between social equals alleviates overwhelming emotions (such as terror and sorrow), thus ending their increasingly injurious solitude; and the bond of affection between the pair stimulates a vision of social contentment in which the benevolence of the human heart corresponds with that of nature.[53] Similarly, in *The Prelude*, conversation with Coleridge and Dorothy helps Wordsworth 'To regulate my soul' (10. 907). Dorothy, above all, embodying both society and nature, and 'Speaking in a voice / Of sudden admonition like a brook' (10. 909–10), rescues Wordsworth from despair by returning him to his more emotionally subdued 'true self' (10. 915).[54] Even when Wordsworth declares in *Lyrical Ballads*' 'Lines written at a small distance from my House' that he wishes to celebrate the beauty of the March sun and 'this one day / . . . give to idleness',[55] his elation is safely enclosed within an address to Dorothy:

> No joyless forms shall regulate
> Our living Calendar:
> We from to-day, my friend, will date
> The opening of the year (17–20).

Expressing a wish to let loose his joy, by calling upon Dorothy for company Wordsworth is careful to avoid the potential danger of the kind of solitary passion that destroys Martha Ray in 'The Thorn'.[56] The poet tells his sister that together they will memorialise the day. The speed with which Wordsworth abandons his initially wild and spontaneous affections for the 'silent laws our hearts will make' (29) is startling.

V

Although Wordsworth has to massage Shaftesbury to fit a 1790s Painite attack on poverty and oppression in *Salisbury Plain*, the Whig's theory of self-regulation already amounts to a theory of social criticism. As proposed in the introduction, Whig aesthetics assumes 'that feeling has a critical, or cognitive, component – that it can make judgements, particularly on social, political and philosophical matters'. Not yet advancing the case for professional critics, although anticipating their existence, Shaftesbury praises the worth of wit and raillery imbued with a critical edge. *An Essay on the Freedom of Wit and Humour* warns against the seductiveness of ideas:

> We may be charg'd perhaps with wilful ignorance and blind Idolatory, for having taken Opinions on Trust, and consecrated in our-selves certain *Idol-Notions*, which we will never suffer to be unveil'd, or seen in open light. They may perhaps be Monsters, and not Divinitys, or Sacred Truths, which are kept thus choicely, in some dark Corner of our Minds: The Spectres may impose on us, whilst we refuse to turn 'em every way, and view their Shapes and Complexions in every light (*C* 1. 38).

Like philosophical dialogue, when allied with the protocols of polite society wit and raillery can have a moderating influence and debunk fanciful notions. It even appears that intellectual sobriety and politeness are more important to Shaftesbury than ideas themselves when he writes that 'A mannerly Wit can hurt no Cause of Interest for which I am in the least concern'd' (*C* 1. 55). Virtue is achieved through sociable politeness. Consequently, any notion that looks to become anti-social through its own zeal cannot be in the interest of the good. For Shaftesbury, ridicule serves reason, which in alliance with affection orders individuals and society in keeping with God's benevolent wishes.

Two poems in the 1798 *Lyrical Ballads* demonstrate Wordsworth's awareness of this Shaftesburean lesson. In 'Expostulation and Reply', a friend berates Wordsworth for idling his time away in daydreams when he could be reading – drinking in the '["]spirit breath'd / From dead men to their kind["]' (7–8).[57] Nonplussed, Wordsworth responds trenchantly to this criticism. There is no need to read, he argues, when nature will teach anyone patient enough to receive her knowledge:

> 'Think you, mid all this mighty sum
> Of things for ever speaking,
> That nothing of itself will come,
> But we must still be seeking['] (25–8)?

If this were the end of the matter, it would hardly be polite: the poet silences his interlocutor, has the last word, and his theory of 'wise passiveness' wins a rhetorical victory. However, the sister poem, 'The Tables Turned', restores equilibrium between the two sides. This time it is Wordsworth who cajoles his bookish friend: 'Up! Up! My Friend, and quit your books; / Or surely you'll grow double' (1–2). The friend does not speak in this poem, but his censorious words of the previous poem seem to have scored a hit, as the poet sounds shrill and bullying:

> Books! 'tis a dull and endless strife,
> Come hear the woodland linnet,
> How sweet his music; on my life
> There's more of wisdom in it (9–12).

It is possible to take this comment at face value. But the rhyme of 'linnet' with 'in it' signals that the manner in which Wordsworth has conveyed his position is trite, if not belligerent. For all the exuberant Romanticism of everything that follows, an awareness of Wordsworth's Shaftesbureanism activates the poem's profound irony. The description of the throstle as 'no mean preacher' (14) is too clichéd to be an oversight; and when Wordsworth makes his most hyperbolic claim, the reader properly grasps the poem's carefully staged drama:

> One impulse from a vernal wood
> Can teach you more than man;
> Of moral evil and of good,
> Than all the sages can (21–4).

This statement is both delightful and absurd. What is more, neither of the speakers in the two poems can be said to be wholly correct. Daydreaming and study both have their place – but to condemn one in favour of the other is, in essence, impolite, and risks a blind commitment to either intellect or the natural heart. With some wit, the poems show the folly of zealousness or 'The enthusiastic imagination [that] reifies the existence of its own representations.'[58]   Nevertheless, the poems do not simply advocate polite negotiation and compromise. Assessing the relative benefits of both muted and clamorous feeling in these poems, Wordsworth renders affect *critical* – that is, he transforms feeling into thought, and does not simply follow the Shaftesburean line that it is best to smooth over strong emotion. Having already succeeded in hitching Shaftesbury to his republican agenda in *Salisbury Plain*, Wordsworth here begins the bolder task of thinking Shaftesbury dialectically – or *radicalising* the philosopher. In 'Expostulation and Reply', poetic enthusiasm criticises rationalist regulation; in 'The Tables Turned', regulation is a critique of enthusiasm. Neither stance can be said to win out, as the efficacy of each instance of thinking-feeling is dependent upon context.[59] It is worth remembering, however, that while Wordsworth's (dialectical) experiment with affect appears to represent a departure from Whig aesthetics, it also depends in large part upon continuity with Shaftesbury. Nowhere is the ambiguity of Wordsworth's relationship with civic humanism more pronounced than in his use of Shaftesbury's idea of *taste*.

VI

Shaftesbury objects to any behaviour that conflicts with order, including religious fanaticism. He dislikes the zealot, but provocatively extending the application of the word *enthusiasm* in support of his Whig criticism of the Church, Shaftesbury also refers to the dogmatic Christian as 'a cruel Enthusiast, . . . [a] *Bigot*, a Persecutor' (*C* 1. 249) – a man who is as harmful to the natural, sociable order as a libertine. Yet religious belief is only one of the foundations of his thinking. The moral sense is not autonomous, although if given a free rein it may try to become so, and must be regulated by reason or conscience. The man who commits a crime is tortured by 'ill Remembrance and displeasing Consciousness' (*C* 1. 248), which he either ignores, with the result that he is miserable because sinful, or acknowledges in order to become virtuous and happy. Having risked the possibility that his writing could be interpreted as implicitly democratic in its assertion of a shared human nature, Shaftesbury henceforth begins to retrieve the notion of social distinctions and hierarchy. To this end, he links conscience to *taste*. As Pierre Bourdieu points out, 'Social subjects . . . distinguish themselves by the distinctions they make': those who exercise taste display the liberty that has allowed them to cultivate good taste – their social privilege.[60] The remainder of this chapter explores how, in his attempt to establish himself as simultaneously unique and universal, Wordsworth's use of the concept of *taste* again borrows from Shaftesbury. Unencumbered by the social values of the civic humanist gentleman, however, Wordsworth once more loosens Shaftesbury's work – this time his discourse on taste – from Whig class commitments to further extend its potential philosophical, political and aesthetic reach.

What Shaftesbury usually describes as *reason, regulation* or *conscience*, he occasionally calls *taste*. In *The Moralists*, he proclaims: 'How long e'er true *Taste* is gain'd! How many things shocking, how many offensive at first, which afterwards are known and acknowledg'd the highest *Beautys*!' (*C* 2. 105). *Taste* implies the happy cohabitation of the natural and artificial, and the word's rarity in Shaftesbury's writing points to an anxiety about the inherent contradiction of the notion. Taste regulates and modifies natural pleasures into a 'plausible *Enthusiasm*, a reasonable *Extasy* and *Transport*' (*C* 2. 104).[61] A subject lacking taste, and in the grip of the luxury made possible by new wealth, not only floats free from the formal constraints of the social strata he was born into, but is also unproductive. Shaftesbury evokes conscience and taste, then, to call the subject back to his true social position and rightful form of activity. Without action and work, '*the Body* languishes, and is oppress'd' (*C* 1. 252).

Expanding upon his view of work, Shaftesbury makes distinctions between the kinds of employment appropriate for different people. Those with good breeding and inherited wealth are neither suited to, nor obliged to take, the rougher occupations, but must still find 'something of fit and proper Imployment' (*C* 1. 253) to keep them from 'Disorder of the Passions' (*C* 1. 254). Raised with a '*Liberal Education*' (*C* 1. 220), the aristocrat should turn his attentions to 'Letters, Sciences, Arts, Husbandry, publick Affairs, Oeconomy, or the like' (*C* 1. 254) – diversions appropriate to his station. The noble is not born with an impeccable sensibility, but perfects his taste with effort and pains, 'strict Attention, and repeated Check' (*C* 1. 210). Everyone, theoretically, can accomplish the aristocrat's level of sophistication, but in practice only he has the freedom to properly foster his taste. The lower orders, it follows, must settle with their assigned roles. The newly moneyed, Shaftesbury cautions, do not have the highly developed taste that will allow them to safely enjoy wealth, and the general population must be reined in by its betters.

The threat for Wordsworth is the growing literary marketplace rather than new money. He argues that the experimentation characterising *Lyrical Ballads* derives in part from a desire to 'give a full account of the present state of the public taste in this country, and to determine how far this taste is healthy or depraved' (*PrW* 1. 120). This could not be acheived 'without pointing out, in what manner language and the human mind act and react on each other, and without retracing the revolutions not only of literature alone but likewise of society itself' (*PrW* 1. 120). The revolutionary dimension of the Preface lies in the authority it places in plain language – the kind of language believed to be untouched by commerce, luxury or vice. McGann contends that for Wordsworth 'the debasement of contemporary culture represents a falling away from a natural condition of "organic" healthfulness'.[62] By thus presenting the state of literature and the state of society as somehow interdependent, and subsuming this interdependence beneath the umbrella term *taste*, Wordsworth 'is implicitly arguing that the eighteenth century's traditions of sensibility are in themselves "healthful"'.[63] As counter-intuitive as it seems, the phrase 'rustic language' aligns Wordsworth's poetry with eighteenth-century aesthetics and, among other things, Shaftesbury's virtuous and disinterested citizen. For all Wordsworth's insistence on being an ordinary man speaking to men, he also claims to be 'possessed of more than usual *organic* sensibility' (*PrW* 1. 126; my italics) – that is, the owner of a 'gentlemanly' sensibility unadulterated, and uninfluenced, by contemporary culture's passing fashions.

Bourdieu constructs the philosophical pronouncements of Romanticism in both Britain and Continental Europe as, in part, a response to the 'development of a veritable culture industry'.[64] Wordsworth is himself acutely aware of the competition facing his work:

> . . . the increasing accumulation of men in cities, where the uniformity of their occupations produces a craving for extraordinary incident which the rapid communication of intelligence hourly gratifies. To this tendency of life and manners the literature and theatrical exhibitions of the country have conformed themselves. The invaluable works of Shakespear and Milton are driven into neglect by the frantic novels, sickly and stupid German Tragedies, and deluges of idle and extravagant stories in verse (*PrW* 1. 128).

The problem, as he sees it, is the explosion of mass literacy, and its accompanying culture of journalism and 'popular' literature. In Bourdieu's terms, there is only one way to respond to the situation: Wordsworth must ignore the economic imperative by which success in the domain of mass culture is measured.[65] He has to separate *Lyrical Ballads* from such an economy, and generate another form of capital in a necessary but also strategic refusal to regard his writing as simply one commodity among others in the cultural marketplace. In form a disinterested – or Shaftesburean – meditation on poetics, the Preface is also deeply invested in the benefits of presenting Wordsworth's verse as above and beyond commerce.[66] Wordsworth both brandishes the word *taste* in order to assert the gentlemanly purity and refinement of his labours and, at the same time, firmly distinguishes his work from the products of popular printing presses and his other literary rivals. Constructing *Lyrical Ballads* as polite and independent, Wordsworth politely claims his independence from commerce *and* Shaftesbureanism, all the while quietly harnessing the conflicting values (and sentiments) of trade and civic humanist aesthetics. Wordsworth turns to his advantage one of the most reactionary areas of the Whig's thinking – his reflections on taste – and thus extends the 'empire' of his art (*PrW* 1. 141). From now on, poetry will no longer have to esteem regulated feeling to the exclusion of the 'vulgar' sensations associated with the marketplace. Open to the full spectrum of affect, the poet can bring the passions into dramatic, and critical, dialogue with one another.

Each philosophical or theological scruple of *An Inquiry* is designed to bolster the Whig social order. New bourgeois wealth is demonised, the role of the civic humanist elite celebrated (as only the leisured can be truly virtuous), and the subjection of the lower orders to the law of their social superiors is justified. Without adequate time for taste, the masses have to be coerced into an acceptance of their lot through the spectacle of law:

> For in the Publick Executions of the greatest Villains, we see generally that the Infamy and Odiousness of their Crime, and Shame of it before Mankind, contribute more to their Misery than all besides; and that it is not the immediate Pain, or Death it-self, which raises so much of Horrour either in the Sufferers or Spectators, as that ignominious kind of Death which is inflicted for Publick Crimes, and Violations of Justice and Humanity (*C* 1. 220).

Shaftesbury believes that the villain is improved by the realisation that he has acted against society and, by extension, the natural law of God. The worker must be terrified into obedience by state displays of violence, whereas the aristocrat's feeling for justice and humanity is cultivated in the liberty of his library. The casual acceptance of the use of violence in the above passage reveals the true nature of Shaftesbury's thinking. *The Inquiry* is a complex reworking, in the new language of Sensibility, of an endangered ruling elite's right to govern. The paradoxical, at times frantic, ideology of taste it outlines – the 'universally available' property of the few – is at once its most dynamic and most problematic gift to later Whig aesthetics. In the next chapter, it will be seen that the contradictions latent in Shaftesbury's aesthetics surface dramatically in Edmund Burke. Maintaining close contact with his civic humanist heritage, Wordsworth seizes upon this further elaboration of the possibilities of Whig affect to propel his most innovative poetics.

2
Burke, Wordsworth and the Poet

In order to police feeling and maintain social order, Shaftesbury inclined towards a notion of taste that was shared by his peers through tacit, 'intuitive', class understanding. As the eighteenth century progressed, however, Whig aestheticians sought to put the regulation of affect onto a more transparent footing. Hume, Gerard and Burke, among others, demanded greater rigour of the philosophical discourse on aesthetics, and even suggested that the task required experts who specialised in the discipline – critics. This work of clarification revealed significant problems with the Whig project, but it also provided Wordsworth with added opportunity and material for his study of affect.

This chapter explores how thinkers in the second half of the eighteenth century addressed the increasingly unworkable knots in Whig aesthetics – the contradictory claim that feeling is both healthy and poisonous, in particular – by constructing taste as an *institution* rather than the function of an accident of breeding. If this tactic promised to bring greater precision to a cloudy term, the resort to specialists conflicted with Shaftesbury's devotion to the disinterested gentleman, the elegant Whig embodiment of the non-specialist. Edmund Burke's attempts to balance Shaftesburean reservations about expertise (such as its bourgeois provenance, lack of organicism and tendency towards enthusiasm) with calls for a more abstract aesthetics often led to anguished intellectual gymnastics. Indeed, what Ian Haywood calls Burke's 'longstanding fascination with political violence' frequently brought him to the exploration of affects far too impolite to have detained Shaftesbury.[1] Although primarily concerned with providing an overview of Burke's aesthetics that will seed discussion of Wordsworth in the rest of the book, this chapter also draws out some of the political implications of the poet's peculiar reception of Whig philosophy after Shaftesbury. In *The Borderers, Letter to the Bishop of*

Llandaff and *The Convention of Cintra*, Wordsworth (pragmatically) annexes Burke's objections to theory and the individual, and praise of custom and tradition, for his own 'affective analysis' of contemporary politics. Having already elaborated a dialectical reading of Shaftesburean affect, he finds in Burke's *Philosophical Enquiry into the Origin of our Ideas of the Sublime and Beautiful* a spectacular new terrain of feelings with which he will come to question and, perhaps, escape the restrictive dogmas of both Whigs and republicans. Moreover, by way of Gerard and Burke, Wordsworth begins to discern – or at least is professionally invested in suggesting – that the Poet has a special role in advancing the critical aspects of affect.

I

The idea of taste in the eighteenth century is so widespread that it can be seen as general cultural currency. Ernest Tuveson argues that it is not just one of the most important terms in Shaftesbury's work, but 'a key word of the age itself'.[2] Shaun Irlam suggests that 'taste establishes itself as a badge of class membership', that it is 'what completes [a] man, confers upon him "manhood" or, in a tradition of classical humanism, humanity itself'.[3] For Barrell, the discourse of civic humanism within which theories of *taste* were expounded 'was the most authoritative fantasy of masculinity in early eighteenth century Britain'.[4] Luxury and effeminacy were to be regulated by the class and gender distinctions established through the debate on taste.[5] Indeed, it is the gentlemanly labour required to discuss what counts as taste, rather than the effeminacy implicit in subjection to a finalised definition, that gives the discourse of taste its strength, albeit a precarious one.

In his 1757 essay, 'Of the Standard of Taste', Hume writes that 'It is natural for us to seek a *Standard of Taste*; a rule by which the various sentiments of men may be reconciled; at least a decision afforded confirming one sentiment, and condemning another'.[6] There is an acknowledged need for better agreement about this commonly used term. For Hume, taste can only be defined by appeal to its culturally accepted meaning:

> Wherever you can ascertain a delicacy of taste, it is sure to meet with approbation; and the best way of ascertaining it is, to appeal to those models and principles which have been established by the uniform consent and experience of nations and ages.[7]

Hume, like Shaftesbury, contends that taste is available to everyone and can be cultivated, 'as nothing tends to increase and improve this talent, than *practice*.[8] In fact, he is more insistent than Shaftesbury on the objectivity of taste. For Hume, taste is ultimately concerned with the disinterested study of fine art, and the subject with good taste needs to 'forget, if possible, . . . individual being, and . . . peculiar circumstances'.[9] In order to understand creations of the past, the subject has to cast off the manners and ideas of his age, and become as open to the work as possible, 'for prejudice is destructive of sound judgement, and perverts all operations of the intellectual faculties'.[10] Hume's prescriptive essay reveals the central role taken by taste in debates about social cohesion, and signals the relocation of the judgement of taste from the private conscience of the Shaftesburean gentleman to the more public 'institution' of criticism. The multitude of full-length studies on aesthetics in the period placed great stress on the public dimension of taste, and it is to some of these I now turn.

Shaftesbury's already considerable reputation within Britain was enhanced by a number of his students, among them Alexander Gerard.[11] Gerard takes up the main threads of Shaftesburean aesthetics, but in a form modified by his reading of Hume. In *An Essay on Taste* (1759), Gerard agrees with Shaftesbury and Hume that taste 'derives its origin from certain powers natural to the mind' (*ET* 1). At first, taste is crude, but 'Every exertion of it, if properly applied, wears off some defect, corrects some inaccuracy, strengthens some of its principles', polishes it (*ET* 92). Good taste, by definition henceforth, 'supposes not only *culture*, but culture *judiciously applied*' (*ET* 96). Like Shaftesbury, Gerard makes good taste universally attainable, but limits access to those with the leisure to develop it adequately:

> Many, by being confined to incessant labour for the necessities of life, or by being engaged in pursuits which give all their thoughts a different direction, are prevented from ever bestowing the smallest attention on productions in the fine arts; in many, taste has not received sufficient culture by education, practice and reflection, in many its native relish has been perverted by prejudices, by injudicious imitation, wrong habits, corruption of manners, and the like . . . (*ET* 226).

Yet Gerard diverges from Shaftesbury in his opinion on the relationship between taste and virtue. Gerard sees no direct connection between the two: 'a careful examination of the moral faculty, would probably lead us to derive it from other principles than those from which taste has been explained' (*ET* 189). Taste may be innate, but it is by no means necessary to virtue. Indeed, it is difficult for Gerard to say what taste actually is. Admittedly, Shaftesbury only implies that there is a definition of taste: he does not actually produce it. Gerard, by contrast, denies the possibility of a definition. Like Hume, he describes how taste is fostered, privileging practice over description, ultimately viewing it as a bridge between mind and world. It is 'something internal, . . . derived from general principles of human nature' yet remaining almost imperceptible (*ET* 220). It has no qualities of its own, but mediates between the subject and aesthetic experience. Thus, where Shaftesbury hints at what good taste would amount to, Gerard readily obscures access to it. Aesthetic experience cannot act as a neutral vantage point from which to examine taste as, in Gerard, 'aesthetic experience is already figured by taste'.[12]

Through taste, 'The mind receives pleasure or pain, not only from the impulse of external objects, but also from the consciousness of its own operations and dispositions' (*ET* 1).[13] While it enables the mind to reflect upon its motions, taste is not itself available for study. Indeed, Gerard's notion of taste departs from Shaftesbury in other ways. Gerard's thought has much in common with that of Adam Smith: taste is 'subject to the law of *habit*', but it 'derives its efficacy solely from the force of custom' (*ET* 92).[14] *Habit* is familiar from Akenside, but the term *custom* implies a more generous model of society than the very carefully delineated notion of sociability in Shaftesbury. The subject who believes that, through attention and habit, he has good taste will not pronounce upon a work of art 'without waiting for the public suffrage' (*ET* 239). The beautiful is that which pleases generally, and must be authorised by the consensus of others.

Gerard looks to specialised critics to say what does and does not comply with good taste, rather than bow to the dictates of an aristocratic elite. The critic devotes himself to questions of the aesthetic and can therefore be said to have improved his taste to the fullest degree, through hard graft. Trained to feel more acutely than others, he takes 'the lead in pronouncing concerning works of taste' (*ET* 245). Experience and the sheer weight of concentrated effort are finally the qualifications required, as 'moderate difficulty gives higher pleasure than facility' (*ET* 260). It is only the critic prepared to take the necessary time who reaps the rewards that such demanding objects can bestow. Thus, everyone can enjoy works of taste on their own terms, but only the community of dedicated critics can make judgements. There is some evidence for seeing Gerard (as well as Shaftesbury) behind Wordsworth's assertion in the Preface that poets are 'possessed of more than usual organic sensibility'.[15] In Wordsworth, the Poet, like Gerard's critic, has 'thought long and deeply' in order to refine his taste, perfect his craft and possibly even be seen as a professional (*PrW* 1. 126).

Such ideas about the specialist status of the Poet in the period have received considerable attention. Clifford Siskin, for one, sees the Preface not only as a declaration that the Poet has a unique role in national life but also as symptomatic of a change in eighteenth-century social and economic organisation – namely, the increase of specialisation. Despite its appeal to the Poet's organic affections, for Siskin the Preface is a document of the division of intellectual and manual labour. Calling for a 'natural' poetics, Wordsworth 'naturalises', or mystifies, the balkanisation of work by in fact redescribing writing as a specialist field.[16] Through a perverse logic, 'disciplinarity became the proper path to truth, professionalism became an unavoidable product of economic development, and the selection we know as Literature became the transcendent output of the human imagination'.[17] Having made the Shaftesburean claim that the Poet is a disinterested non-specialist, Wordsworth now 'valoriz[es] literature',[18] and poetry specifically, as the primary, or unifying, discipline, 'the breath and finer spirit of all knowledge' (*PrW* 1. 141). Furthermore, his enquiry into 'that sort of pleasure and that quantity of pleasure [that] may be imparted' by poetry draws upon, as shall be seen in the next chapter, Burke's idea that local affections, bonds of love and pleasure, are naturally extended to constitute national unity (*PrW* 1. 118). Poetry comes to be regarded as a deep space in which all thought and feeling is gathered up into a unified and implicitly national representation of community. Radically enlarging the scope of his art of feeling, Wordsworth ambitiously offers himself, in the specialist role of National Poet, as the fulfilment of Literature's grand purpose.[19]

Wordsworth, his poetry and his readership create the conditions for harmonious community. The Preface, then, makes a case for the qualities that separate the Poet from getting and spending while also appealing to his professional vocation. Politely representative of Britain, and consequently of political significance, he is also permitted the specialist's licence to *fathom 'improper' experience*. Suggesting that the Poet has a contract with the reader – he is an expert, the reader a client (*PrW* 1. 122) – Wordsworth brings Shaftesbury's aristocratic emphasis on the importance of self-regulation and Akenside's promotion of habitual attendance to 'natural' objects into line with the eighteenth century's middle-class accent on professionalism and more official consensus. Wordsworth thus again unfastens eighteenth-century aesthetics from its social and political origins, and opens it to possibilities it would once have wished to close down.

Although his mediated reception of the Whig civic humanist tradition of thought on affection allows him to democratise poetry for bourgeois practice, Wordsworth remains true enough to the spirit of Shaftesbury to endeavour to curtail the full potential of such a move:

> while Wordsworth claims to have what is in effect special expertise earned through a specialised training process, he also tries to mitigate the kind of 'rationalisation' or specialised division of labor . . . associate[d] with professional projects.[20]

For Shaftesbury, the universal is all, and he only endorses that which offers 'true *Resignation*, or Submission to the Rule and Order of THE DEITY' (*C* 1. 127). The private zealotry he finds behind specialisation is allowed no place in his thought. He requires that 'a whole Species of Animals contribute to the Existence or Well-being of some other' – particularity only being valuable if one participates in God's harmonious totality (*C* 1. 198). In conformity with Shaftesbury, Wordsworth's Preface therefore takes pains to resolve the contrary demands of professionalism and universality. It is not until *The Prelude*, though, that Wordsworth devotes his full energies to synthesising these antithetical demands.[21]

While Shaftesbury promotes refined nobles as the council of taste, Gerard separates taste from questions of ethics through his conception of a professional community. This apparent de-politicisation of aesthetics makes taste and the affective experience it regulates accessible to the middle classes, such as Wordsworth, that Shaftesbury and other Whig civic humanist writers suspected.[22] However, Gerard's dismissal of a theoretical grounding for taste implies an awareness of the ideological tensions that inhabit its status as both universal and given to hierarchy. While the need for a definition of taste is undisputed, the failure of taste to adequately embody the regulation its own ideology requires is feared. The political dimension to this wariness of theory is clear in the work of arguably the most important eighteenth-century aesthetician, and the single greatest Whig influence on Wordsworth – Edmund Burke.

II

For all his efforts to situate Burke in the context of eighteenth-century aesthetics, J. T. Boulton stresses that Burke was to a degree 'isolated in his originality and boldness' (*PE* xxxii).[23] He and Gerard were contemporaries, but 'Gerard's *Essay on Taste* appeared too late to influence the *Enquiry'*, which had been published two years earlier in 1757 (*PE* xxxiii). Boulton does propose, however, that because of his opposition in the *Enquiry* to some of Hutcheson's ideas, Burke later read Gerard's *Essay* appreciatively, albeit 'with some scepticism' (*PE* xxxiii). Nevertheless, although it did not immediately make 'a major contribution to contemporary discussion', Burke's text reprises many of the themes dominating aesthetics in the middle of the eighteenth century – especially the interest in taste (*PE* xxx). Boulton even argues that 'it may have been to oppose Hume's views on taste that Burke's "Essay" [the "Introduction on Taste" at the beginning of the 1759 second edition of the *Enquiry*] was written' (*PE* xxviii–xxix). The *Enquiry*, then, engages directly with the work of Hume. F. P. Lock contends, furthermore, that Burke's definition of beauty as 'Variety and uniformity' in a 1744 letter to Richard Shackleton demonstrates an intimate acquaintance with Hutcheson, Shaftesbury and the British aesthetic tradition in general.[24]

The 'Introduction on Taste' announces itself as the latest in a series of eighteenth-century attempts to establish aesthetic judgement as a universally innate human capacity:

> . . . it is probable that the standard both of reason and Taste is the same in all human creatures. For if there were not some principles of judgement as well as of sentiment common to all mankind, no hold could possibly be taken either on their reason or their passions, sufficient to maintain the ordinary correspondence of life (*PE* 11).

From the outset, Burke regards the rational and the aesthetic as socially significant: their universality binds the otherwise disparate elements of society. Reason, taste, and sentiment almost seem to precede the social for Burke, in fact, being the condition of possibility of society and communication itself. The same could, perhaps, be said of Wordsworth, who in the Preface predicates communication between himself and the reader on his ability to impart pleasure (*PrW* 1. 118).

Burke asks himself why a philosophical enquiry into the idea of the aesthetic is necessary if it is, apparently, impossible; and he acknowledges the paradoxical nature and seeming redundancy of his enterprise by stating that the failure to properly appreciate the full importance of the aesthetic might make his *Enquiry* seem a 'useless, if not an absurd undertaking, [a fabrication of] . . . rules for caprice, [the legislation] . . . of whims and fancies' (*PE* 12). Still, the entire project is justified by the need to prove that Taste is *natural*, and that a more formal approach to aesthetic, and by extension social, questions is inappropriate.

For Jean-Francois Lyotard, Burke's *Enquiry* reflects a change in the function of the aesthetic in the late eighteenth-century. As a consequence of the decline of the artistic patronage of both Church and state in the period, 'the artist ceases to be guided by a culture which made him the sender and master of a message of glory: he becomes, insofar as he is a genius, the involuntary addressee of an inspiration come to him from an "I know not what"'.[25] In the period's reformulation of the question put to an artwork, from '"How does one make a work of art?", . . . [to] "What is it to experience an affect proper to art?"', Lyotard identifies an epistemological shift.[26] But Bourdieu avers that the artist's altered role in the eighteenth century necessitates a 'process of differentiation', that the advent of theoretical reflection in the field of art is due solely to the pressures imposed by entry into 'an anonymous market'.[27] Despite his thesis that the eighteenth century marks a transformation in the concept of the aesthetic, Lyotard's thinking remains blinkered by too great a fixation on the epistemological aspects of aesthetic experience. A new emphasis is placed upon sensation in art at this time – and is obviously vital to Burke's text (and Wordsworth's poetry) – but Lyotard is mistaken to suggest that the concern with aesthetic autonomy that arises with the end of patronage and the beginning of professionalisation replaces 'didactic forms' of art with a-social and disinterested philosophical aesthetics.[28] The abstruse flights of Burke's work on universalism and sensationism 'reproduce the prior differentiation of the social structures in the initial abstraction by which they are constituted'.[29] The *Enquiry* is marked, at all levels, by the political: its own abstraction corresponds to that of the social sphere.[30] Indeed, the eighteenth-century obsession with sensation might be regarded as a response to the impoverishment of experience that accompanies the advent of modernity. Wordsworth's work, as I propose in the next chapter and the remainder of this study, is both indebted to eighteenth-century aesthetics and an exploration of what might be called its 'repressed' – fears about both certain kinds of affect and a general withering of feeling, for instance.

Reinforcing his 'common-sense' stance, Burke argues that 'A definition may be exact, and yet go but a very little way towards informing us of the nature of the thing defined' (*PE* 12). The only way to know an object, without the interference of theory, is to register the impact it has on the body, the senses:

> We do and must suppose, that as the conformation of their organs are nearly, or altogether the same in all men, so the manner of perceiving external objects is in all men the same, with little difference.

> We are satisfied that what appears light to one eye, appears light to another; that what appears dark and bitter to this man, is likewise dark and bitter to that . . . (*PE* 13).

Affect is the single guarantee of shared experience: 'the pleasures and pains which every object excites in one man, it must raise in all mankind' (*PE* 13). This insistence on the truth of feeling effectively discredits anything that cannot be 'proved' through recourse to the senses. Ideas are disarmed and rejected as without content or foundation, and thus taste is erected as the final judge of truth. However, the *Enquiry* does exhibit anxieties about the slippage of sensation into luxury already familiar from Shaftesbury. William Galperin even suggests that the bodily and 'profane burlesque' that is the Revolutionary mob in the *Reflections* is a return of anxieties about bodily feeling in Burke's earlier aesthetics (*R* 161). The perverse body of the mob becomes the National Assembly, 'an *institution* of the profane' – an horrific legislature comprised of the sensually corrupt.[31]

III

As the political implications of Burke's aesthetics become plain, so do some of the stresses underlying his thinking about affect. He reiterates the idea that physical sensation is shared by all, and that pleasant sensations are the foundation of sociability:

> Pleasure of every kind quickly satisfies; and when it is over, we relapse into indifference, or rather we fall into a soft tranquillity, which is tinged with the agreeable colour of the former sensation (*PE* 34).

There is a sexual aspect to this description of pleasure and feeling good, but Burke's focus on the mimetic element harboured in his sensationist, affective, aesthetics is more important because it reveals contradictions at the centre of his thinking that will be taken up by Wordsworth's poetics of affect.[32]

In the *Enquiry* there is very little difference between an object and a subject's perception of that object. Frances Ferguson writes that 'Burke's procedure in discussing the sublime and beautiful and our thoughts about them, is to treat mental images first as if they were the *affective* traces of objects and then as if they were objects themselves'.[33] In this way, Burke hopes to resolve the tension between the physical and mental in his aesthetics. He does, however, seek to determine which objects produce pleasurable feelings. The greatest pleasure is derived from society:

> . . . the pleasure of any particular social enjoyment outweighs very considerably the uneasiness caused by the want of that particular enjoyment; so that the strongest sensation, relative to the habitudes of *particular society*, are sensations of pleasure. Good company, lively conversations, and the endearments of friendship, fill the mind with great pleasure . . . (*PE* 43).

Burke's discussion of the pleasure of society soon draws upon his theory of beauty. Good society gives the subject pleasure, thereby generating physical affects, which ultimately demarcates the subject from other subjects and enables him to achieve a degree of independence. Yet the pleasurable appeal of society is subsequently internalised – it becomes an 'innate' assumption, a *second nature* – with the result that the subject automatically sympathises with the feelings of others: 'For sympathy must be considered as a sort of substitution, by which we are put into the place of another man, and affected in many respects as he is affected' (*PE* 44). This aspect of sympathy is articulated in accordance with what Tom Furniss has called Burke's 'aesthetic ideology', and later in the eighteenth century is described by Adam Smith as a powerful form of imaginative sympathy:[34]

> The frame of my body can be but little affected by the alterations which are brought about upon that of my companion: but my imagination is more ductile, and more readily assumes, if I may say so, the shape and configuration of the imaginations of those with whom I am familiar.[35]

A subject sympathises with others using exactly the same faculty requisite for the enjoyment of artworks that 'transfuse their passions from one breast to another, and are often capable of grafting a delight on wretchedness, misery and death itself' (*PE* 44). Taste enables the reception of pleasure (of which art and society are the exemplary causes) and is itself a product of, and unthinkable without, mimetic sensualism – the ability to imagine, and then actually experience, what another, similar, person feels.

In Burke's view, sympathy has a mimetic extension. It 'makes us take a concern in whatever men feel, [and] . . . this affection prompts us to copy whatever they do' (*PE* 49).[36] Imitation affords more pleasure, and has the effect of binding the members of society still closer together. In this respect, Burkean imitation, or mimesis, is very close to Shaftesburean regulation in that it forestalls enthusiasm or an egotistical sublime:

> It is by imitation far more than by precept that we learn every thing; and what we learn thus we acquire not only more effectually, but more pleasantly. This forms our manners, our opinions, our lives (*PE* 49).

However, the discussion of imitation through sympathetic feeling leads Burke in some odd directions, and exposes his difficulty – shared by other civic humanist writers – in moderating the subversive potential of affect and pleasure. In 'Of the effects of TRAGEDY', he suggests that tragedy gives pleasure because it is only an *image* of calamity, 'And indeed in some cases we derive as much or more pleasure from that source than from the thing itself' (*PE* 47). Tragedy obtains its power by portraying terror and suffering realistically, but without actually being real. In effect 'the only vehicle of testimony about the world that Burke admits, sensory experience, has been shown to become duplicitous whenever it develops narrative extension'.[37] Fiction and reality lose their distinctiveness as mimetic sensualism responds vigorously to both.

For the same reason that other eighteenth-century writers attempt to resist the democratising tendencies of taste, Burke is compelled to reassert the difference between the affects of tragedy and reality. He describes a theatre audience:

> . . . just at the moment when their minds are erect with expectation, let it be reported that a state criminal of high rank is on the point of being executed in the adjoining square; in a moment the emptiness of the theatre would demonstrate the comparative weakness of the imitative arts, and proclaim the triumph of the real sympathy (*PE* 47).

Francis Ferguson remarks that the execution puts the spectators in an almost impossible position: it 'calls for . . . emotions on behalf of someone who is, presumably, being executed for having acted with some indifference to such sympathetic response'.[38] For Burke, it is not chiefly sympathy for the criminal that is of importance, but the community of feeling experienced by the spectators before the spectacle of the death.[39] He uses the example of a public execution to differentiate between the authentic sympathy elicited by 'reality' and the deceptive sympathy produced by the theatre – and it has the effect of compromising his argument.[40] Trying to limit the arbitrary production of sympathy, through the stimulus of representation rather than the 'real', he draws upon a case where the entire category of sympathy is erased. Public sympathy at an execution is a function of the criminal's anti-social refusal to modify his actions out of feeling for the general public good. This manifestation of sympathy can only be thought of as contradictory. Sympathy and imitation – mimesis – do not necessarily order society simply and neatly.

Whilst guarding against the 'arbitrary' machinations of theory, Burke seeks authenticity and universality through bodily sensation, only to discover truly binding feeling in the 'prospect of immediate death'.[41] Execution punishes by striking at the affective 'ground' of being, but of course terminates any hope of continued sensual mimesis by inflicting an absolutely unique, unrepeatable, and unrepresentable experience upon an individual – the arbitrariness of death. 'Univocal sensation can be imaged only as a by-product of the total loss of sensation' in a one-off act, which therefore cannot admit habit or allow for mimesis.[42] Sociability depends upon the habitual repetition of sympathy, as second nature, through sensual mimesis, but is founded at the same time upon single, unrepeatable and unfeeling acts. Burke's regulated sensationism, then, incubates a disconcerting contradiction within itself, and this appears as death, the arbitrary itself. Attempting to manage the potentially anarchic affects produced by theatre, Burke thus introduces the suspicion that the beautiful could itself fragment the simple unity it is supposed to establish.

It is the task of the Burkean sublime to discipline the affective immoderation that might be caused by the mimetic operation of the beautiful. Unchecked imitation could lead to social paralysis. Burke writes:

> Although imitation is one of the great instruments used by providence in bringing our nature towards its perfection, yet if men gave themselves up to imitation entirely, and each followed the other, and so on in an eternal circle, it is easy to see that there could never be any improvement among them (*PE*, 50).

To counter his initial worry that sensationist aesthetics might encourage dissipation, Burke now attaches the sublime to the dictates of distinction. *Improvement* in this context means the creation of a civilised society through increased differentiation among men.

What is required is something that authoritatively differentiates a man from his fellows and thereby fosters a productive desire for competition.

Ambition for Burke, *pace* Bourdieu, is the 'passion that drives men to all the ways we see in use of signalising themselves, and that tends to make whatever excites in a man the idea of this distinction so very pleasant' (*PE* 50). Without distinction 'we begin to take a complacency in some singular infirmities, follies, or defects of one kind or another' (*PE* 50). It is complacency that Burke demonises in this passage, and which with his definition of the sublime as something far more powerful than the (mere) sensation of 'swelling and triumph' common to ambition (*PE* 50) he works against.[43] Burke's solution to one problem with feeling tends to create fresh complications.

IV

A Burkean rejection of theory drives the Wordsworth's attack on 'capricious habits of expression' (*PrW* 1. 124) in the Preface and the description of his spiritual crisis in Book 10 of *The Prelude*.[44] But it is in *The Borderers* – discussed shortly – that one sees most clearly how the attack on unfeeling individualism that motivates the anti-theory stance of the *Reflections* impresses the poet.[45]

Burke laments that the French Revolution represents a break with the past, achieved in large part through its fetishisation of cold theory. The end result is a paper constitution that has 'no connection with French history or experience'.[46] He holds that theory is arbitrary, having no grounding in nature. Thus, with some sophistry, Burke shuns the false seduction of 'formal method' publicly in his writing (*R* 60). In *An Appeal from the New to the Old Whigs* (1791), he states that

> Nothing universal can be rationally affirmed on any moral, or any political subject. Pure metaphysical abstraction does not belong to these matters. The lines of morality are not like the ideal lines of mathematics (*OW* 19).

In their commitment to – their enthusiasm for – the 'fanaticism' of Parisian philosophy, the Revolutionaries shun this wisdom (*OW* 99). Their assumption that Revolutionary discourse is 'Adamic', that 'every word is the creation of world',[47] renders them extraordinarily arrogant in their approach to government, and provokes Burke to exclaim: 'I cannot conceive how any man can have brought himself to that pitch of presumption, to consider his country as nothing but *carte blanche*, upon which he may scribble whatever he pleases' (*R* 206). Thought is fallible and its monopoly on political life risks fatal error.[48] A dependence upon reason, without due attention to the lessons of experience, positively encourages the reproduction of old mistakes in new forms:

> Whilst you are discussing fashion, the fashion is gone by. The very same vice assumes a new body. The spirit transmigrates; and, far from losing its principle of life by the change of its appearance, it is renovated in its new organs with the fresh vigour of juvenile activity. It walks abroad; it continues its ravages; whilst you are gibbeting the carcass, or demolishing the tomb (*R* 190).

Practices should precede theories: 'They are not often constructed after theory; theories are rather drawn from them' (*R* 220).

Civil society, in Burke's view, is founded on the surrender of personal rights:

> We are not the converts of Rousseau; we are not the disciples of Voltaire; Helvetius has made no progress amongst us . . . We know that *we* have made no discoveries; and we think that no discoveries are to be made, in morality; nor many in the great principles of government, nor in the ideas of liberty, which were understood long before we were born . . . (*R* 137).

Burke insists that the 'stock in each man is small, and that individuals would be better to avail themselves of the general bank and capital of nations, and of ages' in order to create a civil society (*R* 138). The philosophy of the rights of Man, which drives the Revolution, is therefore unacceptable to Burke. He regards the formulation of a system of rights as a mistake because, as a theoretical invention, it must be arbitrary and without a natural foundation in the affections. The French have given men 'imaginary rights', plucked out of thin air, rights which are the fiction of reason rather than based on the living and breathing truth of experience (*OW* 112).[49] Burke still stands by his claim in the *Enquiry* that 'there is rather less difference upon matters of Taste among mankind, than upon most of those which depend upon the naked reason' (*PE* 24). In this he shows himself to be in agreement with Hume who argued for politics 'as an ongoing dialogue between conservators based on the land and innovators based upon commerce'.[50] Their thinking shaped by civic humanism, Hume and Burke seek to preserve the fine balance between landownership, manners (or sentiment) and commerce that is overseen by the steadying influence of traditional political institutions. Burke interprets the way the French have jettisoned their previous system of government as a disaster, a 'wild attempt to methodise anarchy; to perpetuate and fix disorder' (*OW* 112). The politics of 'reason' will, he predicts, render chaotic the once harmonious interplay of the economy and social order – hardly the conditions for so-called natural rights to flourish.

With its scorn for the past, the French Revolution only allows itself the 'shell and husk of history' (*R* 190) for guidance. Any decisions, as a result, are nothing but the 'chimeras of a monstrous and portentous policy' (*R* 264). They represent an unnatural development, a turn towards that 'which is spurious, fictitious, and false' (*R* 315).[51] Burke sees this wilful entry into the realm of the arbitrary production of meaning as a rejection of Divinely ordained natural order. Reason has revolted against the social organisation that Burke would claim is God's will, and the French Revolution is thus a kind of satanic rebellion against 'the author of our place in the order of existence' (*OW* 121):

[God] has marshalled us by a divine tactick, not according to our will, but according to his, he has, in and by that disposition, virtually subjected us to act the part which belongs to the place assigned us. We have obligations to mankind at large, which are not in consequence of any special voluntary pact. . . . On the contrary, the force of all the pacts which we enter into with any particular person or number of persons amongst mankind, depends upon those prior obligations (*OW* 121).

The French have vainly gone against the divine telos of history, which in Burke's opinion also happens to accord with the improvement that leads to civil society. God's law is a living tradition, whereas the doctrine of the National Assembly is 'a dead letter. Dead and putrid'.[52] The claims Burke makes for his aesthetic, sentimental, vision of nationhood effectively allow him to appear 'to have transcended politics just as he claims to have transcended history'.[53] He contrasts true history with the squalid history managed by men – that of 'pride, ambition, avarice, revenge, lust, sedition, hypocrisy, ungoverned zeal, and all the train of disorderly appetites' (*R* 189).

Burke's critique of the Revolutionists' enthusiasm for theory is central to the portrayal of Rivers in *The Borderers* (1797–9). In his introduction to the play, Wordsworth remarks that 'ch[a]sing a phantom, [Rivers] . . . commits new crimes to drive away the memory of the past'.[54] Through 'extravagant speculations' (p. 66) – as opposed to more preferable 'mild effusions of thought' (p. 64) – Rivers deliberately attacks the 'craft of age' (II. iii. 389) and severs himself from history. With a mind potent enough to 'clothe the shapes of things' (I. ii. 100), he throws off any sympathetic, or mimetic, relationship that would connect him to society and its customs. This callous and 'perverted reason' (p. 67), writes Wordsworth using a Burkean locution, tricks Rivers into error:

> Happy are we
> Who live in these disputed tracts that own
> No law but what each man makes for himself.
> Here justice has indeed a field of triumph (II. i. 52–4)!

Rivers escapes 'the tyranny / of moralists and saints and lawgivers' and embraces 'the immediate law / Flashed from the light of circumstances / Upon an independent intellect' (III. v. 28–9; 31–3). Rather than discover truth, identity and community, however, all he achieves is an illusory, loveless and ultimately criminal freedom: the unmoored and numb 'strangeness' (p. 65) of a nameless patch of land.

V

Despite accepting Burke's critique of reason, Wordsworth does not join the Irishman in full-throated acceptance of Whig ideology. As Lucy Newlyn points out, even in the Burkean critique of the intellectual implicit in the description of Rivers, Wordsworth indentifies with the 'radical intellectual' and 'expands our sympathy by giving Satanic depth and grandeur to Rivers's consciousness'.[55] Wordsworth might launch a Burkean protest against his protagonist's intellectual vanity, yet he still finds Rivers' language 'compelling and persuasive'.[56] Explicit praise of Burke in Wordsworth's writing does not appear until late in his career. In 1850, Wordsworth famously added an explicit homage to the 'Genius of Burke!' to *The Prelude*:[57]

> I see him, old but vigorous in age,
> Stand, like an Oak whose stag-horn branches start
> Out of its leafy brow, the more to awe
> The younger brethren of the grove (7. 519–22).

And he goes so far as to ask himself: how

> Could a Youth, and one
> In ancient story versed, whose breast had heaved
> Under the weight of classic eloquence,
> Sit, see, and hear, unthankful, uninspired? (7. 540–3)

A private letter of 1831 to Benjamin Robert Haydon contains the following expression of support for the views of Burke: 'I am averse (with that wisest of the Moderns Mr Burke) to all hot reformations; i.e. to every sudden change in political institutions.'[58] Wordsworth's 1818 *Address to the Freeholders of Westmoreland* publicly pronounces Burke 'the most sagacious politician of his age . . . Time has verified his predictions; the books remain in which his principles of foreknowledge were laid down' (*PrW* 3. 158).

Indeed, it seems remarkable that Wordsworth would endorse Burkean views at all when one recalls that in the unpublished *Letter to the Bishop of Llandaff* (1793), he states that

> Mr Burke rouzed the indignation of all ranks of men, when by a refinement in cruelty superiour to that which in the East yokes the living to the dead he strove to persuade us that we and our posterity to the end of time were riveted to a constitution by the indisoluble compact of a dead parchment, and were bound to cherish a corse at the bosom, when reason might call aloud that it should be entombed (*PrW* 1. 48).

The poet condemns Burke's allegiance to what he regards as deadening tradition. Whereas Burke sees tradition as a vehicle in which 'the goods of fortune, the gifts of Providence are handed down, to us', Wordsworth judges it a prison (*R* 84). He even goes on to associate tradition with the principle of primogeniture that keeps the status quo in place. He believes that oppression can often be traced to economic roots, and asserts that the republican legislator

> will banish from his code all laws such as the unnatural monster of primogeniture, such as encourage associations against labour in the form of corporate bodies, and indeed all that monopolising system of legislation whose baleful influence is shewn in the depopulation of the country and in the necessity which reduces the sad relicks to owe their very existence to the ostentatious bounty of their oppressors (*PrW* 1. 43).

In Wordsworth's view, Burke's politics endorse an economic disparity that is shored up by a conservative ideology of tradition and charity.

Yet notwithstanding its vocal republicanism and direct attack on Burke, the critical approach of the *Letter* sometimes also appears to derive from an agenda informed by Whiggism. Burke's primary dispute with the revolutionists in France is that their 'mechanic philosophy' – as opposed to the sensual, fecund and organic tradition he would promote – gives them a form of government that has no roots, and exercises 'arbitrary power' (*R* 129; 86). 'Arbitrary power' is a phrase often found in republican tracts, of course, but usually in a context disparaging of despotic monarchies. The monarch was thought to have no qualification for rule, other than the blood in his veins, and was held by radicals like Paine to be the figurehead of a corrupt system that 'supported a host of titles, honours and privileges, and rejoiced in creating artificial and unjust distinctions between men who were naturally equal'.[59] When Wordsworth shows his allegiance to the Revolution by arguing that it seeks 'to destroy arbitrary power and to erect a temple to liberty on its ruins', it is reasonable to surmise that he is taking a thoroughly republican stance (*PrW* 1. 35). But the proximity of terminology allows republicanism easily to mutate into Burkeanism, and vice versa. The existence of a Whig 'republican' tradition, furthermore, means that the revolution controversy can often be read as a complex and tangled debate between Whig 'republicans' and defenders of French republicanism.

Burke would be the first to separate the (arbitrary) person from the office of the monarch, insisting that kingship is strengthened by the very fact that it cannot be undermined by any one individual – that the person of the monarch is ultimately the *function* of tradition. In the *Letter*, Wordsworth claims that the French king found himself in a 'monstrous situation that rendered him unaccountable before a human tribunal' (*PrW* 1. 32). At this point, Wordsworth appears to be expressing an opinion compatible with Whig opposition to absolute monarchy. While Whigs agreed that the sovereign was not a divine appointment, Mark Philp points out that

> a range of writers on politics whom we see as republican saw no difficulty in characterising some states with monarchs as republics. For example, the popular definition [of republicanism] was frequently ignored in Britain by post-Restoration political theorists, many of whom believed that a mixed government, involving the combined rule of king, nobility and commons, was not just a form of, but the best form of republican government.[60]

As Whiggism and republicanism are inchoate and entwined ideologies, it is difficult to separate Wordsworth's republicanism from his Whig attitudes. He makes the claim that the situation, and background, of the person of the monarch 'precludes him from attaining even a moderate knowledge of common life and from feeling a particular share in the interests of mankind' (*PrW* 1. 33). It appears here that secreted within Wordsworth's republicanism is an assumption about the importance of *familiarity* – in this case, the (sentimental) familiarity of a monarch with his people – an idea derived from the Whig civic humanist politics of affection. At its very origin, Wordsworth's republicanism is well disposed to an eighteenth-century notion of affection traceable to Shaftesbury and narrowed by Burke to primarily mean tradition.

To return again briefly to *The Borderers*, 'On the Character of Rivers', the introduction to the play, repeatedly describes the protagonist's rationalism as a bad habit. To propose that habit (a key term in Burke's writing) can be harmful suggests that Wordsworth retains a significant amount of independence from the Whig philosophy he draws upon. Indeed, by distinguishing between 'good' and 'bad' habit, Wordsworth injects a remarkable elasticity into Burke's ideas.

This reading of Burke reappears a few years later in 'Ode: Intimations of Immortality' (1802–4). Wordsworth describes life as the deadening accumulation of habit: 'earthly freight, / And custom lie upon thee with a weight, / Heavy as frost' (129–31).[61] James Chandler asserts that although the 'Ode' regards superficial habits as an impasse, it subscribes to Burke's ontology of deep 'habit-based early sentiment', or second nature.[62] Wordsworth substitutes superficial, albeit profoundly damaging, habits with the habitual sentiments that form the self, 'Thoughts that do often lie too deep for tears' (206). However, the association of what Chandler identifies as Burkean second nature with tears – even if only to say that it is *beyond* tears – makes such a claim overly neat. Paul Hamilton conjectures (after Coleridge) that a poem's meaning is its afterlife of often violently opposed interpretations, its 'self-destroying perpetuation' among readers.[63] Rather than a paean to second nature, then, the 'Ode' might be understood as a poem that uses Burke to counter earthly habit while refusing an uncritical commitment to Burke's sentimental ideology of second nature.[64]

The Convention of Cintra (1809) is similarly 'pragmatic' in its adoption of Burkeanism. Expressing his belief that the people of Spain can survive their current occupation by Napoleon, Wordsworth writes:

we estimated *their* character with partial and indulgent fondness; – thinking on their past greatness, not as the undermined foundation of a magnificent building, but as the root of a majestic tree recovered from a long disease, and beginning again to flourish with promise of wider branches and a deeper shade than it had boasted in the fullness of its strength. (*PrW* 1. 228)

Wordsworth's metaphor suggests that a nation's past, its felt sense of tradition, nourishes the present – that the present is organically related to the past. Like a tree, a nation has roots, which make future growth possible and provide a foundation that ensures continuity through time.

According to Tim Fulford, since Locke had 'used the oak to illustrate organic unity . . . Oaks' longevity, rootedness and strength made them suitable emblems for writers who portrayed an ancient constitution secured in the heritable property of land and capable of gradual change as a growth of English soil'.[65] In the 1790s, Edmund Burke revived this image, and 'depicted Britain's form of government as tree-like, of ancient growth'.[66] He likened the people to 'great cattle reposed beneath the shadow of the British oak' (*R* 181). Wordsworth not only employs the figure of the oak, but also assumes Burke's Whig civic humanist ideology of affection and sympathy. He calls for 'the reception and establishment of that knowledge which is founded not upon things but upon sensations; – sensations which are general, and under general influences' (*PrW* 1. 304–5). He even agrees with Burke's insistence in the *Reflections* that

> To be attached to the subdivision, to love the little platoon we belong to in society, is the first principle (the germ as it were) of public affections. It is the first link in the series by which we proceed towards a love of our country and to mankind (*R* 97–8).

Like Burke, Wordsworth believes that nations are founded on local affections writ large. However, if Burke for the most part emphasises the institutions and national customs that unite a country, Wordsworth focuses on people, arguing that nations are 'nothing but aggregates of individuals' bound by 'dispositions of *love*' (*PrW* 1. 267; italics mine).[67] Wordsworth thus agrees with Burke's emphasis on the importance of affection, but makes it available for a more capacious politics.[68]

Wordsworth employs Burke to make an essentially republican point. The result is a blend of Burke and republicanism that, in effect, liberates what is usually suppressed in Whig civic humanist thinking for Wordsworth's critical purposes. In Burkean vein, *The Convention* directly attacks political systems that are founded on theoretical principles. Wordsworth regards the Spanish people's retention of their traditions and culture

> as more human – more social – and therefore as wiser, and of better omen, than if they had stood forth the zealots of abstract principles drawn out of the laboratory of unfeeling philosophists (*PrW* 1. 229).

He concurs with Burke's 'prophetic' warning against the theory-led 'reverses of the French Revolution' (*PrW* 1. 229), and makes a classic civic humanist 'gesture of freedom against the constraints of form and system' – against specialisation, in other words.[69] After Burke (and Shaftesbury), Wordsworth associates theory with the vanity of excessively powerful individuals who, dangerously cut off from affection, people and tradition, 'assume too much credit to themselves' (*PrW* 1. 305). Careerist statesmen, 'contending ambitiously for the rewards and honours of government, are separated from the mass of society to which they belong' (*PrW* 1. 305). A politics that is not naturally felt is made up of 'abstract principles', which have to be taught (*R* 174); and, in Wordsworth's opinion, 'the tendency of such education [is] to warp' (*PrW* 1. 305). Wordsworth's denigration of theory and individualism, and his praise for the regulatory influence of organic and sympathetic affection, certainly marks him out as Burkean. Significantly, though, the poet criticises theory in the name of *ordinary* Spanish people and their way of life rather than as a supporter of monarchy, the Church and established wealth.

Intermixed with his celebration of tradition, in parts of *The Convention* Wordsworth's interest also lands on affects no Whig would sanction. His admiration for trans-individual customs and rituals once again partially assents to Burke's vision of a nation bound by tradition and fellow feeling:

> the visible and familiar occurrences of daily life in every town and village; the patient curiosity and contagious acclamations of the multitude in the streets of the city and within the walls of the theatre; a procession, or a rural dance; a hunting, or a horse-race; a flood, or a fire; rejoicing and ringing of bells for an unexpected gift of good fortune, or the coming of a foolish heir to his estate; – these demonstrate incontestably that the passions of men (I mean, the soul of sensibility in the heart of man) . . . do immeasurably transcend their objects (*PrW* 1. 244).

Nevertheless, the above passage is fascinated by the same enthusiastic transports that greatly trouble Burke. This 'poetic' section of the *Convention* (focussing on theatre, processions, dance, games and music) co-opts Burkean traditionalism and nationalism for the republican cause, and recognises that passion can extend the political reach and constituency of affect. Wordsworth bestows a patrician regard upon affect in the manner of Shaftesbury and Burke, but also delights in the way it can be used to increase the happiness of the wider population.

Drawing heavily on Whig aesthetic ideology, yet equally admiring of the 'excesses' of affect that eighteenth-century aestheticians so feared, Wordsworth is a middle-class poet compelled to assert his professional autonomy in a competitive marketplace. Although he nurtures the civic humanist gentleman's misgivings about the specialist, he also brandishes his professional status in order to pursue otherwise prohibited feelings. Changes in the economic situation of poets, along with the profound entanglement of eighteenth-century Whiggism and republicanism, enable Wordsworth to take an extraordinarily independent-minded stance towards politics. The next chapter explores the poetic licence Wordsworth takes with the Shaftesburean and Burkean discourses to which he owes a large part of his freedom.

3
Poetry and the Liberty of Feeling

If the *Enquiry*'s attempt to provide a philosophical ground for taste is intricately bound up with an attack on reason, Burke's theory of language exposes additional contradictions in his work. Identifying language as one of the main repositories of the affective associations that underpin national tradition (along with the Church and monarchy, for example), he opposes republican efforts to establish just representation and rational debate by purging political discourse of emotion – its mimetic, or poetic, elements. In effect, dismissing republican language as a cold and arid calculus that is divorced from reality, Burke claims for his own discourse a close proximity to natural feeling. Yet, as he affirms the importance of the affective content of his politics – by extolling verse in the *Enquiry* and composing what amounts to prose poetry in key sections of *Reflections on the Revolution in France* – Burke reveals that the positional (rationalist, synthetic, a-historical) and mimetic (feeling, real, traditional) components of language are entwined. At significant moments, his writing neither conserves, restores nor reflects feeling, but *produces* – that is, 'unnaturally' posits – the emotions he claims to find.[1] Hoping that poetic language will provide a secure ground for his traditionalism, Burke becomes in fact less traditionalist than 'visionary'. Rather than augment affectionate links with the past, his own poetic language invents affects that it wishfully projects onto the past, thereby rendering his conservative view of the future (and its ties to the past) a fantasy.

This chapter contends that although Burke would suppress the role of positional language (and the thought and feeling it makes possible) in his writing,[2] he cannot conjure it away. What he does do, however, is attempt to smother it beneath increasingly hysterical assertions that what he feels (or, as I suggest, the feelings that he posits) has a reality that precedes his eloquence. Burke's reading of Milton was perhaps *the* major influence on discussions of the poetic sublime in eighteenth-century Britain, and was certainly familiar to Wordsworth and Coleridge. Having earlier demonstrated that Wordsworth derived his understanding of feeling, and the affective virtues of both the 'aristocratic' and professional poet, from competing strands of Whig aesthetics, I argue that he builds his poetic house on the fruitful antagonism between the mimetic and positional characteristics of language he discovers in Burke. Coleridge's trenchant objections in *Biographia Literaria* to what he perceives as the Preface's valorisation of poetic language over poets themselves suggest his belief that Wordsworth fully realises the implications of the Irishman's foray into prosody and linguistics. After Burke, although travestying his intent, Wordsworth holds that poetry *creates*, as well as reproduces and reflects, feeling. In fact, poetry's adroit handling of the mimetic and positional aspects of language (the 'natural' and 'unnatural', in Burke's terminology) heightens its 'consciousness' of the truth-content of feeling. For Wordsworth, the relative autonomy of poetry gives it a unique ability to 'think' feeling. No longer cultivating affect in order to apply it to ideology-critique, he apprehends that only in *poetic* language is affect truly critical and philosophical.

I

Burke's declaration of the presence and value of the past is, like his aesthetics, closely associated with the body. But in a move already familiar from Shaftesbury, Burke takes pains to shift the emphasis of his aesthetics away from the body. Reducing the role of direct feeling, in the *Reflections* Burke insists on the importance of habit as expressed in manners and customs. Initially, he is concerned with the small-scale habits and affections of the individual. Developing the *Enquiry*'s idea that the beautiful binds society, Burke describes how familiar modes of life prompt love in the subject:

> We begin our public affections in our families. No cold relation is a zealous citizen. We pass on to our neighbourhoods, and our habitual provincial connections. These are inns and resting-places. Such divisions of our country as have been formed by habit . . . (*R* 244).

Love for our own small associations – such as family and locality – develops 'not by a sudden jerk of authority' (*R* 244), but metonymically into something far greater: 'It is the first link in the series by which we proceed towards a love to our country, and to mankind' (*R* 97–8).

As already noted, in the Preface to *Lyrical Ballads* Wordsworth borrows Burkean organicism to instate himself as a representative – albeit a representative critical of aspects of Whig thought – of the nation. For Burke, the routines and habits of everyday life become heightened until we project that love onto the routines and habits of our nation – its customs. In the *Reflections*, custom acts as the beautiful that binds a nation's subjects together. Indeed, Burke justifies the maintenance of tradition by finding in custom the 'natural' continuity of the nation's present with its past. He is even able to present this traditionalism as more representative, although not more democratic, than the revolutionary politics of France.

It is not enough, however, for Burke just to assert the importance of tradition, and assume that events abroad will bear out his faith in its value. The French Revolution has actively taken a stand against the past, and the threat of contamination this poses to England rouses him to seek a way to preserve or even re-establish the presence of the past. A main topic of debate in the literature of the period, language also becomes one of Burke's central themes. As will been seen shortly, Wordsworth joins this same debate when he makes a case for 'real' language in the Preface.

For 1790s republicans, 'to represent power (to give it a visible form) is to render it essentially harmless'.[3] As language is the most important medium of representation, it is no surprise that a writer like Thomas Paine considers 'Speech . . . one of the natural rights of man'.[4] In *The Rights of Man* (1791–2), a main point of disagreement with Burke concerns the fact that Britain does not have a written constitution.[5] Burke's defence of Britain's 'constitution' of heredity is regarded as 'cant' so long as there is no actual document.[6] A constitution that is formulated from principles open to examination, rather than a rhetorical appeal to vague superstitions, as in Burke, is essential to the political rights and liberty of a people. For Paine, 'The American constitutions were to liberty what a grammar is to language: they define its parts of speech, and practically construct them into syntax'.[7]

Burke himself is aware of the dangers inherent in too much public debate and in language itself. At the beginning of the *Reflections*, he disingenuously claims that he cannot address his 'letter' to the National Assembly because he writes 'without the express authority of the government under which I live' (*R* 57). He thus simultaneously implies that others should not make unauthorised announcements, and presents his thoughts as improvised and candid.[8] Yet his text is driven by serious political concerns, of course, particularly regarding the activities of the

Revolution Society and the republican Richard Price. Burke is worried by Price's sermons, and the effect they might have on public opinion. According to Burke, Price believes debate is intrinsically good:

> Dr. Price advises ... [his congregation] to improve upon non-conformity; and to set up, each of them, a separate meeting-house upon his own particular principles ... His zeal ... is not for the propagation of his own opinions, but of any opinions. It is not for the diffusion of truth, but for the spreading of contradiction (*R* 63).

Price has embraced the spirit of the times: 'It has been the misfortune (not as these gentlemen think it, the glory) of this age, that everything is to be discussed' (*R* 142). Nothing is held sacred and all 'truths' are open to interpretation and revision. Burke discerned, Thomas Pfau notes, that the talkers and the 'literati ... exposed the inauthentic and hence vulnerable fabric of tradition'[9] – a view Wordsworth shares in his lament that 'frantic novels ... [and] sickly and stupid German Tragedies' (*PrW* 1. 128) are obliterating Shakespeare and Milton with ease. Burke states in the *Preface to Bissot's Address to his Constituents* (1794) that the revolutionaries use words to fashion a new reality: 'Massacre is sometimes *agitation*, sometimes *effervescence*, sometimes *excess*; sometimes ... an exercise of *revolutionary power*' (*R* 512). Nonetheless, despite this relativist moment in his thought, Burke's work on language generally seeks to guarantee a stable view of history and tradition.

As an eighteenth-century writer on the sublime, Burke inevitably bears the influence of Longinus and his insights into the affective, or mimetic, dimension of language. For Longinus, the sublime is essentially 'a certain Eminence or Perfection of Language'.[10] He retains the conventional idea of the sublime as an experience of extreme passion or even violence, but adds that this is merely one aspect, and that it is accidental and limited to what he calls 'the Gifts of Nature'.[11] By far the most common manifestations of the sublime in this tradition are linguistic. For example, sublime boldness and grandeur is to be found in the apt expression of thoughts – a period that perfectly suits, or mimics, its content; and powerful emotion is evoked by the 'skilful Application of Figures'.[12] It is through the manipulation of rhetoric and style, indeed, that the majority of sublime effects are achieved. Longinus encourages a 'noble and graceful manner of Expression, which is not only to chuse out significant and elegant Words, but also to adorn and embellish the Stile, by the Assistance of Tropes'.[13] The structure and composition of a piece is said to greatly assist its impact. As early as

Longinus, it is difficult to fully separate language that engenders (posits) feeling from that which expresses (mimics) it.

Burke acknowledges that, along with painting, poetry is one of the 'affecting arts', and so is certainly aware of the force of words (*PE* 44). In a section of the *Enquiry* he briefly becomes a disciple of Longinus by insisting on the significance of language. Arguing that fear is one of the primary passions aroused by the sublime, Burke airs his learning in order to show that 'Several languages bear a strong testimony to the affinity of these ideas' (*PE* 58):

> They frequently use the same word, to signify indifferently the modes of astonishment or admiration and those of terror . . . The Romans used the verb *stupeo*, a term which strongly marks the state of an astonished mind, to express the effect either of simple fear, or of astonishment . . . ; and do not the French *etonnement*, and the English *astonishment* and *amazement*, point out as clearly the kindred emotions which attend fear and wonder (*PE* 58)?

Words confess their intimacy with the sublime through their multiple meanings; and by exploiting this polysemy it is possible to generate profoundly affecting expression. Abstract words, such as those Burke cites, obtain their strength through the might of the situations with which they are associated. Thus, any literal meaning is secondary to the enormous emotional content they carry and that it is advisable to supervise:

> When words which have been generally so applied are put together without any rational view, or in such manner that they do not rightly agree with each other, the stile is called bombast. And it requires . . . much good sense and experience to be guarded against the force of such language; for when propriety is neglected, a greater number of these affecting words may be taken into the service, and a greater variety may be indulged in combining them (*PE* 166).

Essentially, Burke is talking about language's talent for confounding rather than explaining, for manufacturing emotion rather than disclosing genuine feeling or truth. With strict qualifications, all the same, he is prepared to employ this kind of language for his own ends. Burke does not, though, spell out the difference between the 'true' and 'false' affects of the associations that congregate around abstract words. Furthermore, when he suggests that only he (or a man, like him presumably, with 'much good sense and experience') can tell them apart, it appears that Burke's model of language is sometimes motivated by expediency as opposed to theoretical rigour.

In the *Enquiry*, one of the causes of the sublime is said to be obscurity: 'To make a thing very terrible, obscurity seems in general to be necessary. When we know the full extent of any danger, when we can accustom our eyes to it, a great deal of the apprehension vanishes' (*PE* 58). The anticipatory political resonance is immediately apparent. The republicans use reason to extinguish the mystery of tradition and its representative, the monarch. Hence 'Those despotic governments, which are founded on the passions of men, and principally upon the passion of fear, keep their chief as much as may be from the public eye' (*PE* 59). This may seem more like description of Burke's own mystifying ideology than a critique of Oriental despotism. But the power that Burke wishes to protect is a tempered sublime, the mixed constitution of a sublime already predicated on the beautiful. Obscurity is not, therefore, only of use to 'the heathen [whose] temples were dark' (*PE* 59).

The abode of obscurity is language. Not just any form of language, however, but its most affecting form: poetry. Poetry has 'a more powerful dominion over the passions than the other art' (*PE* 61) – a view that Wordsworth will put forward in the Preface. Burke locates this power in language's vagueness, the obscurity arising from its necessary generalisation, particularly as poetry. He thus further develops his associative theory of language:

> No body, I believe, immediately on hearing the sounds, virtue, liberty, or honour, conceives any *precise* notion of the particular modes of action and thinking, together with the mixt and simple ideas, and the several relations of them for which these words are substituted . . . (*PE* 164; emphasis mine).

Some words are emotive because they summon up complex associations of thoughts and passions to the detriment of conceptual precision. This gives them their power. Clearly, such power can be perverted, but Burke continues to emphasise that when engaged in metrical composition words are at their most potent.

Poetry affects 'rather by sympathy than imitation' (*PE* 172). On this point, Burke is close to his contemporary, Alexander Gerard, who writes in the appendix to his *Essay on Taste* that 'Its employing language, or instituted signs renders . . . [poetry] absolutely incapable of being in this sense imitative' (*ET* 163). Mimesis loses out to the sublime once again as 'words undoubtedly have no sort of resemblance to the ideas for which they stand' (*PE* 173). In this way, verse, as opposed to painting, relieves civic humanist aesthetics of its anxiety about the visual and its 'vulgar crowd of divergent sensations'.[14] Again, a nervousness about the body, shared at times by Wordsworth, is the subtext of theoretical distinctions. Later, instead of attempting to defeat the republicans with their own reason, *Reflections* constructs the Revolution in such a way that the arbitrary insinuations of theory give way to a poetry that complicates, and perhaps obscures, rather than represents a simple reality. Burke's language induces a cultivated myopia, and makes it difficult to judge between 'a clear expression, and a strong expression' (*PE* 175).

An idea of the political use to which Burke puts poetry can already be found in the *Enquiry*. He states that poetry's affects translate passions from one person to another, and give pleasure (*PE* 44). He quotes liberally in order to establish the affective nature of poetic obscurity, and regards the description of Death in *Paradise Lost* as the finest example of sublime vagueness. As Lucy Newlyn notes, 'It was Burke's *Philosophical Enquiry* that succeeded in establishing Milton's description of Death as the touchstone for sublime language.'[15] Indeed, the profound influence of this volume on subsequent writers cannot be overestimated.[16] Marilyn Butler sources the 'intense focus upon the intimate and local' in Coleridge's conversation poems – written during the period of his most intense collaboration with Wordsworth – to the *Enquiry*,[17] an observation supported by Philip Cardinal's impressive demonstration that 'The Nightingale' contains 'virtually every aspect of the Burkean sublime.'[18]

Burke quotes the following passage:

> *The other shape,*
> *If shape it might be called that shape had none*
> *Distinguishable, in member, joint, or limb;*
> *Or substance might be called that shadow seemed,*
> *For each seemed either; black he stood as night;*
> *Fierce as ten furies; terrible as hell;*
> *And shook a deadly dart. What seemed his head*
> *The likeness of a kingly crown had on.*

In this description all is dark, uncertain, confused, terrible, and sublime to the last degree (*PE* 59).

Death is a theme to which Burke often resorts in his anatomy of the sublime and beautiful, and it is hardly surprising that it reappears in the discussion of poetry. The word *death* is, he argues, again quoting Milton, a sure way to elicit a sublime affect:

> Here is displayed the force of union in
>   *Rocks, caves, lakes, dens, bogs, fens and shades;*
> which yet would lose the greatest part of their effect, if they were
>   not the
>   *Rocks, caves, lakes, dens, bogs, fens and shades-*
> -*of* Death (*PE* 174).

The frequent conjunction of the sublime and death, though, is less remarkable than the thrice-repeated occurrence of the word *shape* in the first passage from Milton. In order to make an important point, Burke highlights a section of *Paradise Lost* that is not simply an example of the repeated use in poetry of what he calls '*compounded abstract* words' (*PE* 164) – those words that carry considerable associative, and thus affective, freight. *Shape* both imposes and defies definition; abstract and inchoate, it also invites empirical, visual, verification. *Shape* implies that what it asserts in the abstract is actually *there* (if obscured in darkness) and amenable to re-presentation. To put it another way, the word is speculative while also implying that it has made contact with something as real as death. For Burke, *shape* does not simply posit: it also mimics. He is careful, however, to home in on a Miltonic term that, while it alludes to visual reality, does not succumb to what civic humanism perceives as the material chaos of 'minute and infinitely nuanced definitions'.[19] Yet the repetition of *shape* three times in Milton's verse is troubling. For Paul de Man, repetition in poetry 'rhythmically articulates what is in fact a disarticulation'.[20] A poem's 'monotonous' pressure towards meaning also undercuts determinate meaning. De Man's thesis about the necessarily 'disfiguring' effect of figurative language is neither Burke's conscious nor unconscious goal. Where the two writers might agree, nevertheless, is on the positional power of words – that is, the anti-mimetic side of language.[21] A discussion of Wordsworth's interest in this aspect of language comprises much of the second half of this chapter.

In an extended aside on poetic metre, de Man argues that '"measure" separates from the phenomenal aspects of signification . . . and stresses instead the literal and material aspects of language'.[22] Measure (and language in general, de Man suggests) reveals the tendency of linguistic matter to 'extinguish and bury' what words claim to represent.[23] Language 'means', quite simply, by repeatedly insisting that it represents or expresses something actual, that what it says is true. For de Man, the imposing power of language derives from the institutional – or iterative – and arbitrary nature of its signs. But this repetition is hypnotic and induces a 'forgetting' that signification is just but the invention of a 'machine' that is 'beyond the polarities of chance and determination'.[24] Moreover, not only do speakers forget that language posits, knowing nothing before or after language they have no awareness of the 'violence' inherent in its blind, and fundamentally senseless, positional *force*.[25]

Our immersion in language might erase any sense of the 'violence of position', but when we hear poetry's measure (and other instances of the 'thing-ness' of language) we remember that the only reality words present is that of their own existence.[26] De Man calls this poetry's 'negative knowledge'.[27] It sometimes 'knows' that it can only be certain of itself. Still, enchanted by the sensual substantiality of its own music, poetry once again forgets that it posits the apparently tactile reality it seems to represent, to mimic. In short, language is repeatedly deceived into, and awoken from, the belief that its 'literal and material aspects' reflect the literal and material facticity of the non-linguistic.

De Man develops his literary philosophy to advance what is at this stage of his career a politically ambiguous argument about epistemological doubt; but Burke's utilisation of such a notion, in the form of his avowal of poetry's *affecting* obscurity, is always for conservative purposes. As has already been observed, he often employs quotations from poetry for rhetorical emphasis and to illustrate his argument. Milton is the English writer who makes the most appearances in the *Reflections*, his status as the finest English poet adding authority to Burke's treatise, although Shakespeare and Dryden are also cited. It is no coincidence that these are the three authors Wordsworth mentions, or alludes to, most frequently. The poetry most commonly found in the *Enquiry*, however, is the Latin verse of Virgil, Horace and Lucretius. In this way, Burke drastically limits his eighteenth-century readership. Burke's text can thus be seen to contribute to a very specific debate with a particular, and particularly educated, readership in mind.

When considering Burke on the affective obscurity of language, then, it is essential to remember that his work is meant for a highly select readership and not for general consumption. I proposed in the previous chapter that Wordsworth might also attempt to limit the social availability of poetic language in the Preface, in his case by claiming that poetry is a vocation. Nevertheless, Wordsworth's expansion of the definition of tradition to include the middle class, and his emphasis on pleasure, not only indicates that his reading of Burke is filtered through his republicanism but also prepares the way for his use of affect to criticise eighteenth-century aesthetics.

While the nebulousness of poetic language, Burke implies, displaying a debt to Shaftesbury, is a source of delight for the highly cultivated reader, it should not be loosed on the undiscriminating general public. If for the educated man the subtle affective resonance of language is a harmless delight, in the hands of a demagogue poetic language is an invitation to dangerous interpretative or persuasive licence. Accordingly, Burke dismisses the rhetorically loaded pronouncements of his political adversaries as dishonest rabble-rousing. Yet he permits himself the liberty of exploiting the poetic and rhetorical resources of English and Latin (or at least an English regulated by Latin) in the *Reflections* in order to present the Revolution in his own terms. Following a line of reasoning that is at best paradoxical, Burke writes in his most affecting manner so he can shut down the interpretative options of the Revolution's observers. To discredit his foes, he accuses them of deceitful rhetoric, declaring that only his words are politically responsible while simultaneously using every trick of language available. Burke thus attempts to produce the definitive account of the Revolution, the one that will be accepted as fact. The deployment through language of the disciplinary sublime will, he hopes, rescue English opinion from the anarchic French mob and return it to the more 'productive' old guard.

The seizure of the French king and queen is, therefore, rightly considered the climax of the *Reflections*. It is the place where Burke's protest against the Revolution is articulated with the greatest passion, and it is also where he makes his most concerted attempt to undermine the appeal of Revolutionary anarchy. The section is written in Burke's melodramatic signature style, and was perceived by his critics to abandon any commitment to historical truth. It contains the kind of 'literary' writing that incited Paine to tell the author 'to recollect that he is writing history, and not *plays*, and that his readers expect truth, and not the spouting rant of high-toned declamation'.[28] Yet, as Elizabeth Samet suggests, 'Burkes himself conceived of his deliberately affective tragic history as a response to what seemed to him a French farce in which both poetic and political justice were being thwarted'.[29] He sees his poetical prose, in other words, as a true agent of historical 'correction'.

Burke offers the reader a picture of the innocent queen disturbed in her bedroom by marauding revolutionaries:

From . . . [her] sleep the queen was first startled by the voice of the centinel at her door, who cried out to her, to save herself by flight – that this was the last proof of fidelity he could give – that they were upon him, and he was dead (*R* 121).

The mob enters her room and a symbolic rape occurs: 'A band of cruel ruffians and assassins, reeking with blood, rushed into the chamber of the queen, and pierced with an hundred strokes of bayonets and poniards the bed' (*R* 121).[30] For Burke, this scene is emblematic of how the Revolution strips power bare and leaves nothing but the rags of arbitrary government:

> All the decent drapery of life is to be rudely torn off. All the super-added ideas, furnished from the wardrobe of a moral imagination, which the heart owns, and the understanding ratifies, as necessary to cover the defects of our naked shivering nature, and to raise it to dignity in our own estimation, are to be exploded as ridiculous, absurd, and antiquated fashion (*R* 128).

The queen, like the state, is robbed of all mystery and reduced to the ordinary: 'On this scheme of things . . . a queen is but a woman; a woman is but an animal; and an animal not of the highest order' (*R* 128). Nothing remains of the queen to admire when she is reduced to this condition.

For some commentators, Burke conspires here in the very thing he deplores. It is his 'text rather than the Revolutionary "mob" that exposes the queen';[31] and the 'sublime' power of the passage could be said to unwittingly make the Revolution an exciting experience for the reader. However, the stripping of the queen is an example of a false sublime – one that works against nature by giving women the volition of men or, in this instance, cheating them of their beauty. When the sublime presses too close, and takes a bodily form, it becomes grotesque. Rather than use the event as a way of achieving a cheap sensationalism, Burke puts on the force of this corrupt sublime in order to reactivate his own 'ethical' sublime. In this context, the part of the authentic sublime that encourages self-preservation will extend its rule. But it will not be the self of an individual that is restored. It will, instead, be the self of an entire nation.

The Revolution has removed the government's sublime obscurity, an event Burke presents as a violation of the body of the queen. The monarch carries colossal symbolic importance for Burke. To violate the royal person, therefore, amounts to attacking the customs and manners of the country, and ultimately the way of life of its inhabitants. Burke takes it upon himself, then, to return dignity to the queen and all her subjects, and he does so by means of his highest style. He remembers the queen at her most magnificent and beautiful:

> I saw her just above the horizon, decorating and cheering the elevated sphere she just began to move in, – glittering like the morning-star, full of life, and splendour, and joy (*R* 126).

No attempt is made at faithful description, as Burke's rhetoric has a political agenda. In the decade before the Revolution, radical Dissenters, such as Lord George Gordon, had been involved 'in a politico-pornographic smear campaign levelled at the body and morals of Marie Antoinette . . . [that] linked Dissent to a new libertine egoism antithetical to the chivalric manners and domestic virtues of European civilization'.[32] There are many possible readings of this campaign, but Iain McCalman's analysis of the situation is especially plausible: Marie Antoinette had become a symbol for the 'feminine traits of secrecy, greed and ruthlessness that had supposedly infected the courts of the *ancien régime* since the time of Louis XV'.[33] Decadence was associated with a general feminisation – or effeminacy – of the court, where intrigue behind closed doors watered vice and injustice. Burke intends his paean to the queen to chivalrously and discretely adorn her body with poetry. Indeed, covering Marie Antoinette with words and praising her beauty, Burke allows the queen's femininity, so crudely exposed by radical activity, to be displaced by something resembling the more masculine sublime. The apparent secrecy of women, exploited by the revolutionaries, is transformed by Burke into the sublime mystery of the monarchy.

Inevitably, Burke's gambit can appear hysterical. Falling back on exclamation, his fluency almost deserts him: 'Oh! what a Revolution! and what a heart must I have, to contemplate without emotion that elevation and that fall!' (*R* 126). The queen floats over the ground of representation on the hot breath of the writer as he makes her treatment during the Revolution an episode that 'did draw tears from me', like a work of imaginative literature. She is a fantasy in which Burke, the author, finds the poetry needed to bestow grandeur upon the monarch once again.

Poetic language here has two functions. It allows Burke to adorn the monarchy in the sublime drapes required for his version of respectable and respected government; and it begins the process of reviving the values of the monarchy and its traditions that for him are more representative than French democracy. By aggrandising the monarchy with the sublime artifice of language, Burke tries to revive the disciplining influence of tradition, the living history 'who keeps a durable record of all our acts' and in which a nation finds its authentic self (*R* 121). The kinds of books in circulation are similarly important in determining a country's present opinions and sustaining memories, and Burke is concerned that the reading of the wrong texts is encouraged by radical debating societies. Books can dictate the 'character of the age', and it is the complacent acceptance of incorrect authors that has sent France off course:

> We continue, as in the two last ages, to read more generally, than I believe is now done on the continent, the authors of sound antiquity ... They suffer us to be more than transiently amused with paradoxical morality (*R* 312; 318).

Again, as in the *Enquiry*, Burke asserts the value of classical writers. He holds that truly great literature and the accumulated wealth of great libraries contains 'the force and weakness of the human mind' (*R* 210). It is necessary to keep these writings alive, these 'grand monuments of the dead ... [to] continue the regards and connexions of life beyond the grave' (*R* 201): literature derives its authority from and contributes to the continuation of 'antient manners' (*R* 130). The creation of a modern, alternative canon in the French revolutionaries' adherence to the works of Rousseau, and the English radicals' consumption of self-penned political writings, severs the present from the revered guidance of the past. By implication, Burke thinks a popular reading public is a dangerous thing: the books that should be read are those of the ancients, and are therefore only accessible to the classically trained minority who, by definition, have nothing to gain and everything to lose from modern radicalisms. If it is necessary to read English authors, Burke recommends Milton or *Cooper's Hill* by 'our political poet' Sir John Denham – a writer of confirmed royalist credentials (*R* 166).

Burke's representation of the Revolution through a prism of literature labours to redirect the sublime and beautiful to their proper functions, so correcting the distorted versions brought about by the French Revolution. Through this realignment of the sublime and beautiful, he hopes to restore the present to its organic relation with a past that has almost been erased. Despite his impressive display of the rhetorical power and variety of English, though, Burke discourages others from trying the same. Having given a lesson in English style, he waves his readership to the Classical or English poets he favours.

Rewriting the Revolution in the episode on the seizure of the king and queen returns Burke's work to a contradictory assertion of a 'natural' politics by means of an ideologically loaded aesthetics. He intends to regulate, for example, the proliferation of 'arbitrary' theorisation that is latent in the *Enquiry* and violently explicit in the French Revolution, by bringing it under the governance of his aesthetic theory, that in turn is sustained by a highly theologised model of tradition. Of course, Burke does not halt the Revolution with poetic prose, but he defines politics as a question of the conflict between 'natural', organic, form and 'arbitrary' reason.

This adoption of the aesthetics of the sublime by Burke and others (including Wordsworth) provides writers with an immense persuasive resource:

> On the one hand they could celebrate the principle of confusion and decidedly antirationalist expressive convention; on the other, and precisely as exponents of the sublime, they could inscribe themselves into a posture of control and thus of . . . superiority.[34]

The literariness, in both style and genealogy, of an aesthetic ideology founded on the sublime, places the literature that follows in a central, yet contradictory, position. The aesthetic is posited as natural, true and timeless, yet at the same time potentially the incubator of theory, dissenting politics and materiality. After Burke, it is difficult to argue that the imprecision and rhetoric of literature is natural rather than, as he claims of theory, unnatural. However, to say that literature has an ideological element is not the same as declaring it false. The truth-content of literature and literary language that emerges from Burke lies in its disclosure of an excess of affect that occurs on 'natural' aesthetics' watch. Literature does not dutifully fulfil the task Burke assigns it. It has a double character as both ideology and the exposure (or critique) of ideology.

II

Wordsworth's work exhibits a similarly double character. His Romantic poetics of 'emotion recollected in tranquillity' owes a large debt to Shaftesbury, and his republican politics is shot through with Burkeanism. Yet, whereas Burke is uneasy about the ambiguities he inhabits, for Wordsworth conflict is a source of possibility. It is in the light of Coleridge's objections to the Preface that the full profundity of Wordsworth's *transformation* of Whig civic humanist aesthetics is revealed.

The celebration of poetry as the 'spontaneous overflow of powerful feelings' (*PrW* 1. 148) is at least as important as the idea of 'recollection' in the Preface. Poetry is both the repeated overflow and the regulation of emotion – the two activities being inseparable, and without final resolution. Benefiting from his sense of the fault lines running through the thought of Shaftesbury and Burke, in the Preface Wordsworth develops a dialectical reading of the aesthetic tradition he inherits. Regulation and tradition criticise the anarchy of overflow but, equally, overflow is a critique of the potentially impoverishing restraint that is central to civic humanist ideas of order. As discussed in Chapter 2, the Preface contributes to the 'democratisation' of politeness – a liberation, in effect, of the dialectical underside (or 'repressed') of eighteenth-century aesthetics.

Aside from 'emotion recollected in tranquillity' and the 'spontaneous overflow of powerful feelings', the other most discussed tenet contained in the Preface is Wordsworth's claim to be employing 'the real language of men' (*PrW* 1. 122). Pressing on with his contention that pleasure and sensation are the true ends of poetry, he argues that rural life provides the ideal language for the production of verse:

> Low and rustic life was generally chosen because in that situation the essential passions of the heart find a better soil in which they can attain their maturity, are less under restraint, and speak a plainer more emphatic language (*PrW* 1. 124).

The civic humanist inspiration behind his valorisation of 'plain' and 'simple' language has already been examined, but it is pertinent to further explore the significance for Wordsworth of rural life in particular. He explains that in rural life 'elementary feelings exist in a state of greater simplicity . . . [and] are more easily comprehended' (*PrW* 1. 124). Eighteenth-century writers of sensibility intended the aesthetics of affection to 'naturalise' the social structure from which they profited, but their investigations also turned affection into a category that could aid thinking critical of the status quo. Thus, when Coleridge writes *Biographia Literaria* (1818), he distances himself from Wordsworth precisely over the political ambiguities integral to the Preface's elaboration of the aesthetics of sensation and departure from its usual eighteenth-century remit. In part, Coleridge's assault on the Preface identifies some of the anti-Whig implications of Wordsworth's poetics. However, according to Cardinal, Coleridge's critical allusions to Milton in the 'Nightingale' betray a wish to distance 'himself from Burke's (and Wordsworth's) humanistic vision of the sublime to elaborate a more orthodox religious idea of the aesthetic'.[35] Coleridge's critique of the Preface, then, arguably stems from an awareness of the *un*-Burkean consequences that follow from Wordsworth's all-too-faithful reception of Burke and the Whig tradition.

Coleridge couches his objections to the Preface in a vocabulary that belies the seriousness of his complaints. He writes that 'in a poem . . . it is not possible to imitate truly a dull and garrulous discourser, without repeating the effects of dulness and garrulity'.[36] He remarks that adherence to the language and thoughts of 'ordinary' life and people will not generate a poetry anyone might actually care to read. The kind of people inhabiting *Lyrical Ballads* do not often exhibit 'the best part of human language, properly so called, [which] is derived from reflection on the acts of the mind itself'.[37] The conclusion of this statement censures Wordsworth for not fully committing to his (Shaftesburean) prescription of poetry as 'emotion recollected in tranquillity'.[38]

There is nothing authentic, Coleridge continues, in the 'vulgarity' of the so-called real language of men. He shuns the eighteenth-century's value-laden equation of language with the level of a speaker's 'soul and civilisation':[39]

> . . . a rustic's language, purified from all provincialism and grossness, and so far re-constructed as to be made consistent with the rules of grammar . . . will not differ from the language of any other man of common-sense, except as far as the notions, which the rustic has to convey, are fewer and more indiscriminate.[40]

He sees the peril lurking in Wordsworth's praise of the rustic's language of feeling. Not only does Wordsworth assume that rustic language is somehow prelapsarian – hence signalling a dangerous attraction to the 'excessive', rather than regulative, dimensions of poetry, and intimation of friendship with revolutionary transparency – he also, more crucially, runs the risk of undervaluing himself.

Coleridge calls for a consideration of the language of the rustic:

> If the history of the phrases in hourly currency among our peasants were traced, a person not previously aware of the fact would be sur-prized at finding so large a number, which three or four centuries ago were the exclusive property of the universities and the schools; and at the commencement of the Reformation had been transferred from the school to the pulpit, and thus gradually passed into common life.[41]

This theory of transmission – focussing on the 'documentary', rather than experimental, aspect of Wordsworth's 'ordinary' language – seeks to place the learned at the top of the linguistic tree, and so goes against the standard 1790s liberal views contemporary with the publication of *Lyrical Ballads*. In the 1780s and 90s, Joseph Ritson's 'researches into the origins of the ballad and popular song led him to draw a distinction between the popular entertainer who travelled "about from place to place, singing and playing to the illiterate vulgar" and the more aristocratic minstrel who entertained in the houses of the great'.[42] In short, Ritson argued for the existence of a popular tradition that was separate from, rather than a poor cousin of, an aristocratic tradition: popular tradition 'amounted to a complete alternative culture replete with its own version of history enshrined in the ballads and folklore'.[43] The idea that, while related to other discourses and common life itself, poetry is also relatively autonomous comes to play a vital part in Wordsworth's work.[44] Proposing that the parts of *Lyrical Ballads* 'which have been spoken in . . . [Wordsworth's] own character, are those which have given, and which will give universal delight', Coleridge hopes to confirm the poet as the origin of a cultural output that should appeal to all but which is broken and divided from itself when corrupted into a more populist form.[45] He worries that the (relatively autonomous) ballad tradition from which Wordsworth draws signifies above and beyond the person of the poet. He thus implies that it is the poet's role to enrich the language by providing linguistic counters for others to use, and rejects the idea that poetic form itself 'thinks'. Wordsworth, Coleridge argues, is foolish to claim that he is using the language of the rustic when it is, in fact, that of the poet's '*good sense* and *natural feeling*'.[46]

Still concerned that he has not protested his case forcefully enough, Coleridge introduces another theory of language: 'Every man's language has, first, its *individualities*; secondly, the common properties of the *class* to which he belongs; and thirdly, words and phrases of *universal* use'.[47] He states that when Wordsworth presents the language of the rustic as '"real" . . . we must substitute *ordinary*, or *lingua communis*'.[48] Coleridge's emphasis on the social dimension of language is based on a Shaftesburean suspicion of enthusiasm. In his *Miscellaneous Reflections*, Shaftesbury distinguishes between 'a *Legitimate* and a *Bastard-sort*' of enthusiasm (*C* 2. 161). The difference, he explains in *Sensus Communis*, is between an enthusiasm that leaves a man with 'nothing before his Eyes' but his passion, and an enthusiasm that renders him still a 'good sociable Man' (*C* 1. 52). Coleridge voices here a concern about the anti-mimetic, the ability of poetic language to break free of regulation, and fashion (rather than simply reflect) the world.[49] Disputing rustic language's advantage over other forms of language,

Coleridge reveals the fundamental tension upon which the Preface is constructed. Wordsworth is attempting to assert authenticity, the essential universality of his poetic discourse, and at the same time allow for the emergence of the new. He is certainly no unbridled enthusiast in the Preface – wishing as he does to study affect, to *think* feeling – but neither is he resolutely committed to staying within the bounds of regulation, habit and tradition. Wordsworth is dedicated to both the civic humanist project and an anti-mimeticism that is its critique. In fact, he encourages their antagonism, regarding it as a means to liberate affect.

To extend, or even universalise, the reach of his work, Wordsworth's appeal to feeling is, as I have suggested, directed by eighteenth-century aesthetics. Likewise, his promotion of 'real' language links true feeling with a mode of expression said to be available to all. He thus accentuates, although in a more democratic spirit than that found in the Whig tradition, the socially binding (that is, regulatory) role of poetry. However, at this point in the Preface Wordsworth also differentiates between a superficial, debased feeling and a deeper, more authentic kind. By arguing that the poet's language might be the locale of this authentic language of feeling, Wordsworth makes very large claims for himself and poetry. In essence, he presents his poetry as a *discourse of authenticity* – a language that brings to light a reality otherwise hidden, or even short-circuited, by the 'degenerate' chatter of the everyday. One could accuse Wordsworth of an 'elitist' proclamation of access to truth – that he takes back with one hand the democracy of poetry he has offered with the other. But it is necessary to add, once more, that this move represents a decisive break with the Whig poetics of regulation. The answer to one of the questions posed in the introduction – 'What happens to the theories of affect debated in the prose writings of Whig aestheticians when they enter Wordsworth's lyric and narrative poetry?' – begins to appear. Constructing his own poetic language as both the representation of the authentic and authenticity itself, Wordsworth intimates that poetry not only uncovers what is already there but also exceeds the common round of the 'sayable'. Poetry becomes the site of the 'unsayable' or, to use a more utopian terminology, the 'as-yet-unsaid'.[50] As the Preface seeks to uncover the real and regulate the passions, it also looks to break free of the quotidian in order to create the conditions in which to imagine a future undimmed by the past.[51]

For Coleridge, there is an enormous problem simply with Wordsworth's praise of rustic language, as it does away with the singular status of the poet. After all, if rustic language is so potent there is no reason why the age's great writers should not come from that class of men, instead of

from the professional class of poets in which Wordsworth and Coleridge
place themselves. Coleridge is defiant on this point:

> . . . how difficultly hidden, the powers of genius are; and yet find
> even in situations the most favorable, according to Mr. Wordsworth,
> for the formation of a pure and poetic language; in situations which
> ensure familiarity with the grandest objects for the imagination;
> but *one* BURNS, among the shepherds of *Scotland*, and not a single
> poet of humble life among those of *English* lakes and mountains;
> I conclude, that POETIC GENIUS is not only a very delicate but a
> very rare plant.[52]

He has little patience with any attempt to bestow the potential for
'poetic genius' on everyone. Just as later eighteenth-century aestheticians introduced the notion of taste to regulate the egalitarian drift of
theories of Sensibility, so Coleridge insists on a poetics that mystifies,
rather than undermines, the social position of the Poet.

Coleridge extends his attack on Wordsworth's poetics with further
remarks on language. Continuing to disagree with the idea that rustic
language be awarded any kind of privilege, he argues that

> poetry is essentially ideal, that it avoids and excludes all *accident*;
> that its apparent individualities of rank, character, or occupation
> must be *representative* of a class; and that the *persons* of poetry must
> be clothed with *generic* attributes, with the *common* attributes of the
> class; not with such as one gifted individual might *possibly* possess,
> but such as from his situation it is most probable beforehand, that
> he *would* possess.[53]

Coleridge claims that behind the accidents of class and location, poetic
language draws upon a common linguistic, and abstract, resource: grammar. At this stage in his quarrel with Wordsworth, Coleridge follows
the civic humanist line that 'political authority is rightly exercised by
those capable of thinking in general terms; which usually means those
capable of producing abstract ideas – "decomplex" ideas – out of the raw
data experience'.[54] Lauding the abstract virtues of grammar over the accidents of social rank and experience, Coleridge tries to wrestle the poetic
away from the 'vulgar' rustics Wordsworth favours, and hand it back
to those whose education allows them to 'transcend' the limitations of
their empirical situation. In agreement with Shaftesbury, Coleridge
contends that although all language draws upon grammar those with

the leisure to read widely can cultivate grammatical superiority. As is the case with his eighteenth-century forebears, Coleridge's judgements about language turn out also to contain judgements about class. Rustics can speak a grammatically correct English, but it will be limited in its breadth by circumstance. The educated, however, 'are familiar with the great works of various times and various tongues', and so have superior grammatical resources.[55] Preserving 'the authoritative status of the culture of the cultivated classes', Coleridge thereby protects the specialist status of the poet from the slide in the Preface towards the democratisation of poetic genius.[56] Nevertheless, regardless of Coleridge's spirited accusations, Wordsworth's Preface does still uphold differences between poetry and prose, middle-class poets and writers from other classes, while concurrently promoting poetry's capacity for authenticity and invention.

III

Wordsworth's aversion to the affectations of eighteenth-century poetry in the Preface is, at one stage, presented as a critique of the distinction between poetry and prose. Having accepted that metre is the defining characteristic of poetry, he then disputes the idea that metre is, as a result, an artificial addition to verse:

> If in a poem there should be found a series of lines, or even a single line, in which the language, though naturally arranged and according to the strict laws of metre, does not differ from that of prose, there is a numerous class of critics who, when they stumble upon these prosaisms as they call them, . . . exult over the Poet as over a man ignorant of his own profession (*PrW* 1. 132).

Wordsworth regards this crass identification of poetry with verse as a sign of the debasement of the contemporary production and judgement of the art. As a poet hostile to arbitrary ornament, he has cut himself off 'from a large portion of phrases and figures of speech which from father to son have long been considered as the common inheritance of poets' (*PrW* 1. 132). The radical refuses the idea of primogeniture, even when it is confined only to questions of writing. Furthermore, he supports his case with an entire theory of the Fall of poetic language into a condition of unthinking slavery to tradition.

In the 1802 Appendix to the Preface, Wordsworth offers his version of the degeneration of poetic language:

The earliest poets of all nations generally wrote from passion excited by real events; they wrote naturally, and as men: feeling powerfully as they did, their language was daring, and figurative (*PrW* 1. 160).

These first poets wrote sincere and authentic poetry that produced figures derived from natural feelings. Later, however, the practice of poetry became institutionalised:

Poets, and Men ambitious of the fame of Poets, perceiving the influence of such language, and desirous of producing the same effect without being animated by the same passion, set themselves to a mechanical adoption of these figures of speech, and made use of them, sometimes with propriety, but much more frequently applied them to feelings and thoughts with which they had no natural connection (*PrW* 1. 160).

Wordsworth favours the natural over the mechanical. The language of '[g]enuine passion', he states, was replaced by the mechanical repetition of 'poetic' figures, which ultimately led to a 'distorted language' soon to be mistaken for true poetry (*PrW* 1. 160; 1. 161).[57] Poets 'carried the abuse still further, and introduced phrases . . . altogether of their own invention' that masqueraded as expressions of true feeling (*PrW* 1. 161). The result was that poetry became a 'wanton deviation from good sense and nature' (*PrW* 1. 161). Although he disparages such language, Wordsworth implicitly acknowledges that the anti-mimetic (or positional) aspect of language generates meanings and affects worthy of attention.

At the same time that he contests the notion of poetry as an arbitrary mechanism, Wordsworth is also adamant that the repetition necessary for metre is acceptable – although metre is 'a symbol or promise of this unusual language' and often becomes an excuse for 'more of this adulterated phraseology' (*PrW* 1. 161). From this idea of a 'promise' contained in poetic language, and suggestion that poetry is always partly orientated towards the future, he moves on to a consideration of language's past. He explains that the natural language of poetry was forgotten, and that the gaudy baubles of this fallen poetry were 'received as a natural language' (*PrW* 1. 93).

Barbara Johnson is correct to point out the problems arising at this point in Wordsworth's theory:

In this history of abuse, the natural and the mechanical, the true and the false, become utterly indistinguishable. It becomes all the more necessary – but all the more difficult – to restore the boundary line. Each time Wordsworth attempts to do so, however, the distinction breaks down. The natural becomes unnatural, life imitates art, and mechanical inventions are mistaken for the natural language of passion.[58]

Wordsworth cannot prevent the natural from flipping over into the unnatural, and vice versa. Indeed, behind this discussion of affectation in eighteenth-century verse, there is, perhaps, a misgiving about the privilege he has accorded rustic language. His curiosity about how 'natural' language might become 'unnatural', reminiscent of the anxiety in eighteenth-century aesthetics about sensation mutating into a luxury of the body, is more than a civic humanist fear of the 'natural' rustic becoming a poet: it also indicates an interest in how the rustic could break free ('unnaturally', arguably) of the restraint characteristic of the civic humanist gentleman or even the bourgeois professional poet. The definition of poetry as 'emotion recollected in tranquillity' is a Shaftesburean and Whig dictum to regulate emotion with memory, reflection, composition and measure. The rustic poet supposedly has no distance from his emotion which, undisciplined, is similar to enthusiastic excess. Yet, the continued draw that the rustic poet has for Wordsworth suggests his dissatisfaction with dogged obedience to the regulatory aesthetics of the eighteenth century, including Burke's.[59]

Experimenting further with the problem, Wordsworth again tries to introduce distinctions – this time between 'good repetition and degraded, hollow repetition'.[60] However, Wordsworth's theory is not simply a rebuttal of language in favour of 'reality'. The Preface's radicalism, its political commitment, as stated in the Advertisement to *Lyrical Ballads*, to 'the language of conversation in the middle and lower classes of society', and its claim to originality and experimentation, is finely balanced by Wordsworth's civic humanist caution about affective excess (*PrW* 1. 116). He will exploit the 'materiality of the signifier', but only in so far as it helps him to distinguish his poetry from that of others in order to achieve the liberty necessary for the critical exploration of affect. To completely ally himself to a single aspect of language would be to end the spirit of experiment that motivates *Lyrical Ballads* and all of Wordsworth's most compelling work.

Another of Wordsworth's primary justifications for the use of rustic language in *Lyrical Ballads* is that it is impervious to 'social vanity' because of 'the sameness and narrow circle of [the rustic's] . . . intercourse' (*PrW* 1. 124). Rustic language arises out of 'repeated experience and regular feelings' (*PrW* 1. 124). In the following passage, he goes further and proposes a case for his poetry as a good form of repetition:

> . . . our continued influxes of feeling are modified and directed by our thoughts, which are indeed the representatives of all our past feelings; and as by contemplating the relation of these general representatives to each other, we discover what is really important to men, so by the repetition and continuance of this act feelings connected with important subjects will be nourished, till at length, if we be originally possessed of much organic sensibility, such habits of mind will be produced that by obeying blindly and mechanically the impulses of those habits . . . that the understanding of the being to whom we address ourselves, if he be in a healthful state of association, must necessarily be in some degree enlightened, his taste exalted, and his affections ameliorated (*PrW* 1. 126).

Johnson remarks, quite rightly, that the 'astonishing thing about this story is the use of the word "mechanical" – which has had negative connotations everywhere else in the Preface – as the height of poeticality'.[61] For Wordsworth, the superficial repetition of contemporary poetry needs to be replaced by a deeper form of repetition, one that taps into the original scene of poetry and figural language. It may even be the case that *mechanical* is not the most significant word in this passage. Rather than referring to the 'mechanism' of instinctual spasms, the phrase 'habits of mind', and then the recurrence of *habit* one line later, recalls Burke's conviction that habit binds society: '[n]othing is so strong a tie of amity between nation and nation as correspondence in laws, customs, manners, and *habits* of life. They have more than the force of treaties in themselves'.[62]

Wordsworth values metre as something 'regular and uniform' (*PrW* 1. 144). Expanding on his idea of emotion recollected in tranquillity, he increasingly resorts to the thesis that repetition – habit – orders and regulates, or in the idiom of a political radical, maintains bonds of affection between individuals and communities. Wordsworth welcomes the truth-content that emerges from the grain of Burke's writing rather than the Irishman's grand narrative – the living process of his thought, and not its more rigid objective. Wordsworth argues that '[w]ords metrically arranged will long continue to impart such a pleasure to mankind as he who is sensible of the extent of that pleasure will be desirous to impart' (*PrW* 1. 146). So great, in fact, is the excitement produced by rhythmic language, 'an unusual and irregular state of mind', that it always threatens to escalate into something that 'may be carried beyond its proper bounds' (*PrW* 1. 146). Excitement is a portal to the perilous realm of enthusiastic excess: there is always the possibility that passion will triumph over reason, an outcome most commonly associated with religious fanaticism. However, the 'co-presence of something regular', metre, manages emotion, and shapes it into 'something to which the mind has been accustomed when in an unexcited or less excited state . . . [It] has great efficacy in tempering and restraining the passion by an intertexture of ordinary feeling' (*PrW* 1. 146). Metre here has the remedial effect of Shaftesburean solitary dialogue: the mind is divided from its own enthusiasm by the familiar and habitual associations summoned up by metre, is calmed and returned to itself, called back home from its wanderings. But this interpretation is overly Foucauldian. What looks like a Whiggish anxiety about strong emotion is, equally, Wordsworth's introduction of some distance between self and affect so that he can *experience* feeling – that is, keep it conscious.

Metre has a double function: it is a sign and facilitator of heightened emotion, and it is also affect's (benign) regulator. Wordsworth's poetry, as described in the Preface, uses the linguistic turn Burke gives Whig civic humanist ideas of tradition, habit and regularity so that poet and reader can experience the variety of affective states and enjoy 'the perception of similitude in dissimilitude' (*PrW* 1. 148). Despite the origin of Wordsworth's terminology in Burke and Shaftesbury, he only takes from the Whigs what he pleases, coaxing the critical potential from eighteenth-century aesthetics.

The 'Romantic' aspects of Wordsworth's poetry of feeling are put boldly in a vocabulary that, though always reconcilable with the Whig tradition, diverges from its ideological intent:

> I should mention one other circumstance which distinguishes these Poems from the popular poetry of the day; it is this, that the feeling therein developed gives importance to the action and the situation and not the action and situation to the feeling (*PrW* 1. 128).

This is consistent with the views of both a political revolutionary and a traditionalist. The poet seeks situations which coincide with heightened and poetic feelings that he represents as already existent: he is indifferent to situations that do not conform to these prior feelings. According to this view, Wordsworth's poetic theory is one of confirmation rather than critique. However, towards the end of the Preface, he explains that the ballad forms he uses in *Lyrical Ballads* are valuable because they can convey the power of imagination 'to many hundreds of people who would never have heard of it' (*PrW* 1. 150). The simplicity of ballads enables them to communicate in a comparatively transparent way, with the result that the perceptions of readers are altered. The implication is that through poetry a mutable reader is brought into a relationship of understanding with a mutable reality. Metrical writing will be 'read a hundred times where the prose is read only once' (*PrW* 1. 150). Loosed from bondage to a static, ready-made content, Wordsworth envisages poetry as inexhaustible; the reader never tires of Wordsworth's verse because he or she enters into a ceaseless dialectic between the regulation and excess of affect it brings about.[63] Wordsworth's poetry does not *contain* a politics. It is, instead, a relatively autonomous instrument that scrutinises affect in order to lay bare what is living (feeling) and what is dead (unfeeling) in ideology. The next chapter explores how Wordsworth's independent and critical art changes the meaning of the phrase 'political poetry' by becoming, in effect, the condition of possibility of a politics that truly thinks.

4

Wordsworth's Ear and the Place of Aesthetic Autonomy

Unable to control the wayward tendencies of affect by linking it to the 'realities' of the body and language, Burke attempts to ground his aesthetic ideology by reaffirming traditional connections between human feeling and the land. While the body is too excitable, and language according to Burke is an incubator of 'false' and worrisome transports, the apparently irrefutable presence of the land promises to anchor the individual's affections to home and locality, nation and Christendom.

As a number of critics have observed, Wordsworth's assumptions about place, nature and emotion translate well into Burkean terms. The poet not only shares the Whig civic humanist belief in the fundamental importance of affect, he also agrees with Burke's more particular view that a deleterious severance of human feeling from the land (and therefore from the nation and its institutions) has recently occurred. Nevertheless, although there are many similarities between the two writers, Wordsworth has a poetic and political agenda that is not signed up to the Irishman's philosophy. The result is art that is often Burkean in origin yet profoundly un-Burkean in execution and reach.

The 'imprecision' of language does not scandalize Wordsworth, and his assessment of the significance of the commercialisation of land is more sanguine than Burke's. At times, the *Reflections* almost demands the removal of land from the market. Wordsworth, by contrast, appears to accept that land has become irreparably compromised by money and the processes of exchange. Uniting his interest in the role of both poetic language and – increasingly – place in the production of affect, he begins to imagine poetry itself as a relatively autonomous locale in which to restore relations between thought and feeling. Whereas Burke wishes to press land into the service of an abstraction (Whig ideology), Wordsworth conceives of his poetry as a rigorously demarcated arena in which to respond to the specificity of the *thought-of* – the raw material of thinking and feeling. Examining the status of looking and listening in *Lyrical Ballads* and *The Prelude*, this chapter argues that the 'thought' of Wordsworth's poetry is as plastic as its many objects are varied. Attending closely to the dialectical interplay between intellect and the senses that occurs within his poetry, and even to interactions between individual senses, he produces a poetic 'feeling-thinking' that is at once materialist and critical. Through engagement with Burke and the Whig tradition, Wordsworth's dialectical and relatively autonomous verse negates abstraction in a promise to the unique and even, perhaps, impermanent.[1]

I

In the wake of the Revolution, Burke begins a damage-limitation exercise. He appoints himself to the task of repairing the natural relationship between Man and God that the French have dissolved. Burke initially goes about this task by once again considering the significance of the body. But having previously founded the importance of taste on the natural authenticity of sensation, he now insists on the authenticity of a subject's connection with property – a civic humanist position Wordsworth later also adopts.[2] In the Revolution, however, according to Burke, property has lost touch with its true meaning and the subject has become alienated from ownership.

Mary Wollstonecraft recognises that Burke's repeated insistence on the notion of a natural, divine history that is kept in place through the transmission of the paternal name amounts to a defence of heredity and property. His supposedly disinterested quest for truth masks the fact that he has a personal stake in the models of history and politics he defends. Wollstonecraft argues that his talk of God is a cynical exercise, and that it would be more honest for Burke 'to style [himself] . . . the champion of property'.[3] He is not a thinker with any vestige of objectivity. Instead he 'has secured himself a pension of fifteen hundred pounds per annum . . . [from] the Irish establishment'.[4] His livelihood is dependent on the stability of property and the rank that secures it. Thus, Wollstonecraft sees fit to insinuate that Burke's 'respect for rank has swallowed up the common feelings of humanity'.[5] She even insists that the whole apparatus of Burke's attack on the principles of the French Revolution is nothing but a desperate bid to once more mystify the inequality from which he benefits. Reason is his target because if it becomes the basis of political discussion, the continuity of rank and property will be challenged and overthrown. Property is kept in the hands of the few because people like Burke 'guard the temple of super-stition, and prevent reason from entering with her officious light'.[6] Wollstonecraft suggests that by presenting the French Revolution as an unnatural over-production of theory and political systematisation, Burke has made thought itself suspect, thus forestalling attacks upon his entire aesthetic ideology.

The confiscation of property he sees taking place in France is, perhaps, the event that confirms his belief in the wickedness of the Revolution. Property, in Burke's view, is closely allied with the transfer of the pater-nal name across generations – the name that ultimately keeps a nation united with the will of God. Detached from its family name, property is just another meaningless market commodity. To see it torn from its 'proper' owner is, therefore, to witness a kind of blasphemy. The first principle of the Revolution, the equality of man, defies the very condi-tions upon which the security of property depends. But the envious and poor Revolutionaries, driven by a lust for revenge on the wealthy, are unaware of the crime they commit. Burke, in fact, perfectly understands the source of their envious grasping: 'who, immersed in hopeless pov-erty, could regard all property, whether secular or ecclesiastical, with no other eye than that of envy[?]', he asks (*R* 97). Quite simply, the most unsuitable people for the safeguard of land are in power:

> Was it to be expected that they would attend to the stability of property, whose existence had always depended upon whatever rendered property questionable, ambitious, and insecure? Their objects would be enlarged with their elevation, but their disposition and habits, and mode of accomplishing their designs, must remain the same (*R* 94).

Casting out the essence of the nation, the 'natural landed interest' so beloved of civic humanists, the Revolutionaries have 'systematically subverted' the divine principle of property and replaced this natural law with 'their own arbitrary pleasure to determine what property is to be protected and what subverted' (*R* 95; 90; 272).

Burke is astounded by the simplicity of his disagreement with the French over the status of property. Believing that 'some decent regu-lated pre-eminence, some preference (not exclusive appropriation), given to birth, is neither unnatural, nor unjust, nor impolitic', he finds it difficult to understand the logic of the Revolution's confiscation policy: 'I considered that treasure rather as a possession to be secured than a prize to be contended for' (*R* 103; 105). However, he ties himself in knots trying to make property and rank both hereditary *and* fair. He does not wish 'to confine power, authority, and distinction to blood, and names, and titles. No, Sir. There is no qualification for government, but virtue and wisdom, actual or presumptive' (*R* 101). But having proposed this meritocracy, he then states that wisdom itself is acquired and that the privileged are more likely to have had the requisite training and education. Ultimately, the status quo remains unimpaired:

> The characteristic essence of property, formed out of the combined principles of its acquisition and conservation, is to be *unequal.* The great masses [of property] therefore which excite envy, and tempt rapacity, must be put out of the possibility of danger (*R* 102).

The lower orders must not be granted the expectation of wealth, as they are incapable of securing it, and their failure to get rich will inevitably lead to volatile resentment. The transmission of property is not only almost sacred, it is 'that which tends the most to the perpetuation of society itself' (*R* 102).

The stability of property through inheritance is a defence against the over-production that occurs elsewhere due to the system-breeding politics of the French Revolution. The property market that develops in France effects a process of cultural devaluation due to a proliferation of competing, and supposedly more superficial, values. The Revolutionary government has confiscated lands and transmuted the authentic value of such lands into money; and Burke finds this substitution of money into land, the value of which should be defined by its connection to the past through inheritance, nothing short of monstrous. Property loses its true worth and becomes demonically animated by the market:

> it assumes an unnatural and monstrous activity, and thereby throws into the hands of the several managers, principle and subordinate, Parisian and provincial, all the representative of money, and perhaps a full tenth part of all the land in France . . . the greatest possible uncertainty in its value (*R* 238).

The substitution of 'natural' heredity for the false system of the market results in the promiscuous circulation of property that then loses its 'real' value, its historical significance. Thus, Burke again witnesses the arbitrary infiltrate and damagingly overproduce. The property market seems to undermine the course necessary to history, and leads France into a phantom history that lacks depth or value.

II

'Michael' is easily characterised as the work of a Burkean – but, as will soon become apparent, Wordsworth considerably modifies Burke. The beginning of the poem recapitulates the idea, already implied in the Preface's defence of rustic language, that poetry's task is to guarantee the continued transmission of tradition from generation to generation. Wordsworth writes that he will tell the story of Michael

> For the delight of a few natural hearts,
> And with yet fonder feeling, for the sake
> Of youthful Poets, who among these Hills
> Will be my second Self when I am gone. (36–9)[7]

If it is economically impossible to pass on land and the tradition it literally grounds, poetry will continue the process. As David Collings points out, Wordsworth displaces Burke's embodiment of tradition in land and institutions (such as the Church and monarchy) to literature, thereby handing Michael's 'family heritage down to readers'.[8] Wordsworth thus substitutes the 'living continuity' of tradition 'with an abstract idea of it, making it an improper figure for itself, a sign of the symbol'.[9] He relinquishes Burke's grounded traditionalism for an historicism predicated on literature and the vagaries of interpretation. Nevertheless, as Collings points out in his reading of 'Michael', Wordsworth's idea of tradition (and Burke's, for that matter) is already a form of symbolic exchange, in which inheritance is *represented* through Michael's handing of a staff to Luke.[10] Moreover, Michael's land – the objective site of tradition – is only of significance because it is loaded with the symbolic freight of ancestry. On this evidence, the very nature of tradition seems to be the elision of sign and symbol. In parallel to the subversion of traditional landownership by economic forces, Wordsworth is able to substitute one sign system for another, 'poetry' for 'land', as representative of tradition.

While a case can be made for the Burkeanism of 'Michael', Wordsworth's discussion of the poem (along with 'The Brothers', its companion piece in *Lyrical Ballads*) in his 1802 letter to Charles James Fox complicates matters. Burke's influence is shown in the letter's concern about continuity of landownership. Like Burke, Wordsworth believes that the vital bonds of affection between people are predicated on place.[11] He is particularly anxious about the disappearance of the class of landowners known as 'statesmen' – small proprietors whose 'little tract of land serves as a kind of permanent rallying point for their domestic feelings' and 'is a fountain fitted to the nature of social man from which supplies of affection, as pure as his heart was intended for, are daily drawn' (*EY* 314–15). Wordsworth here makes the link between land, affection and social cohesion that is common in Burke's writing.

It would be wrong, however, to describe the letter to Fox as thoroughly Burkean. Wordsworth begins with the observation that the 'bonds of domestic feeling among the poor' are being broken 'by the spreading of manufactures through every part of the country, by the heavy taxes upon postage, by workhouses, Houses of Industry, and the invention of Soup-shops &c. &c. superadded to the encreasing disproportion between the price of labour and that of the necessaries of life' (*EY* 313). This concern for the 'lower orders' is clearly a departure from Burke. One of Wordsworth's principle themes is the alienation experienced by the poor – what he calls 'a rapid decay of the domestic affections among the lower orders of society' whereby

> parents are separated from their children, and children from their parents; the wife no longer prepares with her own hands a meal for her husband, the produce of his labour; there is little doing in his house in which his affections can be interested, and but little left in it which he can love' (*EY* 313; 314).

Such an interest in the relationship between affection and home could be reeled back to support an argument for Wordsworth's Burkeanism. But the letter and the poems it cites reflect a breadth of social sympathy that exceeds such a narrow definition. Wordsworth is concerned, in equal parts, about both the inhabitants of the workhouse and small proprietors like Michael. His politics, therefore, are not limited to either an altruistic or paternalistic concern for different classes of the poor. The bonds of affection between people that, he believes, are assured by place are his abiding concern – in all their structural and social variety. Landownership, then, is just one instance of the relationship between people and place that interests Wordsworth: the daily round of the mendicant described in 'The Old Cumberland Beggar' is another, and just as important.[12] The relative stability of each relationship provides the foundation for 'repeated experience and regular feelings' that Wordsworth affirms in the Preface to *Lyrical Ballads* (*PrW* 1. 124).

In short, although often sharing a rhetoric and thematics usually associated with Burke, Wordsworth's politics in the letter to Fox are not restricted to Whiggism.[13] The poet decries the mechanistic inhumanity of market forces and government policies that – indifferent to the delicate bonds between people and place – ravage communities, dislocate individuals and destroy affection. He argues that social breakdown is the fault of a political system that, through its imposition of arbitrary social policies and institutions (soup shops and workhouses, among other things) from above, subsumes individuals beneath the general category of 'the lower orders'. Once rendered an abstraction, the 'lower orders' are then manipulated in ways that damage both individuals and society.

The poet addresses this argument to Fox in the belief that the politician has a 'constant predominance of sensibility of heart' that enables him to look upon men 'as individuals', and to leave his 'heart open to be influenced by them in that capacity' (*EY* 313). Wordsworth suggests that this perspective is not only exceptional for a politician, but also essential for social and political justice. Thus, perceiving the leader of the Whig opposition as sensitive and humane, Wordsworth justifies writing this literary critical letter on the politics of a poem about an impoverished Cumbrian shepherd and a half-built sheepfold.

III

The force of Wordsworth's diagnosis of social ills in 'Michael' and 'The Brothers' creates the expectation that in the content of the poems there is a proposed cure – an ideological doctrine. But Wordsworth encourages Fox to *read* the poems, thereby undercutting the authority of the letter's exegesis: the implication is that the poems are a process interpretation cannot exhaust. While the concerns expressed in the letter may reflect a 'politics', the poems give rational form to affection without converting affection into an idea.[14] The poems cannot be translated into political theory. They offer art as an experience of the reciprocity of thought and feeling – arguably the condition of possibility of any political theory aspiring to realise human happiness. Theodor Adorno's remarks on music and language are pertinent: 'In contrast to philosophy and the sciences, which impart knowledge, the elements of art which come together for the purpose of knowledge never culminate in a decision'.[15] Pursuing knowledge, but without leaping to the swift abstractions required by instrumental reason, 'Michael' and 'The Brothers' reveal the relationship of thought to feeling as human experience – or life.

Wordsworth explains that 'Michael' and 'The Brothers' were written to 'excite profitable sympathies in many kind and good hearts' (*EY* 315). He restates this idea in 'Michael' itself, and claims that while he was still a boy, the story 'led me on to feel / For passions that were not my own'

(30–1). In his turn, Wordsworth will offer up the tale 'For the delight of a few natural hearts' (36). Although Burkean in appearance, this line and the rest of the surrounding passage reflects the Preface's ideologically fluid discussion about poetry's role in the preservation of people's attachments to one another. There, Wordsworth describes the poet as 'the rock of defence of human nature; an upholder and preserver, carrying everywhere with him relationship and love' (*PrW* 1. 141). Mindful affection is transmitted in poetry, in this way restoring the bonds of feeling that have been distorted and broken by political and economic ideology: 'in spite of things silently gone out of mind and things violently destroyed, the Poet binds together by *passion* and *knowledge* the vast empire of human society' (*PrW* 1. 141; my italics).

In Wordsworth, affection and sympathy for others is produced in the reader through the fine balance his art achieves between the intellectual and the sensual. Wordsworth's poetry gives pleasure, a vital component of affection and sympathy, through the play inherent in its unwillingness to negate itself in the name of an abstract political 'truth':[16]

> We have no sympathy but what is propagated by pleasure: I would not be misunderstood; but wherever we sympathize with pain it will be found that the sympathy is produced and carried on by subtle combinations with pleasure (*PrW* 1. 140).

There is, then, 'an infinite complexity of pain and pleasure' at the centre of Wordsworth's poetry (*PrW* 1. 140). Crucially, however, affection – and by extension Burkean tradition – is not presented simply as a first principle or truth in Wordsworth: it can become poisoned, transfixing individuals if they find its loss impossible to bear.

'Michael' explores the dialectic of affection and alienation by telling the same story twice. Michael's relationships, labour, and expectations are initially described in the context of affection. After the disappearance of Luke, however, they are re-described in the context of alienation. In the first part of the poem, while Luke is still growing up, the relationships, labours and hopes of Michael and Isabel are represented by their cottage, the light that shines from it 'a public Symbol of the life, / The thrifty Pair had liv'd' (137–8). The cottage is known 'by all / Who dwelt within the limits of the Vale, / Both old and young' as 'The Evening Star' (144–6). Furthermore, when Luke is of an age, Michael

> from a winter coppice cut
> With his own hands a sapling, which he hoop'd

> With iron, making it throughout in all
> Due requisites a perfect Shepherd's Staff,
> And gave it to the Boy (190–4).

The staff is another symbol – this time of the bond between Michael, Luke and the land they tend.

However, by the time the poem is written 'The Cottage [...] Is gone, the ploughshare has been through the ground / On which it stood' (485–7), and all that remains is the unfinished sheepfold. The story of Michael's life after Luke's desertion is actually a retelling of the same life, but the tale of affection has now become one of alienation. The cottage and staff have been replaced by the sheepfold: the 'life of eager industry' (124) and permanence symbolised by the cottage and staff is inverted in Michael's solitary visits to the 'straggling Heap of unhewn stones' (17). Alienated from Luke and Isabel (the latter disappearing from the narrative at Luke's fall, only to reappear after Michael's death), the land is no longer a 'rallying point for . . . domestic feelings' through which Michael may express affection for his family. The construction of the sheepfold initially embodies the bond between Michael and Luke. The 'heap of stones, which by the streamlet's edge / Lay thrown together, ready for the work' (327–8) hummed with the kinetic energy of love and hope. That love, indeed, found expression for an instant when the boy 'stooped down, / And, as his father had requested, laid / The first stone of the Sheep-fold' (418–20). But by the end of the poem, Wordsworth reports how ' – 'tis believed by all / That many and many a day . . . [Michael] thither went, / And never lifted up a single stone' (464–6). The power of affection contained in the fold and its heap of stones becomes nothing but a dead weight.[17] Rather than an ongoing project, the incomplete structure is now effectively a ruin – a sign of rotten affection. Languishing in thrall to his failure, Michael is oppressed by the thing that once animated his spirits. In the terminology of the *Essays upon Epitaphs*, Michael's love for his land and his son has become a 'counter-spirit', no longer a phenomenon that will 'uphold, and feed, and leave in quiet', but one that is 'unremittingly and noiselessly at work to derange, to subvert, to lay waste, to vitiate, and to dissolve' (*PrW* 2. 185–8).

The unfinished sheepfold is not simply a melancholy image that reflects the broken covenant between Michael and Luke, however. Containing at the same time a memory of hope and failure, it *mediates* affection and alienation through one another. The sheepfold liberates the conceptual in the mimetic. Neither affection nor alienation is allowed to harden into a brute fact of feeling that prohibits further analysis – and the poem refuses to take a simple republican or Whig position. Here, alienation is predicated on the loss of affection, and affection is predicated on the possibility of alienation. The poem mimetically captures the way affection, through its opposite, itself sustains Michael's sense of loss. Thus, by telling the same story twice, and through the doubled significance of the stone sheepfold, the poem introduces alienation as the dialectical *critique* of affection, while also (and more conventionally) positing affection as the critique of alienation. An interrogation of false affection and false alienation, the poem facilitates hope for the marriage of social life and truth. As Wordsworth's ideal reader, and through the (itself poetic) 'repetition and continuance' of reading poetry, Fox may thus 'be in some degree enlightened, and his affections ameliorated' (*PrW* 1. 129).

IV

According to James Chandler, 'The Ruined Cottage', written before 'Michael' in 1797–8 but not included in *Lyrical Ballads*, contains another important statement on the use of poetry that represents a seminal moment in what he regards as Wordsworth's development of a specifically Burkean conception of poetry and its uses: 'No longer just a natural tale, the poem becomes an illustration of what it means to tell a natural tale – how such a story is produced, how it is received, and what difference its telling makes to speaker and listener'.[18] Chandler's work on the poem is part of his broader analysis of Wordsworth's attitude towards books as vehicles of Burkean tradition – transmitters of 'natural culture . . . that is, of culture as a second nature'.[19]

The Pedlar explains to the narrator that

> [']The poets in their elegies and songs
> Lamenting the departed call the groves,
> They call upon the hills and streams to mourn,
> And senseless rocks, nor idly; for they speak
> In their invocations with a voice
> Obedient to the strong creative power
> Of human passion['] (73–9).[20]

The relationship between art and nature is central to this section of the poem. As representatives of Mankind, poets unite an isolated humanity with an otherwise indifferent nature. Their poetry, the Pedlar says, has the power to call upon nature – which usually remains mute – to mourn human frailty. However, the phrase 'voice / Obedient' suggests that poets address nature in answer to a kind of summons. While it is difficult to be sure who commands and who obeys, the understanding between poets and nature is clearly established.

The narrator goes on to recall how the Pedlar told the 'homely tale [of Margaret] with such familiar power, / . . . / . . . that the things of which he spake / Seemed present' (209–12). Describing the story recorded in the poem as 'homely', Wordsworth suggests that it is not only as plain as the Preface would have it, but is also 'home-like' – that verse can provide the sense of connection and stability usually associated with home. Once transformed into poetry, a tale has something like a redemptive power. Listening to the old man's tale, moved by the tragical history he hears and paralysed by 'the impotence of grief' (500), the poet-narrator learns his vocation. The Pedlar recounts the feelings he once had upon seeing Margaret's decayed cottage:

> [']Amid the uneasy thoughts which filled my mind,
> That what we feel of sorrow and despair
> From ruin and from change, and all the grief
> The passing shews of being leave behind,
> Appeared an idle dream that could not live
> Where meditation was. I turned away
> And walked along my road in happiness' (519–25).

Meditation not only preserves the past, but reduces temporality to merely one of the 'passing shews of being'. We are to suppose that poetry alerts us to Being itself, the unchanging kernel of existence. Indeed, the invitation at the beginning of the poem to escape the summer sun 'beside the root / Of some huge *oak* whose aged branches make / A twilight of their own' (11–13; my italics) attaches poetry to Burke's idea of England's organic tradition.[21] The poet's conservative function is said to dissipate the suffering time induces and restore a sense of permanence amidst change. Thus, one can agree with Chandler's conclusion that the poem might serve 'as a guideline for a literary program because it implies a view of how literature functions within a culture'.[22]

Chandler argues that because the poem 'seeks to promote a specific approach to its own interpretation' it implies that 'books teach as nature teaches only insofar as they teach as speech does'.[23] However, it is not necessarily the case that the poem portrays the situation of storytelling as essentially oral. Clearly, the oral setting plays an important part in Wordsworth's poetics at this time because of its evocation of a traditionalism associated with the ballad. Of more import, though, is the suggestion in the poem that the poet is one who teaches having already *listened* to a teaching. At the end of 'The Ruined Cottage' the narrator and the pedlar sit together on a bench while 'A thrush sang loud, and other melodies, / At a distance heard, peopled the milder air' (532–3). Birdsong dwells in the air, in the same way that people live on land. By listening to the Pedlar's account of Margaret's life – and with her derelict house poignant and impressive nearby – the narrator memorises a domestic tale that, once composed into poetry, he and other listeners or readers can later inhabit like a (natural) home.

Poetry is a form of teaching in *Lyrical Ballads*. The poet advises and disciplines, calling people back to a traditional attitude of humility and responsibility towards nature. In 'The Idle Shepherd-Boys', Wordsworth describes a pastoral scene: 'The valley rings with mirth and joy, / Among the hills the Echoes play /A never, never ending song / To welcome in the May' (1–4). The boys pass the time 'as happy as the Day' (21), apparently oblivious to the sand-lark's chant and the thrush's song: 'They never hear the cry, / That plaintive cry! which up the hill / Comes from the depth of Dungeon-Gill' (30–3). In their play and distraction, the boys are deaf to nature.

During a game, one of the boys notices a lamb 'swimming round and round' in a torrent; but before they can save the creature a poet draws 'it gently from the pool, / . . . forth into the light' (89–90). A lover of brooks more 'than the sages' books', 'the Bard / Those idle Shepherd-boys upbraid, / And bade them better mind their trade' (96–8). In 'Michael', Luke might be kept in check by his father's 'looks or threatening gestures' (203), but the son ultimately transgresses. In 'The Idle Shepherd-Boys', there is no suggestion that the poet's words are ignored. The narrative ends with the reprimand, and no drama follows. The poet is heard where a more conventional figure of authority is not.

While 'The Idle Shepherd-Boys' remarks upon the failure of the boys to notice the sounds of nature, other poems in *Lyrical Ballads* expand upon the theme of hearing, reinforcing its significance. In 'Expostulation and Reply', Wordsworth answers the criticism that he is daydreaming:

> 'Think you, mid all this mighty sum
> 'Of things for ever speaking,
> 'That nothing of itself will come,
> 'But we must still be seeking['] (25–8)?

The frantic 'agency' of the eye is dismissed in favour of a passivity more often associated with the ear; and the rhetorical question Wordsworth asks in reply to his friend stops further discussion, indicating that the poet will tolerate no disagreement. As in 'The Idle Shepherd-Boys', the poet, who listens, insists on being heard.

'The Tables Turned', paired with 'Expostulation and Reply', returns to the same theme. Wordsworth tells his friend to stop reading, to observe nature, and 'hear the woodland linnet, / How sweet his music; on my life / There's more of wisdom in it' (10–12). The throstle is considered a 'preacher', and Wordsworth demands that 'Nature be your teacher' (16). One must listen to nature because upon its breath is a 'spontaneous wisdom' (line 19). 'Meddling intellect', on the other hand, Wordsworth claims, employing a visual metaphor, 'Mishapes the beauteous forms of things' (26; 27). In an image of momentary synaesthesia, Wordsworth asks his interlocutor to 'bring with you a heart / That watches and receives' (31–2) – *watching* implying a passive and receptive stance, as opposed to the more active alternative of *looking*. Critical of books and reading, most of the poem, in fact, can be considered a defence of listening. In his song, the poet – attuned to the wise speech of nature – emphasises the value of the passive ear, rather than the more demanding eye.

IV

In some ways, the above discussion of listening in Wordsworth coincides with prevailing notions of Romantic conservatism. The politics of Romanticism has often been discussed in terms of attitudes towards the self. Many critics have insisted that by opting out of social conflict to seek resolution in the 'natural' and internal realm of subjective imagination, Romantic poetry asserts a fundamentally reactionary ideology.[24] The major recent version of this view contends that in 'Tintern Abbey' Wordsworth closes his eyes to what is in front of him and, abandoning society in order to consolidate his self, turns to private memory and imagination. The case against Wordsworth depends upon the assumption that vision is primary in his work. While Wordsworth favours vision for 'freely embodying internal realities', he dismisses hearing for 'slavishly registering external and mutable fact'.[25] Wordsworth's conservatism is a function of his acquiescence to instrumental reason – that is, a kind of rationality dedicated to preserving human life by bringing a nature perceived as potentially hostile under its rubric. Vision is thus key to the correlation of conservatism with instrumental reason.

If vision is free to embody internal realities, the self is released from the demands of empirical reality and, by extension, society and politics.[26]

Such an over-emphasis on vision leads to a flawed understanding of Wordsworth's politics (and the relationship between politics and aesthetics in his work), whereas an awareness of the importance of hearing in the poetry reveals a writer open to, for want of a better word, otherness. Geoffrey Hartman, for example, submits that listening dissolves the tyrannical subject of the eye, and facilitates the manifestation of something preceding subjectivity, an 'elemental' state that is 'ghostlier . . . yet more living than what is present'.[27] However, Hartman's 'nostalgic', Heideggerian reading could also be used to construct Wordsworth as a fully fledged Burkean – a view brought into question by the discussion so far. The priority of language over subjectivity in Heidegger is remarkably similar to the priority of tradition over the individual in Burke. There is a danger, then, that debate might stall somewhere between an ocular Wordsworth and an equally conservative Heideggerian, perhaps Burkean, Wordsworth.

Latent in Wordsworth's promotion of the aural is an anti-humanism he suspects.[28] In short, the poetry is quietly contradictory: it at once asserts and disavows a politics, using the ear to criticise the eye, yet also declining to give the ear a positive value. Rather than denounce Wordsworth as subject-centred or celebrate his 'inscription' in language and tradition, it is possible to regard the poet's dialectical auto-critique as testimony to his art's relative autonomy. For Adorno, aesthetic autonomy – a work's internal 'logic' – is its politics. More concerned with formal integrity than the expression of content, the artwork's

> detachment from naked existence becomes the measure of the world's falsity and meanness. Protesting against these conditions, the poem proclaims the dream of a world in which things would be different.[29]

Its studied ambivalence towards listening is the poetry's resistance to the absence of harmony in the world. Rejecting conflict by withdrawing into itself, Wordsworth's poetry nurtures and sustains a hope for reconciliation between humankind and nature.[30]

V

What if 'Tintern Abbey' is not founded solely on a philosophy of reflection in which the relationship between subject and object is governed by the eye? Political critics of Romanticism who approach

Wordsworth by way of vision tend to consider art solely in terms of mimesis, with the inevitable result that they scrutinise the poetry of the period for the ideology it is believed to reproduce. Moreover, the model of ideology such critics habitually work with is inadequate when applied to art. Ideology is not synonymous with the falsehoods a social group peddles in order to present its own interests as universal. The concept attempts to both expose and *explain* false ideas, thereby revealing what Adorno calls their 'historical necessity' – the truth of their untruth.[31] If artworks were simply ideology, as it is usually defined, they would be deluded or deceitful failures. In the event, incorporating ideology as material for composition, successful art catches falsehood in the act of masking truth. As Adorno puts it, 'The greatness of works of art lies solely in their power to let those things be heard which ideology conceals. Whether intended or not, their success transcends false consciousness.'[32] The remainder of this chapter contends that Wordsworth does not always use vision to set the subject against the object. Furthermore, it will become increasingly clear that listening is at least as important as looking (or looking away) in his poetry. In essence, listening counteracts vision and then counteracts itself. By following a line of enquiry that does not lead directly to a theory of art-as-mimesis, it is possible to read Wordsworth's poetry with regard to its relative aesthetic autonomy. Thus, elements of ideology that are present in his work can be interpreted in the light of their hidden truth, or 'truth content', rather than simply as proof of political bad faith.

Wordsworth attempts to establish the self's continuity through time, but he does not simply spurn the present or attempt to subsume it under the influence of memory. 'Tintern Abbey', after all, begins with the statement that 'again I *hear* / These waters, rolling from their mountain-springs / With a sweet inland murmur' (2–4). *Behold* in line 5 only appears following the initial auditory experience. Even then, the scene Wordsworth depicts has little of the clarity expected from vision:

>   – Once again
> Do I behold these steep and lofty cliffs,
> Which on a wild secluded scene impress
> Thoughts of more deep seclusion; and connect
> The landscape with the quiet of the sky (4–8).

'Tintern Abbey' can obviously be regarded as an exercise in visionary displacement and sublimation, but the phrase 'quiet of the sky' is responsible for much of the Wordsworthian mystery in the above passage. A moment of similarly affecting discretion, in fact, occurs shortly afterwards:

> Once again I see
> These hedgerows, hardly hedgerows, little lines
> Of sportive wood run wild; these pastoral farms
> Green to the very door; and wreaths of smoke
> Sent up in silence, from among the trees,
> With some uncertain notice, as might seem,
> Of vagrant dwellers in the houseless woods,
> Or of some hermit's cave, where by his fire
> The hermit sits alone (14–22).

It is not just the sight of the wreaths of smoke that evokes Wordsworth's reverie, but also their silence. Imagination is drawn outwards and *into* the scenery by silence: the visionary does not simply erase the real in order to seal up the self. As already seen at the conclusion of 'The Ruined Cottage', listening in poetry enables Wordsworth to experience a real, and precise, sense of place.

Wordsworth's praise of the mood that unlocks memory is also marked by a vocabulary that shifts between the visual and the aural:

> that blessed mood,
> In which the burthen of the mystery,
> In which the heavy and weary weight
> Of all this unintelligible world
> Is lighten'd: – that serene and blessed mood,
> In which the affections gently lead us on,
> Until the breath of this corporeal frame,
> And even the motion of our human blood
> Almost suspended, we are laid asleep
> In body, and become a living soul:
> While with an eye made quiet by the power
> Of harmony, and the deep power of joy,
> We see into the life of things (38–51).

When Wordsworth's breath itself is suspended – his speech hushed, in Shakespeare's idiom[33] – and unfettered by his own hubbub, he gains access to the 'living soul'. The visionary eye is presented in terms of *quiet* and *harmony* – usually aural terms. In the present, Wordsworth only grasps 'gleams of half-extinguish'd thought' (59). When his 'mind's eye' is quietened, though, he retrieves the past in all its sensual plenitude. The eye is not transformed into an ear – but, bewilderingly, when silenced it can perceive harmony.

Both sound and vision are central to 'Tintern Abbey':

> The sounding cataract
> Haunted me like a passion: the tall rock,
> The mountain, and the deep and gloomy wood,
> Their colours and their forms, were then to me
> An appetite: a feeling and a love,
> That had no need of a remoter charm,
> By thought supplied, nor any interest
> Unborrowed from the eye (77–84).

Again, a visionary reminiscence is introduced by a noise. But, in this case, there is something superficial about sight. Although what Wordsworth sees inspires 'a feeling and a love' in him that he equates with the life-affirming quality of appetite, the poem yearns to escape from fretful desire and experience stillness in time. 'Tintern Abbey' expresses an urge to get beyond desire and its regulating dynamic of subject and object. Wordsworth wishes to be 'laid asleep / In body, and become a living soul', reach a silence in which he can hear 'The still, sad music of humanity' (46–7; 92). This tranquil spot, characterised by silence, harmony and music, baffles the subject-object opposition that organises the philosophy of reflection. The power that 'chasten[s] and subdues' (94) Wordsworth is not his sovereign self willing its transcendence of social reality. It is, instead, nature's revelation of Being, the 'spirit, that impels / All thinking things, all objects of all thought, / And rolls through all things' (101–3) – the call towards which the individual self grasps for consolation.

When Wordsworth turns to Dorothy in the final section of 'Tintern Abbey', he first notes 'the shooting lights / Of thy wild eyes' (119–20). By Wordsworth's definition, only the Poet can hear the song of nature. However, he sees in Dorothy a representative of the 'wild', and can hear in her 'The language of my former heart' (118). Her natural speech calls him from his present self to something deeper. Through Dorothy, her mind likened to a 'dwelling-place / For all sweet sounds and harmonies' (141–2), Wordsworth once more hears nature's voice and the call of Being.

VI

In Book 5 of *The Prelude* (1805), Wordsworth pauses to consider the
poem thus far:

> . . . Hitherto,
> In progress through this Verse, my mind hath look'd
> Upon the speaking face of earth and heaven
> As her prime Teacher . . .[34]

He learns his vocation by listening to nature, and states in Book I that he

> . . . yearn[s] towards some philosophic Song
> Of Truth that cherishes our daily life;
> With meditations passionate from deep
> Recesses in man's heart, immortal verse
> Thoughtfully fitted to the Orphean lyre (1. 231–5).

His work aspires to the condition of song, and so the importance of his
voice is emphasised:

> . . . great hopes were mine;
> My own voice cheer'd me, and, far more, the mind's
> Internal echo of the imperfect sound:
> To both I listen'd, drawing from them both
> A chearful confidence in things to come (1. 63–7).

While attending to the song of Being that nature sings, the poet also listens to his own voice. In a gesture of autonomy, Wordsworth replicates,
in his person, the structure upon which his poetic vocation depends.
Thus, he both responds to the voice of nature and, at the same time,
frees himself from a passive stance towards it. In other words, he begins
an attempt to father himself as a poet using his own voice.

Perhaps in illustration of this point, the Winander Boy episode in
Book 5 explores the delicate interplay of speaking and listening. The
boy, an 'apprentice' poet,

> Blew mimic hootings to the silent owls
> That they might answer him. – And they would shout,
> Across the watery Vale, and shout again,

> Responsive to his call, with quivering peals,
> And long halloos, and screams, and echoes loud
> Redoubled and redoubled (5. 398–403).

The initial call seems to originate with the boy, but his cries are themselves 'mimic hootings' – already a response to nature. In fact, the owls' calls are soon impossible to tell apart from echoes. Call and response are virtually indistinguishable.[35]

For Wordsworth, poetry alerts humankind to nature's song, which tells of the sameness-in-difference of Being. He might define the poet as one who sings – with the implication that he is identical with his poetry – but he also suggests that poetry is not identical with itself, as it is made possible by an act of listening. It is, in effect, a special kind of listening. Poetry is dependant on language, which always remains anterior to it; and language itself is dependant on speech, requiring as it does mediation through a speaker. Poetry, nature and language, then, all lack a clear origin, as each predicates, and is predicated upon, the others.[36]

Attention to the status of listening in Wordsworth qualifies the claim that the poetry represents a withdrawal into conservative interiority. Wordsworth's work is founded on an act of listening that necessarily opens it to some kind of exterior – an affirmation of the self's relationship with otherness and difference. However, there is a hidden cost in Wordsworth's openness to the other. The idea that poetry is already a kind of listening grants the poet access to the 'outside' and makes him more responsive to the social, but it also amounts to a breach of the self and concomitant diminution of agency – something akin to Burke's advocacy of submission to tradition.[37] This strategy of undercutting the will in order to achieve a privileged relationship towards Being has long been problematic. Coleridge was alert to an attack on the integrity of the subject in Wordsworth's poetics. In *Biographia Literaria,* he argues that poetry is not 'composition by accidental motives, [but] by an act of the will'.[38] Coleridge quite explicitly 'corrects' the theory of spontaneity in the Preface to *Lyrical Ballads,* emphasising that poetic composition is a '*voluntary* act . . . a union; an interpenetration of passion and of will, of *spontaneous* impulse and *voluntary* purpose'.[39] The Friend jealously defends the freedom of the self that Wordsworth endangers.

If one looks at the 1835 text of 'On the Power of Sound', the problems inherent in Wordsworth's poetics of listening become apparent. The ear is directly addressed in the poem as though, according to the 'Argument', it is 'occupied by a spiritual functionary, in communication with sounds, individual, or combined in studied harmony':[40]

> Thy functions are etherial,
> As if within thee dwelt a glancing Mind,
> Organ of Vision! And a spirit aerial
> Informs the cell of hearing, dark and blind;
> Intricate labyrinth, more dread for thought
> To enter than oracular cave (1–6).

The ear is presented as more potent than the eye in this passage, and Wordsworth appeals for music to provide a model for life: 'O for some soul-affecting scheme, / Of *moral* music, to unite / Wanderers whose portion is the faintest dream / Of memory!' (169–72). Music becomes a metaphor for a desired harmony on earth, and also represents the living memory of everything that has ever been heard – 'From the Babe's first cry to voice of regal City' (163). With the aid of the ear, 'all things are controlled' (178) by sound.

Wordsworth's ethics of sound seems intended to establish a totalising aesthetic ideology. Indeed, at the end of 'On the Power of Sound' music is transformed into the most totalising concept of all: the Creator. In the beginning was a sound – the Word: 'A Voice to Light gave Being', 'the WORD, that shall not pass away' (209; 224). The poem initially uses music as a metaphor in order to express hope for harmony amongst men. However, music is ultimately figured as that which precedes and exceeds Being itself, including human beings. Having already compromised its agency, Wordsworth's poetics of listening appear to tend towards the complete negation of the subject.

Further examination of *The Prelude*, nevertheless, reveals that Book 5 is already unsure about such thinking. Making his mimic hootings to the owls, the Winander Boy sometimes hears nothing:

> . . . And when it chanced
> That pauses of deep silence mock'd his skill,
> Then sometimes, in that silence, while he hung
> Listening, a gentle shock of mild surprize
> Has carried far into his heart the voice
> Of mountain torrents, or the visible scene
> Would enter unawares into his mind
> With all its solemn imagery, its rocks,
> Its woods, and that uncertain Heaven, receiv'd
> Into the bosom of the steady Lake (5. 404–13).

According to Paul de Man, the placement of *hung* introduces an anxiety into this passage. He argues that in Wordsworth *hung* and *hangs* always signal moments when sense is vertiginously postponed, 'as if the earth were suddenly pulled out from under our feet'.[41] It can be added that the positioning of *hung* adjacent to *listening* on the next line encourages a reading that locates indeterminacy specifically in the boy's relation to the calls he awaits. It is while the boy listens that a fall is anticipated.

However, the shift in the verb form from *hung* in line 406 to *has carried* in line 408 suggests that the natural sounds have arrived within the breast of the Boy before the event described at that moment in the poem. Listening, then, does not just render inoperable the opposition between subject and object: it is already determined by the language of nature (the call of Being, to use a Heideggerian vocabulary) that precedes such divisions. It must be assumed, then, that the boy is at one with nature before subjectivity emerges. For Wordsworth, as he writes in 'Ode: Intimations of Immortality', the poet's task is to restore awareness of nature and the authentic realm of Being that 'lie[s] too deep for tears' (206).[42] But the anxiety surrounding his representation of the Boy's intimacy with nature, and the recollection of the Boy's early death that follows in lines 415–16, insinuates a distance between Wordsworth and his poetics of listening.

Even earlier in Book 5, which begins with a lament against time, and compares poetry with living tradition (again, another name for Being), the dream of the Arab carrying a stone and a shell is recounted. The question of Romantic Orientalism is complex, but it is likely that the figure of the Arab is tainted with unease in Wordsworth because the period commonly associated the Orient with the origins of mankind.[43] Thomas de Quincey's *Confessions of an English Opium Eater* (1821), for example, constructs the East not only as the ancient cradle of mankind, but also as infantile, bestial and terrifying:

> I was stared at, hooted at, grinned at, chattered at, by monkeys, by paroquets, by cockatoos. I ran into pagodas: and I was fixed, for centuries, at the summit, or in secret rooms; I was the idol; I was the priest; I was worshipped; I was sacrificed.[44]

The Arab Dream draws upon similar fears. The Arab attempts to save the stone and the shell, representatives of geometry and poetry – the rational and sensual poles of Being – from a flood. When held to the ear, from the shell is heard

> . . . in an unknown Tongue,
> Which yet I understood, articulate sounds,

> A loud, prophetic blast of harmony,
> An Ode, in passion utter'd, which foretold
> Destruction to the Children of the Earth,
> By deluge now at hand (5. 94–9).

The unearthly language of poetry predicts the submersion of the earth by water, the significance of which becomes apparent later in the child-hood memory of the Drowned Man that follows on from the Winander Boy episode.

The Drowned Man section anxiously brings together nature and death by way of an alignment of listening with depth. In a lake near fields that are 'shaped like ears' (5. 457), a man goes missing. A party goes onto the lake, and 'in their Boat, / Sounded with grappling-irons, and long poles' (5. 468–9). The body of a man is recovered from the water:

> . . . 'mid that beauteous scene
> Of trees, and hills, and water, bolt upright
> Rose with his ghastly face; a spectre-shape
> Of terror even (5. 470–3)!

The discovery of the corpse in the depths suggests that the language of nature Wordsworth listens for does not return anyone to fullness.[45] The link between the Arab and the deluge indicates a degree of uncertainty about such a search for origins; and the appearance of the corpse indi-cates that, while the poetics of listening promises a reawakening to the wisdom of nature, what it actually delivers is dread and a loss of self. Locating the Poet's importance in his ability to hear and then communi-cate nature's forgotten and submerged song of Being, Wordsworth defines the 'authentic' subject as little more than a cipher traversed by language. Judging by the evidence of *The Prelude*'s Boy of Winander and Drowned Man, this kind of relationship with language amounts to death.

VII

Although Wordsworth's visionary art has often been considered, if not conservative in a Burkean sense, certainly a subject-centred discourse of appropriation, it is possible to read his poetics of the ear as an opening of the self to otherness. In this way, the poetry can be said to corre-spond to an altogether more socially responsible politics. However, as shown above, a profound anti-humanism stalks the idea of listening in Wordsworth. It seems, then, that these opposing interpretations offer an unhappy choice with regard to Wordsworth's politics: his poetry either suppresses the social or harms, and finally sacrifices, the subject.

Nevertheless, despite the problems discussed, the theme of listening in Wordsworth subverts the distinction between subject and object that motivates many political readings of Wordsworth. Indeed, the fact that listening is simultaneously affirmed and denied in the poetry further complicates the question of Wordsworth's commitments. One could argue, of course, that ambivalence towards the ear implies his disenchantment with politics – a view in keeping with the idea that the poet abandons the social for the aesthetic. However, if the poetry is approached as relatively autonomous art, a different conclusion arises concerning the political implications of the aural in Wordsworth.

For Adorno, bourgeois art is notable for its attempt to constitute 'itself purely according to its own particular laws'.[46] The 1800 Preface to *Lyrical Ballads* – with its efforts to describe the poet's unique qualities, and definition of poetry as the conjunction of passion and metre – witnesses to this assumption of aesthetic autonomy (*PrW* 1. 127; 1. 146). The autonomous work of art 'withdraws' from the world and develops according to an internal law. Henceforth, the formal unity of the work takes precedence over its content.[47] In the case of Wordsworth, the self's separation from nature is the poetry's originating formal principle rather than a problem for its content to overcome.

The idea that Wordsworth's politics can be conjured up from the manifest content of his poetry is misguided. The incompatibility of the visionary and aural relationships with nature is not a sign of political inconsistency or aesthetic failure. That Wordsworth also distances himself from the poetics of the ear indicates that the poetry develops an internal argument it has no wish to resolve. Despite the contradictions that persist and deepen across his *oeuvre*, Wordsworth's desire for harmony with nature remains constant. His poetics of the ear attempts to achieve this unity through the notion that the self is constituted by the song of nature, and therefore at one with nature before the fall into forgetfulness. Yet, the association of listening with death, and Wordsworth's doubts about the ear, further the poetry's withdrawal into itself. An element of mimeticism endures in the fact that the poetry appears to present ideas, but it only *mimes* the problem-solving processes of instrumental reason. The poetry is still always elaborated in accordance with its inner necessity.

This ambivalence about listening reveals the autonomy of Wordsworth's work. Both 'The Ruined Cottage' and 'Tintern Abbey' speak of a sense of alienation: nature seems indifferent to human anguish about time. By learning from nature that there is an aspect of the self that is forever unchanged, the poet bids humankind to overcome its fear of time by living harmoniously with the natural world. But the poetry cannot conclude with a representation of joyful reconciliation. To assert that people live in harmony with nature would be false: the desired intimacy with nature is itself predicated on unrelenting estrangement. Humanity's fundamental separation from nature is not surmounted by the mere statement of its reverse. In Book 5, what the poetry expresses is a continued hope for harmony combined with the realisation that from within a society determined by fearful hostility towards nature and attendant hunt after self-preservation, such unity with nature can only be thought of as death. Without presenting it as propositional content, the formal contradiction of the poetry suggests the impossibility of harmony under present conditions of habitual fear.

At the end of Book 5, Wordsworth recalls the moment

> when first
> My ears began to open to the charm
> Of words in tuneful order, found them sweet
> For their own sakes (5. 576–9).

By listening to the music in words, rather than reading them for their meaning, he learns the pleasure of poetry. Again linking sound and place, Wordsworth goes on to remember how he and a friend spent hours as youths walking around a lake 'Repeating favourite verses with one voice / Or conning more, as happy as the birds / That round us chanted' (5. 588–90). Through song, the two experienced a joy 'More bright than madness or the dreams of wine' and sensed 'That wish for something loftier, more adorned / Than is the common aspect, daily garb, / Of human life' (5. 509–601). The music of verse makes it possible to 'Receive enduring touches of deep joy / From the great nature that exists in works / Of mighty poets' (5. 617–19). Within the affective and intellectual breadth of poetry, Wordsworth explains, one can know more than one knows, transcendence and happiness, and glimpse other possible lives. 1807's 'The Solitary Reaper' recapitulates this movement. Wordsworth hears the woman's 'overflowing' song and 'listen'd, till I had my fill' *because* he is unable to understand the words.[48] It is because he cannot assimilate the encounter to his rules for social listening that Wordsworth feels the curve of own fullness in the woman's song.[49] However, he still does not turn this into the content of his work. Although concerned with the theme of books and reading, Book 5 holds its tongue about 'Their later influence' (5. 632). Longing for a better world, Wordsworth's relatively autonomous art – experimenting with both the ear and the eye – makes of itself a place that cultivates hope by refusing to legislate for the future from the perspective of a damaged present. The next chapter discusses the necessity of Wordsworth's efforts to prevent his poetics, regardless of his labours to construct poetry as a material locale, from succumbing to the pull of abstraction.

5
Poetry and Embodiment

Wordsworth criticises ideologies and abstractions that he believes, by curbing the possibilities of thought and feeling, cause pain and injustice.[1] Profoundly suspicious of ideas, his poetry develops into a materialism that negates political dogma of all hues. It appears, then, that the poet's relatively autonomous art is condemned always to be reactive: defined in opposition to fixed modes of thought and feeling, it cannot imagine anything else and has little substantive identity of its own. This chapter argues, however, that Wordsworth does not remain permanently critical in the years around his 'Great Decade'. Rather, he negates his own negations, and moves beyond endless critique towards a 'positive' idea of poetry. In its negotiations with Burke (and Kant, to a lesser extent), Wordsworth's 'The Sublime and the Beautiful' surmounts the involuntary moment of dialectics (its structural negativity) and begins to theorise a 'primary' poetics.

Exploiting tensions in Burke's writing, Wordsworth benefits from the Irishman's discoveries without submitting to the constraints of Whig ideology. The unmanageable instability of the sublime in Burke's *Enquiry* in fact provides the motor Wordsworth requires to forge an art that has a positive component robust enough to accompany the force of negation treated in the previous chapter. In 'The Sublime and the Beautiful', Wordsworth deploys Kant's ('objective') rationalism against Burke's excessive anti-mimeticism. But instead of encouraging the two thinkers to negate one another dialectically, Wordsworth synthesises Burke's sensationist traditionalism with Kant's subject-centred anti-materialism. 'The Sublime and the Beautiful' posits consciousness as both receptive to affect *and* analytical. Simultaneously *in* and *before* the world, thought for Wordsworth is not simply attuned to context: it is fundamentally shaped by matter – or, in other words, *embodied*.

This has major implications for Wordsworth's conception of poetry. Following Burke's lead, in *The Prelude* Wordsworth applies the categories of the sublime and beautiful to the French Revolution. Burke ultimately uses his aesthetics as a means to configure the Revolution as an abstraction that he can reject on equally abstract (or un-aesthetic) grounds. The poet, conversely, structures his verse around the sublime and beautiful in order to penetrate the complex emotional and intellectual content of the Revolution, and know the affect of events on consciousness. He re-emerges with thinking that is conspicuously inseparable from its incarnation as poetry. Prepared to withhold judgement on the Revolution, for example, *The Prelude* dwells with it in verse and then fashions itself into a parallel 'event' that is motivated by the encounter. Moreover, through the 'spots of time', Wordsworth leaves his critique of Burkean tradition behind and presents *The Prelude* as a history and tradition in its own right. The poem thus becomes a fully embodied *alternative* to the objects of its critique. Breaking with the reactive tendency of Wordsworth's art, *The Prelude*'s radical attentiveness to its own form renders it experimental and hence, by definition, a poetry of the future.[2]

I

For Burke, the experience of the sublime is achieved through engagement with 'terrible objects' (*PE* 39). The fear thus generated is delightful when, rather than pressing too close, it activates 'The passions belonging to self-preservation . . . the strongest of all the passions' (*PE* 40; 51). The subject avoids the annihilation of his subjectivity – always a danger when confronted with the sublime – and maintains a sense of self by following the dictates of the instinct of self-preservation. It is not the fearful element of the sublime, then, that Burke emphasises, but its product – self-love. The sublime's twofold movement begins by jolting the subject, through terror, from the potential complacency of socially binding mimetic beauty discussed in Chapter 2 and ends, having stimulated the instinct of self-preservation, by furnishing him with a sense of self. Thus, the sublime enables an individual to maintain his distinction from other members of society while regulating his emotions.

Although it releases the subject from the amorphousness and potential paralysis of imitation, Burke fears that the sublime itself might lead to another cycle of imitation, or a dissolution of the self at the moment of its elevation. He writes that the shouts of a crowd, for example, can so overwhelm the imagination 'that in this staggering, and hurry of the mind, the best established tempers can scarcely forebear being borne down, and joining in the common cry, and common resolution of the crowd' (*PE* 82). He values the sublime as a subjection to 'a power in some way superior' that differentiates the individual from the group (*PE* 65). Without this imperative, 'Melancholy, dejection, despair, and often self-murder, is the consequence of the gloomy view we take of things in . . . [a] relaxed state of body' (*PE* 135). The kind of sublime that Burke admires also instils in the subject the self-preserving compulsion to work: 'The best remedy for all these evils is exercise or *labour*' (*PE* 135). The sublime, finally, insists on the moral value of improvement and distinction.

As commentators have observed, in Burke the sublime is thoroughly gendered. By token of its fierceness, the role of the sublime has much in common with that of a father:

> The authority of a father, so useful to our well-being, and so justly vener-able upon all accounts, hinders us from having that entire love for him that we have for our mothers, where the paternal authority is almost melted down into the mother's fondness and indulgence (*PE* 111).

The father disciplines the laxity caused by the mother's over-indulgence and, as a consequence of his sternness, is rarely loved with equal affec-tion. Real power is comprised of the awe and respect commanded by a father, tempered by the qualities of a grandfather 'in whom this author-ity is removed a degree from us, and where the weakness of age mellows it' (*PE* 111).

Regarding the sublime as masculine, Burke's expressly male gaze also defines the beautiful. At this stage, the beautiful and 'woman' become analogous within his 'universalist' aesthetics. Frances Ferguson suggests that the link between the sublime and labour, and that between the mimetic beautiful and death, reminds us

> when it was that labor and death entered the world – with the Fall of Man . . . the labour of Burke's sublime is explicitly labelled as a providentially ordered capacity for mitigating the force of the beauti-ful that brought about both the Fall and the very possibility of the Fall, for the fatal flaw that Burke's category of the beautiful uncovers in man is his need for 'social communication.'[3]

Despite arguing for the beautiful's mysterious socialising capacity, how-ever, Burke insists that women are one of its major sources. The associa-tion of beauty with femininity, as well as desire and love, leads him to the conclusion that '[w]e shall have a strong desire for a woman of no remarkable beauty; whilst the greatest beauty in men, or in other animals, though it causes love, yet excites nothing at all of desire' (*PE* 91). Notwithstanding Burke's apparent conviction about the contents of the category of the beautiful, particularly in his description of the aspects of beauty peculiar to women, the distinction he makes between the sublime and the beautiful will not hold. It will become apparent, nonetheless, that for Wordsworth the vitality of the *Enquiry* does not lie in the indeterminacy that so much scholarship has had as its goal.

II

In his comparison of the qualities of a grandfather with those of a father, Burke suggests that the 'good' sublime disciplines beauty but is also softened by it: terror is translated into respect in order to encourage industry rather than incapacitating fear. In a way that he later appeals to in the *Reflections*, beauty moderates the sublime. When the two aesthetic characteristics are harmoniously blended in state institutions, national stability is ensured, Burke claims. The ethical and regulatory qualities of the sublime and beautiful are realised objectively in customs and institutions, and the subject living under their rule accepts them as a second nature. However, the harmony Burke advocates always depends upon his ability to define the sublime and beautiful with accuracy and, just as importantly, keep the two separate. In the *Enquiry*, though, the beautiful begins to be seen not just as a likely source of lethargy, but as dangerously deceptive. At times, indeed, the sublime itself also appears undisciplined.

Burke attempts to isolate what it is that makes beauty in women quite so thrilling, and settles on the idea that 'the beauty of women is considerably owing to their weakness, or delicacy, and is even enhanced by their timidity, a quality of mind analogous to it' (*PE* 116). Whereas the qualities associated with men – 'fortitude, justice, wisdom' – fall under the rubric of the sublime, women attain beauty through frailty (*PE* 110). Perfection is not an essential criterion of beauty:

> . . . where it is highest in the female sex, [beauty] almost always carries with it an idea of weakness and imperfection. Women are very sensible of this; for which reason, they learn to lisp, to totter in their walk, to counterfeit weakness, and even sickness (*PE* 110).

Burke concludes that 'Beauty in distress is much the most affecting beauty' (*PE* 110).

Mary Wollstonecraft's response to the *Reflections* is key to identifying the impact of Burke's discussion of women on his general enquiry into the sublime and beautiful. She regards with abhorrence both the premium Burke places on flawed beauty in women and his casual use of gender stereotypes. She suggests in *A Vindication of the Rights of Men* (1790) that Burke's sensibility is perverse if it can only discover beauty in imperfection, and reasons that if fortitude, justice, wisdom and truth had never been desirable and amiable qualities, everyone would start 'systematically neglecting morals to secure beauty'.[4] Wollstonecraft therefore looks upon Burke with suspicion, and investigates the contorted intellectual manoeuvres he is required to make in order to keep the sublime and beautiful distinct.

Chapter 2 considered the 'natural', social function of mimesis in Burke (frequently linked in the *Enquiry* to the beautiful), and how it is brought into question by dependence upon the arbitrary interruption of death. Burke tries to rectify such worrying difficulties with his theory of the sublime, thus defining beauty as weak and therefore easy to control. In the above passage, however, he clearly implies that women intentionally exploit their appearance of weakness. Essentially, Burke 'credits women with the conscious deployment of feminine artifice', and thus lands on a *dialectical* reading of 'woman' which allows that the masquerade of weakness might, in reality, be a sinister strength.[5] Despite efforts to control the subversive – or 'critical' – effects of beauty through the 'masculine' sublime, the *Enquiry* cannot fully domesticate it.

When he arrives at his analysis of the most beautiful physical characteristics of women, Burke places considerable importance on the female breast:

> Observe that part of a beautiful woman where she is perhaps the most beautiful, about the neck and breasts; the smoothness; the softness; the easy and insensible swell; the variety of the surface, which is never for the smallest space the same; the deceitful maze, through which the unsteady eye slides giddily, without knowing where to fix, or whither it is carried (*PE* 115).

Burke not only foregrounds the deceit inherent in beauty, but also stretches the category of the beautiful to breaking point. Fixing on the breast, the male gaze finds itself in a vertiginous situation. Almost severed from the will of the subject, the eye cannot comprehend what it perceives.

Burke's analysis of the breast reiterates the danger inherent in the lethargy occasioned by beauty: 'the self is undone by the beautiful. Beauty offers no resistance, it seduces without arousing (or offering) force or opposition and so presents no friction against which the "I" might test itself'.[6] Beauty robs the subject of individuality, returning him indifferently to the mass of society. The sublime might be recruited to police the deficiencies of the beautiful, but this section of the *Enquiry* is more than just a repetition of the oft-noted need to safeguard against beauty. Beauty here acts as an incomplete sublime. There is something overwhelming about the sensations elicited by the sight of a beautiful woman's breast. Certainly there is no horror, but it appears that 'the mind is so entirely filled with its object, that it cannot entertain any other, nor by consequence reason on that object which employs it' (*PE* 57). This definition of the sublime, which omits the disciplining quality of the category, could serve as a gloss on Burke's description of the female body.

The constellation of themes associated with sex and gender in Burke's categorisations of the sublime and beautiful is evidently strained. Early on in the *Enquiry*, Burke explains the role of the sublime with regard to sexual reproduction. He concedes that 'the generation of mankind is a great purpose, and it is requisite that men should be animated to the pursuit of it by some great incentive' (*PE* 41). Sexual desire is obviously the animating force, a desire prompted by the beauty of women and their physical attributes. Sex, he continues, is therefore 'attended with a very high pleasure' – but the pleasure must not be exclusive (*PE* 41):

> . . . it is by no means designed to be our constant business . . . The difference between men and brutes in this point, seems to be remarkable. Men are at all times pretty equally disposed to the pleasures of love, because they are to be guided by reason in the time and manner of indulging them (*PE* 41–2).

Brutes are prevented from indulging in continuous copulation by the pattern of their seasons; men, on the other hand, are guided by reason. Without reason, men would indulge their passions and do no work. Over-reproduction, it appears, would cause a lack of production. The sublime acts to incite men to action and divert them from sensuousness, yet over-production of the wrong kind haunts Burke's every turn. Within the beautiful is the danger of a disabling mimeticism, and within the beauty of the breast is a disturbing version of the sublime that, without ethical content, furthers the excesses of beauty. The distinctions that the *Enquiry* needs to keep in place refuse to settle. Yet the disarray that readers usually hail, in their belief that they can thereby contribute to the immobilisation of conservative ideology, is almost beside the point. The crucial issue here is not that the outlines of the sublime and beautiful dissolve, but that Burke's aesthetic categories seem to have an *agency* of their own. Chapter 3 discussed Wordsworth's exploitation of the force of positional language in Burke. What follows proposes that Wordsworth transforms his 'negative' poetics into something more 'positive' by using the energies he discovers in Burke's aesthetics.

III

When Wordsworth liberates the anti-mimetic, positional aspect of language in *The Prelude*, he embraces a linguistic idealism. As a boy, the poet steals a boat and is alerted to his crime by 'the voice / Of mountain echoes' (1. 390–1). Earlier, having stolen some eggs, he is haunted by the voice of nature:

> . . . and, when the deed was done,
> I heard among the solitary hills
> Low breathings coming after me, and sounds
> Of undistinguishable motion, steps
> Almost as silent as the turf they trod (1. 329–33).

Language breaks free of the young Wordsworth's control and takes on an independent life, speaking unintelligibly or, perhaps, in a manner still to be understood by the poet. Nevertheless, imposing itself on the boy, nature also has a disciplinary function in this passage, which would suggest that, in accordance with his Whig inheritance, the poet does not commit wholly to this anti-mimetic dimension of language. After all, such a stance – and this is where I part company with prevailing constructions of Wordsworth – would curtail his ability to experience the full range of affect.

The Wordsworthian sublime is similarly poised between the twin characteristics of language – the mimetic and the positional. Although it exhibits many of the features found in Burke's formulation (excessiveness and lack of regulation, to name two), the poet's sublime is often read in Kantian terms. Lucy Newlyn, for example, argues that the eighteenth- and nineteenth-century sublime is basically subject-centred, 'partly because the status of the subject is at this time deeply unstable – still locked into problems of authority and independence, yet attempting to negotiate independence from a transcendental order'.[7]

Newlyn sees Wordsworth's use of the sublime as always bound up with such questions of authority, including 'his own authority as a writer'; and she effectively empties Burke into Kant with her suggestion that the Burkean sublime seals identity and guarantees the subject.[8] Richard Bourke likewise finds Kant in Wordsworth:

> . . . as a project of coordination and harmonisation, the Wordsworthian sublime, in its aggressively destabilising aspect, becomes a mute hypothesis: for it is always on the way to being something else; it has already been enlisted as a constituent element in the project of consolation.[9]

This is, no less, a description of the Kantian sublime in which the sensory is overwhelmed and sovereignty bestowed on Reason. The Kantian sublime promotes the anti-aesthetic defeat of imagination as a spur to Reason. Regardless of much recent criticism's certainty that Wordsworth is Kantian, though, *The Prelude*'s sublime neither confirms the subject nor establishes the rule of Reason. Wordsworth's Burkean sublime runs counter to Kant: it is predominantly the servant of (often bodily) habit not Reason.[10] However, while Burke's aesthetics of the sublime and beautiful mildly irritate his politics, Wordsworth's sublime boldly oversteps its Whig loyalties.

The climbing of Snowdon in Book 13 has regularly been used as evidence of Wordsworth's Kantianism.[11] But the passage is worth returning to because it *does not*, as many allege, offer a version of the sublime that can be read simply as a Kantian suppression of materiality. The scene has the awful characteristics of the Burkean, rather than Kantian, sublime:[12]

> . . . I look'd about, and lo!
> The Moon stood naked in the Heavens, at height
> Immense above my head, and on the shore
> I found myself of a huge sea of mist,
> Which meek and silent, rested at my feet (13. 40–4).

The bold and giant moon sits ominously in the sky, and a mist threatens to engulf the poet. This sense of admiration and fear is further suggested by the description of uncanny vapours that 'shot themselves, / In headlands, tongues, and promontory shapes' (13. 47–8). One has only to remember Burke's discussion of the obscure sublimity of Milton's use of the word *shape* in the *Enquiry* to be alert to the kind of feeling

Wordsworth is attempting to evoke. Equally, the word *shape* signals that the poetry is trembling, ready for departure, at the limit of the mimetic.[13] Indeed, the fact that the mist is described as 'meek' (13. 44), rather than 'terrible', suggests that Wordsworth does not fear being engulfed. There is almost some comfort in the 'roar of waters, torrents, and streams / Innumerable, roaring with one voice' (13. 58–9), and he fixes upon the rising mist: 'in that breach / Through which the homeless voice of waters rose, / That dark deep thorough-fare had Nature lodg'd / The Soul, the Imagination of the Whole' (13. 62–5). The sublime swamps the poet and deprives him of sight, in this instance, but it also promises a clarity of 'vision' through the sound-conveying gap in the mist – and access to something beyond the bounds of his own subjectivity.

The moment of imagination is not strictly Wordsworth's possession. He is made aware of

> . . . a mighty Mind,
> Of one that feeds upon infinity,
> That is exalted by an underpresence,
> The sense of God, or whatsoe'er is dim
> Or vast in its own being . . . (13. 69–73).

Having begun to suppress the mimetic, Wordsworth claims in this passage that the sublime is nature's mimicry of God's power. Like the Creator – who creates *ex nihilo* – nature is able to mould and dominate 'the outward face of things' (13. 78) until 'even the grosest minds must see and hear / And cannot chuse but feel' (13. 83–4). This power is similar to that which 'higher minds bear' (13. 90):

> . . . They build up greatest things
> From least suggestions; ever on the watch,
> Willing to work and to be wrought upon,
> They need not extraordinary calls
> To rouze them, in a world of life they live,
> By sensible impressions not enthrall'd,
> But quicken'd, rouz'd, and made thereby more fit
> To hold communion with the invisible world (13. 98–105).

Wordsworth speaks here of a vagueness in reality that allows Imagination to flourish. It is difficult not to think of Kant. However, the passive turn of the passage does not suggest the triumph of intellectual or imaginative agency. On the contrary, the motif of submersion continues – only this time it is not concerned with the poet's being literally covered over by the mist, but is an image of the mind submerged in tradition: 'the highest bliss / That can be known is theirs, the consciousness / Of whom they are habitually infused / Through every image' (13. 107–10). Commentary has tended to ignore the fact that in this passage consciousness is inseparable from immersion in habit. In fact, it seems to be the case that the victory of imagination in Wordsworth occurs when consciousness is extinguished and the subject resorts to the deep structures of habit. Burke finally ousts Kant.

The Simplon Pass episode – another part of *The Prelude* that no re-evaluation of the poet can justifiably omit – is similarly predicated upon a sense inundation. Although seemingly an example of the Wordsworthian trope of success-through-failure, the celebration of imagination again cannot be read as a reproduction of the Kantian sublime. At the moment of imagination, Wordsworth is 'lost as in a cloud, / Halted without a struggle to break through' (6. 529–30). Of course, the mind does have a role:

> In such strength
> Of usurpation, in such visitings
> Of awful promise, when the light of sense
> Goes out in flashes that have shewn to us
> The invisible world, doth Greatness make abode,
> There harbours whether we be young or old.
> Our destiny, our nature, and our home
> Is with infinitude, and only there (6. 532–9).

It is not at all obvious that such a passage represents a form of 'transcendental idealism'.[14] The inability to say for sure whether imagination dwells in enlightenment or darkness, and the domesticating association of *infinitude* with *home* in lines 538–9, does not unambiguously suggest the illumined triumph of Kant's sovereign mind. The mind, although 'blest in thoughts / That are their own perfection and reward, / Strong in itself' (6. 545–7), is so overwhelmed that an 'access of joy / . . . hides it like the overflowing Nile' (6. 547–8). This is an example of the sensual, affective sublime more familiar from Burke than Kant. Even so, there is clearly some implication of transcendence in this section. While Burke is hardly supplemented with Kant here, it does appear that Wordsworth modifies – or, at the very least, stresses an element of – the Burkean sublime. In effect, he keeps both Kant and Burke in play. Surprisingly, this has gone unremarked by critics.

Throughout 'The Sublime and the Beautiful', his prose fragment published in 1812 but probably started as early as 1805–6, Wordsworth considers the two categories in terms derived from Burke.[15] He argues that although

> we may observe that it is impossible that a mind can be in a healthy state that is not frequently and strongly moved both by sublimity and beauty, it is more dependent for its daily well-being upon the love and gentleness which accompany the one, than upon the exaltation or awe which are created by the other (*PrW* 2. 349).

He suggests, in Burkean fashion, that the sublime and beautiful have a social function. Yet he also sees the sublime as something prior to the beautiful, that by 'making us *conscious* of its presence' the sublime is the condition of possibility of the beautiful (*PrW* 2. 350; my italics). This interest in consciousness might suggest a Kantian take on the sublime. Yet Wordsworth insists that

> The capability of perceiving these qualities [of the sublime and beautiful], & the degree in which they are perceived, will of course depend upon the state or condition of the mind, with respect to habits, knowledge, & powers, which is brought within the reach of their influence (*PrW* 2. 353).

Discussion of the sublime and beautiful is ultimately subsumed beneath concern for the primary importance of habit: perception of the sublime is founded upon a certain training, rather than the abstractions of Reason. Nevertheless, at the same time that Wordsworth introduces into his model of the sublime a sense of materiality associated with habit (whether it resides in the sonic, that is formal, quality of metre in poetry or in the bodily nature of daily routine), he super-adds ideas of 'bringing-to-consciousness' or 'making-possible'. Such notions, in their future orientation, conflict with Burke's 'backward-looking', traditionalist emphasis on habit.

Wordsworth goes on to state that he admires the sublime because it captures the subject in the contemplation of physical and mental might, with the result that 'the head & front of the sensation is intense unity' (*PrW* 2. 354). Wordsworth's sublime consists in the subject's *consciousness* of his absorption by the object. While this departs from Kant's insistence that the sublime frees the mind from determination by matter, it also differs from Burke in the persistence of a role for consciousness. An awareness of determination replaces Burke's pseudo-unconsciousness of habit and Kant's supra-consciousness of freedom. For Wordsworth, the sublime 'exists in the extinction of the comparing power of the mind' (*PrW* 2. 256) – in the rejection of activity that puts the analytical mind *before*, rather than *in*, the world. Wordsworth highlights the bodily but also – and with breathtaking originality – retains a mental content, at least as something to be tempered into experience.

Theresa Kelly asserts that the real difference between Wordsworth and Kant, with regard to the sublime, is that the poet is interested in 'the mind's capacity to engage in an all-encompassing unity'.[16] Undoubtedly, there is a tendency towards unity in Wordsworth's sublime, characterised by 'humility, modesty, diffidence, & an habitual, kindly, & confident communion with Nature' (*PrW* 2. 360). Wordsworth concentrates on the ordinary, whereas Kant suppresses the sensory in the name of Reason. Wordsworth's sublime, located in a *feeling* of unity accessed through *habit*, stands in the tradition of civic humanism to which Shaftesbury and Burke belong. However, while he resists the anti-aesthetic idealism of Kant, Wordsworth also pulls back from the Whig fear of the body; and rather than commit fully to a traditionalist political philosophy, Wordsworth only briefly entertains the call of the mimetic – the concern with empirical sensuality – that lies quietly at the genesis of Burke's writing. What has gone unrecognised is that, at one moment disembodied and transcendental, at the next exploring materiality, Wordsworth experiments with Kant against Burke in order that he might know the possibilities of the Whig sublime. As he descends into the almost primeval caverns of Burkean habit, Wordsworth rejects *both* society *and* the thinking that enables his retreat from it.

IV

How, then, does Wordsworth's still 'negative' treatment of Burke and Kant – his facilitation of their dialectical contact – become a 'positive' poetics and politics, as I claimed it does at the beginning of this chapter? It is necessary once more to reconsider some very well-known lines. In a way that appears to be prefigured by Burke's *Reflections*, Wordsworth comprehends the French Revolution by reading it through the aesthetic categories of the sublime and beautiful. The young poet is presented as a republican, arriving in Paris eager to visit 'each spot of old and recent fame' (9. 42). However, having not 'chanced / To see a regular Chronicle' (9. 100–1) that would explain events properly, Wordsworth finds himself listening to the hubbub of Paris with 'a stranger's ears'

(9. 55). He attempts to enter into the spirit of the Revolution, but is aware that he is merely acting a part:

> . . . from the rubbish [I] gather'd up a stone
> And pocketed the relick in the guise
> Of an Enthusiast, yet, in honest truth
> Though not without some strong incumbancies;
> And glad (could living man be otherwise?)
> I look'd for something which I could not find,
> Affecting more emotion than I felt (9. 65–71).

At this point, Wordsworth is little more than a tourist, albeit one whose political convictions coincide with political events in France. He wishes to *feel* a connection with Revolutionary France, and does so by making the foreign situation in which he finds himself more familiar. Taking his cue from the *Reflections*, Wordsworth uses the aesthetic as a portal to understanding. Thus, the outward signs of revolution make little impression on him, but a picture does. He is profoundly moved by a portrait, 'the Magdalene of le Brun, / A beauty exquisitely wrought, fair face / And rueful, with its ever flowing tears' (9. 78–80). Wordsworth here begins to mobilise Burke's intricately gendered category of the beautiful. Magdalene's face welcomes him to the Revolution while confirming his male independence.[17] The picture of Magdalene, then, is an object that enables the poet to compose the Revolution into an image that engages his affections.

It is not just the category of the beautiful that helps Wordsworth understand the Revolution. The sublime also plays an important role – yet the Revolutionary sublime does not produce the sense of unity one expects from Wordsworth's definition of the term in 'The sublime and the Beautiful'. He remarks upon his initial feeling of alienation in France:

> . . . I was unprepared
> With needful knowledge, had abruptly pass'd
> Into a theatre, of which the stage
> Was busy with an action far advanced (9. 92–5).

Wordsworth perhaps uses a theatrical metaphor in order to disassociate himself from a youthful episode that, by 1805, may have been politically embarrassing. He resorts to *several* strategies to open some distance between himself and the Revolution, though, one such technique being his figuring of the Revolution in terms of the sublime and beautiful. Just as Burke criticises the Revolution for generating a false sublime, Wordsworth sees a corrosion of the aesthetic order in France.[18] The alienation he describes matches what he regards as a failure of the Revolution at the level of aesthetics – which is to say, and I want to be very clear about this, in its effect on the *relationship between thought and feeling.*

Wordsworth recounts his return to Paris in 1792, 'enflamed with hope' (10. 38) after a period spent in the Loire. With its deposition of the king on August 10, 1792, the Revolution has moved into an increasingly violent mode: 'I crossed (a black and empty area then) / The square of the Carousel, few weeks back / Heap'd up with dead and dying' (10. 46–8). Again he describes his alienation. He gazes upon the sites of murder

> . . . as doth a man
> Upon a volume whose contents he knows
> Are memorable, but from him lock'd up,
> Being written in a tongue he cannot read;
> So that he questions the mute leaves with pain
> And half upbraids their silence (10. 49–54).

He writes of the Terror as if it is a manifestation of the false sublime, as Burke would see it – a sublime enthusiasm made terrible by the absence of the softening influence of the beautiful. The violence plunges Wordsworth into a state of sleepless anguish, and he remarks that 'With unextinguish'd taper I kept watch, / Reading at intervals' (10. 61–2). He is almost feverish with 'substantial dread' (10. 66).

Wordsworth's response to the problem is to attempt an aesthetisation of the Revolution, renew his sense of the interplay between thought and feeling. He turns to Shakespeare, alluding to the 'tragic fictions' (10. 67) of *Hamlet* and *Macbeth*. Wordsworth seems to hope that the marriage of the sublime and beautiful in these texts will somehow recall the Revolution from the excessive sublime Burke sees everywhere occurring. In this way, if not calm, he at least has an intuition that '"Year follows year, the tide returns again, / Day follows day"' (10. 72–3) once more. Literature gives back to Wordsworth the intellectual and emotional perspective that he has lost. If poetry is a kind of refuge from history, it is one that enables him to *sensually think* the Revolution rather than experience it as a featureless or ineluctable force.

The crisis that Wordsworth describes in Book 10 of *The Prelude*, his experiment with Reason, can likewise be read as a surrender to, and recovery from, annihilating fervour. On the one hand, horrified by the Terror, and on the other ashamed of his country (because of the war between England and France [10. 768–9]), he represents himself as seeking answers in Godwinian political theory. Godwin's thought finds a 'ready welcome' (10. 810) with the young poet at a time when 'all things tended fast / To depravation'(10. 805–6):

> . . . What delight!
> How glorious! in self-knowledge and self-rule
> To look through all the frailties of the world,
> And, with a resolute mastery shaking off
> The accidents of nature, time, and place
> That make up the weak being of the past,
> Build social freedom on its only basis,
> The freedom of the individual mind (10. 818–25).

Wordsworth attempts to come to terms with his growing disillusionment with the course of the Revolution by testing alternative worldviews. Thus, Godwin's ideas for a while offer some consolation, until 'Sick, wearied out with contrarieties, / [I] yielded up moral questions in despair' (10. 899–900). He then turns to mathematics:

> . . . for my future studies, as the sole
> Employment of the enquiring faculty,
> [I] turn'd towards mathematics, and their clear
> And solid evidence (10. 901–4).

Mathematics soon also proves as insufficient a solution as Godwinism. He concludes that these travels through various forms of Reason amount to a kind of enthusiasm:

> Thus strangely did I war against myself;
> A Bigot to a new Idolatry
> Did like a Monk who hath forsworn the world
> Zealously labour to cut off my heart
> From all the sources of her former strength (11. 74–8).

The detour is experienced as a combination of division, zealotry, slavery and self-destruction. But what Wordsworth finds most disturbing is the loss of affect he notices. The delight that would be the fruit of sublime and beautiful unity is replaced by a flat response to the proliferation of the Revolution's unintelligible forms. The pleasure derived from both sense and intellect vanishes. The works of historian and poet 'wither'd in my esteem' (11. 93), and nature no longer holds any joy:

> ... – giving way
> To a comparison of scene with scene,
> Bent overmuch on superficial things,
> Pampering myself with meagre novelties
> Of colour and proportion, to the moods
> Of time or season, to the moral power,
> The affections, and the spirit of the place,
> Less sensible (11. 157–64).

His dry passion for speculative Reason – literally a slavery to sight, 'the most despotic of our senses' (11. 173) – ultimately renders him dull and wan.

Wordsworth's rejection of the destructive sublime he witnesses in Paris might still be construed as politically conservative. By representing the Revolution in the *Reflections* as a corruption of the aesthetic order, Burke implies that the answer is a return to the correct kinds of, and balance between, the sublime and beautiful. For a strictly Burkean Wordsworth, the Revolution would be shaped in accordance with a generic literary form – tragedy, for instance – the Terror but a momentary deviation from the proper path, and its error merely a stage on the way to truth.[19] Indeed, this story is necessary if Wordsworth is to demonstrate in *The Prelude* that he has triumphed over his own personal crisis. The aesthetic, therefore, can be read either as a (bad faith) denial of the untidiness of reality or as a way to counter the ugliness of reality. Whilst the latter *may* be no better than mystification, it could also be taken as a protest that is much more generalised and politically ambiguous than the scholarly consensus would allow.

Wordsworth turns to Dorothy in order to rediscover his true condition:

> ... and then it was,
> That the beloved Woman, in whose sight
> Those days were pass'd, now speaking in a voice
> Of sudden admonition like a brook
> That does but cross a lonely road, and now
> Seen, heard, and felt, and caught at every turn,
> Companion never lost through many a league,

> Maintain'd for me a saving intercourse
> With my true self: for, though impair'd and changed,
> Much as it seem'd, I was no further changed
> Than is a clouded, not a waning moon.
> She, in the midst of all preserv'd me still
> A Poet (10. 907–19).

Dorothy is represented in the role of kind admonishment, her gentle but insistent voice disciplining Wordsworth's errant gusto for Reason. She reminds him to see, hear and feel, and not just think, prompting him once again to 'seek . . . / My office upon earth' (10. 919–20) – his role as a poet. Such a development looks, of course, Burkean in inspiration: Wordsworth is brought back from his rational excesses, his self restored to wholeness. However, the comparison with Burke is complicated by the role of Dorothy in this process. In Burke, the sublime and beautiful, although gendered, are essentially institutional. Yet Wordsworth is rescued by a human relationship and a human voice.[20] Jon Mee contends that such sociability is in no way genuine reciprocity with another: 'in the poem as a whole sociability seems reduced to a close-knit circle of friends, primarily Dorothy and Coleridge, who can be relied upon to echo the poet's sentiments'.[21] Mee strikingly names this the '"superstitious" limit' of Wordsworth's 'relations with otherness'.[22] He writes that 'Preserving "a feeling for the whole" is predicated on the exclusion of vast swathes of affective human experience, and it seems any possibility of regulation for those whose enthusiasm discovers itself in an urban context is denied'.[23] Mee's impressive observation rests on the assumption that every event in *The Prelude* is 'sublimated into a higher realm by the act of recollection that pulls them into a narrative of the organic development of the self beyond the exigencies of historical experience'.[24] The implication is that each affective nuance in the poem is ultimately conscripted into the service of the Same. But such a view tends to overlook the local context of an episode, thereby itself restricting nuance. A Burkean-Hegelian interpretative machinery, in short, declares Wordsworth a Burkean-Hegelian. If one holds that Wordsworth's poetry is dialectical, but without synthesis, however, it looks markedly different. As a solution to the encounter with the Terror's mob frenzy and the alienating solitude of his experiment with rationalism, Wordsworth's recourse to the comforting sociability of family affection does not appear quite so deficient. Containing the wish to experience the variety of affect (and affection), Wordsworth's strategy for securing feeling at any particular moment does not translate into a straightforward political position.

V

James Chandler argues that Wordsworth's recovery from his speculative excesses does not

> mean being in an original, naked, or habitless condition, or even an approximation of such a condition. It means being in the condition of one's authentic habits and of their attendant feelings. And this is not a Rousseauist state of nature but a Burkean state of second nature.[25]

Second nature for Burke consists of being situated within one's proper habits, the routines of one's community and the tradition of one's nation. In *Lyrical Ballads* Wordsworth extrapolates from Burke a critique of the alienation and social division that follow when small proprietors lose their property, but without adhering to the Irishman's wider political agenda. The preservation, in the virtual society of poets and readers, of the relationships and affections that are lost is 'traditionalist' without necessarily being conservative.

Asserting his thesis that Wordsworth is fully Burkean, Chandler explains that 'traditionalism . . . depends upon a strongly psychologised view of the world . . . the psychological mode is an aid to showing that tradition has survived despite suspicions to the contrary', and he suggests that *The Prelude* is Wordsworth's attempt, through an autobiographical history, to demonstrate that his core self always remains the same.[26] For Chandler, it is the 'spots of time' that represent 'the triumph not only of mental discipline, but also of discipline-as-tradition, a discipline grounded on what Burke calls prejudice'.[27] The 'spots' arrive under circumstances that correspond to those experienced during a previous event. Chandler uses a visual vocabulary that is inadequate to Wordsworth's equally aural aesthetics.[28] But his description of the structure of the 'spots' as a hermeneutic scenario in which the feelings aroused by a present crisis are given meaning by their similarity to the feelings generated by an earlier incident, which itself is only of significance because of the present event, is invaluable.[29] Past and present are inextricably entwined in the poet's mind. If *poetry* is substituted for *mind*, however, one gets closer to what actually happens in *The Prelude*. In the 'spots', Wordsworth makes poetry its own tradition – an alternative tradition to those offered in the 'real' world of men and action. We are now in a position to answer the introduction's question: 'What difference does it make to say that a poem *is* feeling rather than simply the vehicle of a feeling that "belongs" to author or reader?'

As an example of the disciplining function of the 'spots', Chandler examines the Boat-Stealing episode in Book 1. In his analysis, the Boat-Stealing 'spot' emerges from Wordsworth's confused feelings, at the time of writing, as he relates his theft of eggs from a bird's nest on a high crag:

> . . . Oh! at that time,
> While on the perilous ridge I hung alone,
> With what strange utterance did the loud dry wind
> Blow through my ears! the sky seem'd not a sky
> Of earth, and with what motion moved the clouds (1. 347–51)!

The following 'spot', describing the young poet's pursuit by the mountains as he attempts to row across the lake, concludes with a description of comparably obscure feelings:

> In my thoughts
> There was a darkness – call it solitude
> Or blank desertion – no familiar shapes
> Of hourly objects, images of trees,
> Of sea, or sky, no colours of green fields;
> But huge and mighty Forms that do not live
> Like living men mov'd slowly through my mind
> By day and were the trouble of my dreams (1. 421–8).

Wordsworth converts the discomfort he feels as he recalls plundering the nest into a site of discipline by remembering another event, which has almost the same structure, but that can be read as a scene in which a mountain admonished him as it 'Rose up between me and the stars' (1. 411). However, it is useful to revisit J. H. Prynne's remarks about emphatic language.[30] Registering the division between man's social and natural being, lyric language quotes 'recursively the power of poetic speech itself, calling it in evidence to locate a dialectical convergence of outward and inner sense'.[31] Moments of lyricism register alienation and then mobilise poetry, its relatively autonomous reserve of forms, to attempt reconciliation between man and nature. The lyric 'Oh!', and emphatic outcry that follows in the first passage, indicates that it is *poetry* speaking, and not merely language or Wordsworth.[32] Rather than initiate the disciplinary mechanism that Chandler commonly detects, Wordsworth attempts to bring himself into relationship with a nature he cannot understand. Domination is ruled out, as the poetry is a sign of separation from nature and (good) will towards it only. Poetry is an end in itself and not an instrument of overcoming.

The second passage works in a similar way. These profoundly 'negative' lines do not reinscribe Wordsworth in the fabric of an already assured tradition: removing him from the real, they place him firmly in the poetic. Indeed, the poetry suggests a state of pre-cognition, of forms as yet unnamed. The writing expresses no moment of nostalgia or consolidation, and seems to await fullness of meaning from the future – in essence, from its readers.

The famous 'spot' from Book 11 offers some resistance to this 'utopian', or possibility-orientated, interpretation. Wordsworth describes how as a six-year-old boy he and a servant, James, went riding together. By some mischance, the two companions became separated from each other, and the young boy stumbled upon a place 'where in former times / A Murderer had been hung in iron chains' (11. 289–90). The gibbet was much decayed, Wordsworth explains,

> . . . but on the turf
> Hard by, soon after that fell deed was wrought
> Some unknown hand had carved the Murderer's name.
> The monumental writing was engraven
> In times long past, and still, from year to year,
> By superstition of the neighbourhood
> The grass is clear'd away; and to this hour
> The letters are all fresh and visible (11. 292–9).

Geraldine Friedman argues that Wordsworth's confused disturbance by the monumental writing, and subsequent movement to a visionary scene, enacts a political shift away from support for the Revolution, now linked in letter and law with 'retributive justice', and towards a more Burkean conception of society as an organic place where 'feeling comes in aid / Of feeling, and diversity of strength / Attends us, if but once we have been strong' (11. 326–8) – a society bound by tradition and habit.[33]

There is, however, little evidence in this episode of Wordsworth celebrating a sustaining continuity of tradition. The scene described is, in fact, marked by a 'visionary dreariness' (11. 311), consisting of 'a naked pool and dreary crags' (11. 321). Moreover, the apostrophe to Man that follows the 'spot' is again notable for its despondency. Wordsworth pronounces that childhood experience is the base upon which man's 'greatness stands' (11. 332), and that he himself considers his memories 'the hiding places of my power' (11. 336). But the gateways to this source, while appearing open, close on approach. There is no tangible reawakening of the past. What is available, instead, is poetry:

> . . . I would give
> While yet we may, as far as words can give,
> A substance and a life to what I feel:
> I would enshrine the spirit of the past
> For future restoration (11. 339–43).

The above lines suggest that truth, for Wordsworth, resides in poetry. By speaking only of poetic language – rather than psyche, Mind, tradition or second nature, for example – Wordsworth establishes his art not simply as critical of ideology and abstraction, but as a free-standing counter-tradition of feeling. No longer bent solely on negating both reality and the ideologies that threaten to diminish the scope and potential of affect, the poetry shelters feeling. Yet there is no avoiding the fact that the foundations of this 'positive' poetics are imbued with melancholy. As we shall see in the next chapter, Wordsworth discovers that by constructing poetry as a 'thing-like' refuge for feeling, he risks consigning his art to stasis, isolation and irrelevance.[34]

6
Melancholy and Affirmation

Wordsworth assembles the 'spots of time' into a version of tradition that, even as it focuses on the poet's biography, parallels Burke's model of British tradition and represents an alternative to it. Positing poetry as the reconciliation of spirit and matter, Wordsworth thus preserves the idea that division and alienation can be overcome. While his art serves as a gift of hope to the future, however, this poetic response to a crisis in the 'real world' creates its own problems. Wordsworth discovers that there is a cost to establishing poetry as a relatively autonomous counter-tradition. If art withdraws into itself, how can it substantively engage society? The suspicion arises that the power an artwork acquires through its independence equates to social and political impotence. From as early as the 'Lucy poems', then, much of Wordsworth's work is suffused with melancholy and a concern about isolation.

This chapter examines Wordsworth's attempts to confront the difficulties arising from his poetry's inward – that is, formal – turn. At first, he entertains the idea that by destroying poetry he can rejoin the real world. This itself is a melancholy approach, though, not least because it means sacrificing his art's affective, intellectual and experiential gains. Wordsworth instead seeks an aesthetic solution to an aesthetic problem, and develops a dialectical form of allegory. It is not necessary to choose between poetry's conceivably inconsequential truths and life's comparatively blind activity. In the London books of *The Prelude*, Wordsworthian allegory contacts and knows the world through an intimate mimesis of the perceived abstraction of London, while also preserving the (arguably rarefied) distance requisite for assessing the city. Wordsworth can thus think and feel in poetry without becoming isolated from the extra-poetic. I propose that by plunging in and out of an 'allegorical' London in *The Prelude*, he thereby experiences and understands the *real* metropolis. Dialectical allegory allows Wordsworth to closely read and write urban alienation, ultimately finding in the city the dearth of a happy sociability that yet remains always possible.

Despite his innovations with allegory, Wordsworth resists the notion that the poet speaks from a privileged prospect. He acknowledges the considerable imperfections of relatively autonomous art and does not wish to make prophetic statements from mountaintops. He presents himself as a conduit of meaning, rather than its origin. *The Prelude's* unique material form is as vital to its truth-content as any discourse it might convey. This chapter closes with the suggestion that *The Prelude* avoids empty utopianism by staging itself as a *singular* instance of the (thinking and feeling) experience that is so often missing in London. *The Prelude* is a process for communicating with reality and forging new relationships that are its alone: the poem is not simply a statement (spirit divorced from matter) on the importance of community, thought and feeling. In allegory, Wordsworth speaks publically and politically without succumbing to the temptation of abstracting thought from its material conditions and attempting to legislate for anyone but himself.

I

The 'withdrawal' from the world in Wordsworth's poetry, discussed in the last chapter, comes at a price. Accompanying the 'freedom' of the relative autonomy of the aesthetic is an equal and opposite melancholy, a sense that freedom is paid for with estrangement and powerlessness.[1] Even in *Lyrical Ballads*, Wordsworth appears aware of the danger of disappearance that stalks relatively autonomous art, and he broaches the issue by mounting a series of attacks on poetry itself.[2] In his early work – but without fully pursuing its implications – Wordsworth cultivates a position that anticipates the 'anti-art' aesthetic practices that emerge in force at the beginning of the following century. In essence, whilst holding onto the benefits of aesthetic autonomy, Wordsworth also attacks art in an attempt to reconnect it to the world it otherwise shuns. Alienation and impotence, then, account for the exquisite melancholy to be found in much of the verse Wordsworth published in his first book.

Like many of the poems in both the 1798 and 1800 editions of *Lyrical Ballads*, 'Lucy Gray' is about death. In the poem, Lucy gets lost on the moor, never to be found by her parents. We are informed that she had been a 'solitary child' when alive (4). A child of nature, she roamed out on the 'wide moor' with 'no mate, no comrade' (6; 5) – and in death she leaves only the faintest material impression that she ever existed at all:

> And now they homeward turn'd, and cry'd
> 'In Heaven we all shall meet!'
> Then in the snow the Mother spied
> The print of Lucy's feet (41–4).

The parents track her footprints to a bridge, where these frail signs vanish forever:

> They follow'd from the snowy bank
> Those foot-marks, one by one,
> Into the middle of the plank;
> – And further there were none (53–6)!

Although Lucy's prints inevitably fade, it is possible that she lives on as a ghost:

> . . . some maintain that to this day
> She is a living Child,
> That you may see sweet Lucy Gray
> Upon the lonesome Wild.
>
> O'er rough and smooth she trips along,
> And never looks behind;
> And sings a solitary song
> That whistles in the wind (57–64).

That the ghostly Lucy still sings a '*solitary* song' (my italics) might be taken to suggest art's inability to really touch the world, as well as its persistent (if weak and melancholy) attempt still to do so.

Another of these 'death' lyrics was at the centre of theoretical debates among the American deconstructionists of the 1970s – the most important of which was Paul de Man's contribution.[3] 'A slumber did my spirit seal' focuses upon the modification of the idea of time that occurs across the poem's two stanzas:

> A slumber did my spirit seal,
> I had no human fears:
> She seem'd a thing that could not feel
> The touch of earthly years.

> No motion has she now, no force;
> She neither hears not sees;
> Roll'd round in earth's diurnal course,
> With rocks and stones and trees (1–8)!

For de Man, the break between the two stanzas signifies that death has taken the girl described. Where the first stanza speaks of the living girl as 'a thing that could not feel / The touch of earthly years' (3–4), by the second stanza 'the word "thing" that could be used quite innocently, perhaps even in its playfully amorous way . . . [has become] literally true in the retrospective perspective of the eternal "now" of the second part'.[4] Through death, the girl has become 'a *thing* in the full sense of the word'.[5] The poem is taken to display the movement from an inauthentic forgetfulness of the touch of time, signified by the first line's 'A *slumber* did my spirit seal' (my italics), towards an authentic understanding of time. De Man is quick to point out, naturally, that enlightenment is not fully achieved by the speaker. The ascent from error to truth, provoked by the bereavement – the blunt intervention of time – also envelops the poet himself. That the narrative of the poem itself reflects the truth of temporal unfolding does not spare the poet from the error time makes inevitable. The poem is thus, in the most serious way, ironic. The poet is revealed as, at one and the same time, authentic and inauthentic. For de Man, in fact, 'A slumber did my spirit seal' is an allegory of error – it is *both* a demystification of the illusion of immortality by way of the evidence of time, and illustrative of the way such demystification is itself compromised by its own temporal predicament.

In David Bromwich's view, the gloomy Heideggerian tone of de Man's reading is misjudged. Bromwich suggests that 'The mood [of "A slumber"] is a basking in the good of sensation'.[6] He continues: 'The actual emotion of the poem seems to be a pleasure, tuned down to the lowest imaginable hum or pulse of energy.'[7] We assume that this poem about the death of a girl expresses anguish, as we believe that would be 'right and proper'. But according to Bromwich, Wordsworth is the poet he is because his emotional responses to events are untutored, and therefore unconstrained by conventional social expectations. The poem, in fact, describes how although Lucy is dead (in reality or simply now to the poet) she remains perfect, and perfectly alive, in Wordsworth's memory. She is with 'rocks and stones and *trees*' and not with 'rocks and stones and sticks'.[8] 'A slumber' celebrates what she once was, and continues on in the poet's recollection. Bromwich adds, however, that the poem opens up the possibility that Lucy dies 'because [the poet] . . . has come to the end of a feeling'.[9] No longer loving her, Wordsworth seals up his love in a verse.[10]

In the remainder of this chapter, I want to marry de Man's discovery of irony in Wordsworth to Bromwich's idea that – concentrating on the pleasure of how he truly feels at the moment of attention (including that of recollection), and not on how he *ought* to feel – the poet realises that although poetry contains affection it also, in a sense, kills through abandonment of the world and the people in it.

'Strange fits of passion have I known' is perhaps a clearer articulation of the idea that song – or art – murders through its imaginative trans-formation (or negation) of the world. The poem records the poet's feel-ings when he fancifully makes the sinking moon correspond to Lucy's welfare: '"O mercy!" to myself I cried, / 'If Lucy should be dead!"' (27–8). Yet, there is also a very important suggestion of mockery (directed against the poet's ego) in these lines. One could even conjecture that 'She dwelt among the untrodden ways' similarly draws attention to the vanity of the poet's affections:

> She *liv'd* alone, and few could know
> When Lucy ceas'd to be;
> But she is in her grave, and oh!
> The difference to me (9–12).

This poem is highly affecting. That Lucy's obscure existence could engen-der such love in someone who knew her only slightly witnesses to the importance of a single human life, and reveals the almost unfathomable depth of Wordsworth's humanist vision. For Bromwich, these lines dem-onstrate Wordsworth's willingness to risk feeling in ways that mark 'his separation from what anyone else could feel'.[11] Just because no universal decree can be derived from his feeling does not mean that it lacks signifi-cance. Affect, in Wordsworth, is a pleasurable end in itself and does not necessarily have to be underwritten by an unwieldy idea of community. Nevertheless, the reader moved by the death of Lucy is also struck by the fact of the poet's *display* of his strong sentiments. Indeed, the poem's final lines even seem hyperbolic in their emotional pitch. The suspicion arises that Wordsworth perhaps deliberately pitches his feeling so that it appears slightly precious. The result would be to undermine the dignity of the poet and open these peerless poems further onto the world.

In 'We are seven', Wordsworth probes further into the ironic breach of the poem. The scenario consists of a triangulated relationship between the poet protagonist, the 'little cottage girl' (5) he meets and his 'dear brother Jim' (1). The poet stops and asks the girl how many brothers and sisters she has:

> She answered, 'Seven are we,
> 'And two of us at Conway dwell,
> 'And two are gone to sea.
>
> 'Two of us in the church-yard lie,
> 'My sister and my brother,
> 'And in the church-yard cottage, I
> Dwell near them with my mother' (18–24).

He is bewildered by her insistence that she has seven brothers and sisters when two of them are dead, and takes it upon himself to correct her mistake and try to convince her that the true answer is five. But the girl thinks of death as a sleep rather than the end. Finally, the poet can only articulate exasperation:

> 'But they are dead; those two are dead!
> 'Their spirits are in heaven!'
> 'Twas throwing words away; for still
> The little Maid would have her will,
> And said, 'Nay, we are seven' (65–9)!

What is clear is that whereas the young girl cannot distinguish between the spirits of her quick and dead siblings, the poet sees the dead as mere things that have no role among the living.[12] To a degree, then, 'We are seven' sets up the meeting between the poet and the girl as a confrontation between innocence and experience. But although it seems obvious that the girl represents innocence, the poet's state of experience is one of Blakean ambiguity rather than the supposed clarity of Enlightenment. His shrill and positivist response to the girl's delightful justification for counting her siblings at seven suggests that he does not have access to greater understanding through experience. If anything, the poet is crassly dogmatic in his assertion of the girl's error. His view of life and death is less imaginative than the girl's, and looks limited, if not calcified, in comparison with her apparently fanciful belief. The poem thus demonstrates how 'demystifying' reason can rebound upon the subject, ultimately imprisoning him. Reason is shown to be at times as fatefully unenlightened as naivety.

This dialectical reading of the poem is strengthened by the fact that there is a third term in the equation. The poem is addressed to Jim, who stands in for the reader. Jim does not speak, and offers no opinion on the controversy, but his presence serves to unbalance the potential impasse between the two interlocutors. The authority of the poet figure is undercut by the third presence in the poem. Jim's silence, his refusal to second his fellow adult's argument, effectively adds weight to the girl's claims, and helps make the poet's opinions seem ungenerous. Jim does not, ultimately, occupy a position superior to both the speakers, weighing their arguments and passing judgement; but he does gently rock the oppositional structure the poem would otherwise have, an opposition that the poet's age and stature might easily resolve in his favour. Instead, the presence of a third element *stages* the confrontation between the poet and girl. As a consequence, the girl's ideas, despite appearing to be under the spell of 'myth', are less disagreeable than the barren reasoning of the poet, which begins to look unreflective and without charm.[13]

It is in 'Nutting', though, that Wordsworth's immanent critique of autonomous art finds its most profound expression. The young poet, dressed in rags suitable for a ramble, travels 'Among the woods, / And o'er the pathless rocks' (12–13) until he finds a 'dear nook / Unvisited' (14–15), where the drama of the poem takes place. Captivated by its secret beauty

> . . . – A little while I stood,
> Breathing with such suppression of the heart
> As joy delights in; and with wise restraint
> Voluptuous, fearless of a rival, eyed
> The banquet (19–23).

The scene is striking because of the lack of any sense, derived from either Shaftesbury or Akenside, that nature offers an environment in which to regulate enthusiasm. Instead, the boy's pioneering attitude is emphasised. Having arrived in virgin territory, the young Wordsworth is patently excited. He takes great pleasure in the fact that no rival is nearby. However, the mood of the poem soon changes from one of active exploration to passive receptiveness. The boy observes the 'sparkling foam' (32) and listens to the 'murmur and the murmuring sound' (36) of the stream; the narrator notes that at such moments of peace 'The heart luxuriates with indifferent things, / Wasting its kindliness on stocks and stones, / And on the vacant air' (39–41). The boy has become an idolater.[14] Whereas once the copse represented adventure and discovery, it now resembles a self-sufficient artwork that is coldly unconcerned with the boy it enchants.

In another of the poem's revolutions in temper, the young poet suddenly brings the wood into relationship with himself:

> . . . – Then up I rose,
> And dragg'd to earth both branch and bough, with crash
> And merciless ravage; and the shady nook
> Of hazels, and the green and mossy bower,
> Deform'd and sullied, patiently gave up
> Their quiet being (41–6).

He vandalises the bower, forcing Nature to surrender whatever it is she so jealously guards, bringing the previously 'aestheticised' nature and man into contact. The young Wordsworth exults in his power, 'rich beyond the wealth of kings' (49). Yet the poet recalls that 'I felt a sense of pain when I beheld / The silent trees, and saw the intruding sky' (50–1). Relationship does not just end with the young poet. The copse, no longer enigmatic and withdrawn, now communes with man, earth and sky. Autonomy has given away to heteronomy. But the poem is not finished – there is another *volte-face* to bewilder interpretation. 'Nutting' ends with advice to a maiden to tread lightly 'for there is a Spirit in the woods' (53). This piece of moralistic counsel is, obviously, very peculiar in the context of a narrative that has featured boyhood adventure, the boy's feeling that he is an impotent spectator, and his consequent act of destruction.

So why does Wordsworth terminate 'Nutting' in this at best incomprehensible, at worst inane, fashion? For Bromwich, the spiritualisation at the end of the poem is intelligible because 'The boy [is] . . . portrayed as a spectator, but his composing of the scene requires him to enter into it, to change it and to say, as a result of his visible effect, how his appetite has connected him with others'.[15] The violence of the poem is the wrench that sweeps the boy from solitary prostration into upright sociability.[16] The last lines of the poem can be read as a genuine expression of the glory achieved by the boy's actions. However, because the words to the Maiden are prefaced by the admission that the boy feels pain (a pang of jealousy, arguably) it is difficult to completely swallow their apparently calm sincerity. Because of this discord, one must surmise that the ending of the poem attempts to both restore the copse to its former integrity *and* continue in the effort to open it out onto the world. Melancholy about art's withdrawal from the world, Wordsworth's gestures towards an 'anti-art' position are highly ambivalent. While he wants an art that, autonomous and free, can think and feel without impediment, he has an equal wish for an art that can touch the extra-aesthetic. These poems show something of the bind in which Wordsworth finds himself. The question his poetry faces is whether to remain melancholy or to self-destruct.

The unexpected, and almost absurd, spiritualisation that occurs at the end of 'Nutting' also reveals Wordsworth's attitude towards extracting general knowledge from personal, affective experience.[17] The 'lesson' of the poem – that 'there is a Spirit in the woods' – has the form of a universal imperative, but obstinately will not translate into a rule. The truth of the last line is radically contingent – valid only at the moment the poet, wood and poetic utterance converge. In short, 'Nutting' offers a miniature glimpse of the way Wordsworth attempts to think *with* affect – taking the thought of feeling seriously, but always aware of just how much the subjective is intermixed with the grander claims of objectivity. In his suspension of the truth-content of both subjectivity and objectivity, mimesis and cognition, Wordsworth thinks the subject and the object, feeling and thought, the particular and the universal, without emptying one term into the other. In *The Prelude*, this dialectical mode of thinking and feeling enables him to find a way out of the deadlock between aesthetic melancholy and anti-art.

II

Wordsworth does not rest content with the idea that secreting splinters of an 'anti-art' stance within his poetry is the best response to the melancholy sense of detachment that results from relatively autonomous art's negation of the world. Just as he thinks the dialectical mediation of subjectivity and objectivity, feeling and thought, so too does he think melancholy and separation dialectically – by mediating them, in the London books of *The Prelude*, with joy and contact. Whereas in *Lyrical Ballads* Wordsworth takes on the melancholy induced by aesthetic autonomy through an 'attack' on art, in *The Prelude* he begins to regard melancholy as a negative foreshadowing of joyful relationship with the world. In other words, joy and sociability are anticipated in melancholy solitude through their very absence.

Wordsworth is chary of the city almost from the beginning of his career.[18] In the 1800 Preface, he most famously bemoans

> the increasing accumulation of men in cities, where the uniformity of their occupations produces a craving for extraordinary incident which the rapid communication of intelligence hourly gratifies (*PrW* 1. 128).

This association of the city with dissipation and a 'degrading thirst after outrageous stimulation' is characteristic of the widespread suspicion of luxury in the eighteenth-century, particularly among the Whig aestheticians discussed in Chapters 1 and 2. Luxury, in fact, was one of the social phenomena against which the civic humanists defined themselves. As John Barrell notes, for writers such as Shaftesbury and Burke, the virtuous gentleman was characterised by the economic independence that freed him from desire and the consequences of desire.[19] In effect, it was only the wealthy Whig landowner who possessed the qualifications needed for virtue. And with virtue came power – for from his lofty prospect above the fret of daily business, the disinterested gentleman was in the ideal position to observe society and guide its course.

Jon Mee reads Wordsworth's response to London in Book 7 of *The Prelude* as that of a Shaftesburean 'confronted with the infectious proximity of the crowd'.[20] London makes such a compelling assault on the poet that 'Only a deep training in a version of Shaftesbury's techniques of regulation, above all, an ability gained through habitual practice in solitude to relate the confusion of the senses to a larger harmonious whole, ultimately preserves Wordsworth from "the endless stream of men and moving things"'.[21] In this reckoning, Wordsworth's rejection of London in favour of the peace of Grasmere and its environs reveals a classic civic humanist attitude towards modernity.

Without focussing on Shaftesbury, civic humanism or Whiggism, other critics have arrived at similar conclusions about Wordsworth's political outlook, identifying Book 7 of *The Prelude* with a high distain for the market and a 'conservative' critique of the excesses of capitalism. Ross King, for example, synthesises some of the major theoretically informed writing on Book 7 in an attempt to clarify Wordsworth's politics. To add weight to his contention that the poet rejects London in order to safeguard, or re-establish, a prospect that distinguishes him from the common mass of men, King cites Mary Jacobus' thesis that Wordsworth abhors London because it puts 'the this-worldly profits of the eye in place of the other-worldly gains of the mind'.[22] In a footnote, King also borrows from Neil Hertz's psychoanalytic reading of *The Prelude*:

Hertz suggests that the modes of experience elsewhere so appropriate to the text – 'seeing and gazing, listening, remembering, feeling' – are finally baffled in Book 7th, where the billboards and tradesmen's signs are intended to be legible, not merely visible, and consequently must be read or deciphered rather than experienced phenomenologically.[23]

Like Jacobus, Hertz provides tacit agreement with King's proposal that Wordsworth flees London because unable to achieve 'the perspective required for an ordering, all-embracing view' – such a 'perspective' resembling the civic humanist prospect in both form and function.[24] All the same, rather than link Wordsworth with Whiggism, King concludes that 'in *The Prelude* London is for the most part the corrupt metropolis condemned with rhetoric recalling that of Queen Anne Toryism'.[25]

By contrast, in 'Lamb, Lloyd, London: A Perspective on Book 7 of *The Prelude*', Lucy Newlyn brilliantly argues that, for the most part, Wordsworth presents 'the city as a formative experience – as crucial as the country in moulding his imagination, just as exciting as the "changeful language" of the "ancient hills"'.[26] Remarking on the poet's success in writing about the city not simply as '"the quick dance / Of colours, lights and forms", but with an awareness of things purely human', Newlyn eludes the anti-aesthetic prohibitions of historicist criticism.[27] Nevertheless, she closes her piece in step with critical orthodoxy: 'Wordsworth retreats from the implications of his most imaginative writing. The last section of Book 7 is astonishing in its apparent insensitivity to the claims that have gone before'.[28] Ultimately, Newlyn agrees with Mee and King that in Book 7 Wordsworth recoils, in the name of reactionary self-preservation (or 'conservation'), from the disorientating influence of the commercial capital.

It is my contention, however, that Wordsworth's view of London is not simply that of a Whig or Tory appalled by the vulgarity of capitalism. Despite outlawing it in the Preface, Wordsworth deploys allegory in *The Prelude* to not only convey the alienating character of the city, and the law of the market dominating it, but also to comprehend London's social, affective and imaginative potential. In other words, I contest the assumption that, flying from the 'craving for extraordinary incident' he sometimes believes characterises London, Wordsworth establishes in nature a sense of visionary harmony compatible with a conservative politics. But the critique of capitalism Wordsworth presents in the London books of *The Prelude* does not correspond with an easily identifiable ideological position. Now ecstatic, now sorrowful, the poem is interested in the full diversity of feeling, even the frequently unsettling sensations aroused by London. This points to an answer to the introduction's question: 'What are the political implications of poetry that enables readers to experience a range of feelings perhaps otherwise inaccessible?' *The Prelude* strains affect – including joy and melancholy – for its prompts to consciousness. These books, in other words, see Wordsworth constantly searching for ways to further expand the palette of experience and imagine what a good life would feel like.[29]

III

In the Preface to *Lyrical Ballads*, Wordsworth declares that the language of his poetry is natural, that it resembles conversational language rather than the elevated idiom of his eighteenth-century forebears. With the expression 'personifications of abstract ideas', he makes particular reference to writing that comes under the umbrella of allegory, and insists there are no such figures in his work:

> Except in a very few instances the Reader will find no personifications of abstract ideas in these volumes, not that I mean to censure such personifications: they may be well fitted for certain sorts of composition, but in these poems I propose to myself to imitate, and, as far as is possible, to adopt the very language of men, and I do not find that such personifications make any regular or natural part of the language (*PrW* 1. 30).

Wordsworth implies that allegory and personification (a version of allegory) are of a different order to what he takes to be natural, ordinary, or common language. He rejects these figures because they are grafted arbitrarily onto the 'real language of men' (*PrW* 1. 18): mere ornament, a sign of passion rather than passion itself, they render poetic expression inauthentic. As Chester F. Chaplin points out, the attack on abstract personifications in the Preface to *Lyrical Ballads* was part of Wordsworth and Coleridge's attempt to distance themselves from the kind of verse associated with Erasmus Darwin – a poetry that, by simply dressing prosaic thought in poetic ornament, failed to authentically unite language and feeling.[30] In *The Prelude*, however, there are episodes that skilfully employ such 'artificial' language. Personification suits Wordsworth's youthful appraisal of Cambridge University as stultifying in Book 3:

> . . . Shapes of spurious fame, and short-liv'd praise
> Here sate in state, and fed with daily alms
> Retainers won away from solid good;

> And here was Labour, his own Bond-slave, Hope
> That never set the pains against the prize;
> Idleness, halting with his weary clog;
> . . .
>   . . . The Idol weak as the Idolator;
> And Decency and Custom starving Truth;
> And blind Authority, beating with his Staff
> The Child that might have led him; Emptiness
> Followed, as of good omen; and meek Worth
> Left to itself unheard-of, and unknown (3. 628–44).

Just as Cambridge scholarship seems barren of any purpose other than self-perpetuation, so personification – with its fantastic desertion of reality in favour of an infinitely expanding universe populated exclusively by words – battens on an unwholesome parody of nourishment. Through the brittle convention of personification, Wordsworth represents the university as an airless place, overcrowded with dull, self-serving language and customs.

Recalling his studies, Wordsworth writes that he was initially unaware that he favoured 'the more homely produce' (3. 602) of the countryside. Only with hindsight can he

> . . . smile in many a mountain solitude
> At passages and fragments that remain
> [. . .]
> Of that inferior exhibition, play'd
> By wooden images, a theatre
> For Wake or Fair (3. 604–9).

He states plainly that as a student, he would often leave the town and seek tranquillity in nature: 'Oft did I leave / My Comrades and the Crowd, Buildings and Groves, /And walked the fields, the level fields, / With Heaven's blue concave rear'd above my head' (3. 97–100). Far from the press of the colleges and streets, and with a benign sense of his place on earth, Wordsworth achieves a kind of prospect: he can distance himself from the rush and roar, and secure a still point of watchful repose. In this condition, Wordsworth claims he

> . . . look'd for universal things; perused
> The common countenance of earth and heaven:
> And, turning the mind in upon itself,
> Pored, watch'd, expected, listen'd; spread my thoughts,

> And spread them with a wider creeping; felt
> Incumbences more awful, visitings
> Of the Upholder, of the tranquil Soul,
> Which underneath all passion lives secure,
> A steadfast life (3. 110–18).

Finding the commotion of the university town bewildering, the young Wordsworth is soothed by this natural prospect, and able to attend to the 'incommunicable powers' (3. 188) of mystery and spirit.

Even in this book of *The Prelude*, though, Wordsworth does not introduce nature in bald opposition to the urban. It is only while in Cambridge, far 'from those shapes sublime / Wherewith I had been conversant' (3. 102–3), that his mind begins to penetrate the surface of things: nature is not hailed, simplistically, as an antidote to the apparent malaise of town. On the contrary, Wordsworth values the alienation he experiences in Cambridge as a negative index of a possible – and joyful – plenitude. Wordsworth does not regard alienation as something to be fled: it is, instead, essential to harmony, either as a spur to reconciliation or as a marker, a memory, of its loss.

Having escaped the troublesome air of Cambridge, and discovered the ameliorating influence of nature's eternal forms, Wordsworth represents himself as able to return refreshed, and hungry for delight. He is elated at the sight of

> So many happy Youths, so wide and fair
> A congregation, in its budding time
> Of health, and hope, and beauty; all at once
> So many divers samples of the growth
> Of life's sweet season (3. 221–5).

'To me, at least, / It was a goodly prospect' (3. 228–9), he recalls. The kind of solitude and perspective Wordsworth has enjoyed shares little with the will-to-isolation implicit in the civic humanist prospect or 'conservative' retreat into nature. The young poet is conspicuously sociable: 'if a throng was near / That way I lean'd by nature; for my heart / Was social, and lov'd idleness and joy' (3. 234–6). Nature facilitates sociability.

If Wordsworth rejects Cambridge's university primarily, rather than the town itself, he emphasises that he did not therefore also slight books:

> That were to lack
> All sense; but other passions had been mine

> More fervent, making me less prompt, perhaps,
> To in-door study than was wise or well
> Or suited to my years (3. 371–5).

It is not even scholarship that repels him. He loves to read, but also enjoys the physical pleasures of the countryside; he likes talk, yet is glad of his own company. What Wordsworth objects to in Cambridge is the slavery to intellectual *competition* – the principle that dominates the colleges and tarnishes otherwise pleasing activities:

> I griev'd to see among the Band
> Of those who in the field of contest stood
> As combatants, passions that did to me
> Seem low and mean; from ignorance of mine,
> In part, and want of just forbearance, yet
> My wiser mind grieves now for what I saw.
> Willingly did I part from these (3. 511–17).

The University becomes a sign of modernity. The culture of (mental) antagonism and battle that defines the academy spreads beyond its bounds, inevitably shaping the spirit of the town. The University's influence, however, does not necessarily distort the town. On the contrary, it renders Cambridge a representative city: 'in dwarf proportions were express'd / The limbs of the great world, its goings-on / Collaterally pourtray'd, as in mock fight, / A Tournament of blows, some hardly dealt' (3. 616–19). A wondrous stage for the exploration of human creativity and potential, Cambridge and its halls is also an alienating sink of fateful struggle and brutish competition.[31]

IV

De Man defines allegory as a mechanical and arbitrary figure, in which the allegorical signifier is structurally divided from its signified. In other words, there is nothing natural, or motivated, about the allegorical sign:

> The relationship between the allegorical sign and its meaning (*signifié*) is not decreed by dogma . . . We have, instead, a relationship between signs in which the reference to their respective meanings has become of secondary importance. But this relationship between signs necessarily contains a constitutive temporal element; it remains necessary, if there is to be allegory, that the allegorical sign

refer to another sign that precedes it. The meaning constituted by the allegorical sign can then consist only in the repetition (in the Kierkegaardian sense of the term) of a previous sign with which it can never coincide, since it is of the essence of this previous sign to be pure anteriority.[32]

Although the meaning of secular allegory is, in effect, determined in advance, there is no fixed code for either its composition or interpretation. The allegorical sign does not realise an identity with the earlier sign. Meaning is produced, rather, by the difference between the two signs, indeterminacy resulting from the allegorical sign's ceaseless appeal to the authority of an anterior sign that is never perfectly revealed. Thus, de Man suggests, 'allegory designates primarily a distance in relation to its own origin, and, renouncing the nostalgia and the desire to coincide, it establishes its language in the void of this temporal difference'.[33] Defined by time, allegory demystifies the illusory identifications of language. Yet its critical purchase does not allow allegory to transcend such illusions: it is forever negative, exposing untruth without making an appeal to positive terms. Although able to reveal the falsehood of identity, it is a language of disillusion and disenchantment that is unable to convert 'knowledge' into truth. Translated into the terms of Ross King, it might be said that allegory undermines – or even destroys – all claims to a disinterested and objective perspective. This point can be further clarified by an example de Man takes from Baudelaire – that of a man who laughs knowingly as he slips in the street. Splitting himself into two – an empirical, bodily self, and a conscious (that is, ironic and linguistic) self – the man believes he overcomes the 'thingness' to which the fall might reduce him. A sense of pride ensues from this new awareness of frail inauthenticity. Such self-regard, indeed, is almost forgivable when others are walking around oblivious to the danger lurking on the pavement. However, de Man points out that the superiority felt by the man who laughs as he falls is misplaced, 'for to know inauthenticity is not the same as to be authentic'.[34] Allegory and irony might acknowledge error, but as their insight is bound up with failure it can never claim objectivity, disinterest or truth.

In Book 7 of *The Prelude*, however, allegory does not always perform the self-dissolving critique of perspective (or the civic humanist prospect) described by de Man. Its Wordsworthian form maintains an air of superiority, examining the activities in the streets and markets of London from above. Wordsworth recognises that allegory's enslavement to arbitrary conventions (its 'perverse' self-referentiality) is analogous to what looks to be the fruitless and self-replicating circulation of people and commodities. At this stage, he seems to use allegory's disclosure of inauthenticity as a badge of his own authenticity. Wordsworthian allegory does, in this instance, seem to work to 'conservative' effect when deployed with conscious deliberation: abstracted from its ephemeral objects, the poet's allegory passes judgement upon the depravity of capitalism from on high.

At the beginning of Book 7, Wordsworth portrays his younger self as naive in his expectations of the capital:

> Marvellous things
> My fancy had shaped forth, of sights and shows,
> Processions, Equipages, Lords and Dukes,
> The King and the King's Palace, and not last
> Or least, heaven bless him! the renown'd Lord Mayor,
> Dreams hardly less intense than those which wrought
> A change of purpose in young Whittington (7. 108–14).

The youthful poet anticipates discovering London a place out of popular history and fairy tale. The reality, inevitably, is very different: in the capital, 'men lived / Even next-door neighbours . . . yet still / Strangers, and knowing not each other's names' (7. 118–20). The city is chaotic, its 'Babel din' (7. 157) impossible to measure into a simple pattern or master from any perspective or prospect. 'The endless stream of moving men and moving things' (7. 158) defies comprehension and the maintenance of distinctions. There is little difference between the movement of people and goods, as both are 'unnaturally' animated. As Theresa Kelley writes, either men 'are pushed, or move of their own will, or . . . are so cleverly mechanised that they seem to move on their own', like automata.[35] Wordsworth can neither distinguish between people and goods, nor fathom the origin of the power that propels them.

He recalls, in what Shaftesbury might call a state of 'Phrenzy, and Distraction' (*C* 1. 255), the crowds, the visual impression of the shops, and the over-stimulation that consumes subjectivity:

> Here, there, and everywhere, a weary Throng!
> The Comers and the Goers face to face,
> Face after face; the string of dazzling Wares,
> Shop after Shop, with Symbols, blazon'd Names,
> And all the Tradesman's honours overhead;

> Here, fronts of houses, like a title-page,
> With letters huge inscribed from top to toe;
> Stationed above the door like guardian Saints,
> There, allegoric shapes, female or male;
> Or physiognomies of real men,
> Land Warriors, Kings, or Admirals of the Sea,
> Boyle, Shakespear, Newton; or the attractive head
> Of some Scotch Doctor, famous in his day (7. 171–83).

People and objects are difficult to tell apart, individual faces substitute with other faces and, in turn, become interchangeable with shop fronts.[36] Wordsworth cannot even say whether the shop fronts themselves bear allegorical designs or are human. But allegory allows him to reveal the seeming misery of reality whilst retaining some distance from it: he can describe London as hell because it structurally resembles a reviled trope. Although figure and reality are an undecidable blur, Wordsworth composes the allegory: understanding how it works, he thus appears to occupy a guaranteed spot – a disinterested perspective or prospect.

Wordsworth observes the way London distils national and racial characteristics into abstract personifications:

> The Italian, with his Frame of Images
> Upon his head; with Basket at his waist
> The Jew; the stately and slow-moving Turk
> With freight of slippers piled beneath his arm (7. 229–32)!

People are defined by the goods they peddle: commodity and vendor bleed into one another. Again, a slippage between the real and its allegorical figuration occurs. Nevertheless, even in such circumstances there is hope: a memory of the bright and energising sociability Wordsworth enjoyed in Cambridge endures. For all the anxiety London causes him, the poet is clearly invigorated by the demonic energy trade unleashes, and the new relationships, thoughts and feelings it creates.[37]

Still, the city remains an unsettling theatre in which nothing means anything in itself; definitions are always caught up in an economy of circulating and mutually defining objects. Entertainers, like 'saw Singers, Rope-dancers, Giants and Dwarfs, / Clowns, Conjurers, Posture-masters, Harlequins, / Amid the uproar of the rabblement, / Perform their feats' (7. 294–7) before an audience consisting of individuals who dissolve in the spectacle. The city is a place where subjects are transformed into objects, inseparable from the things they sell or consume. Even the actor playing Jack the Giant-killer bears the sign *invisible* on his chest, as though himself another shop front.

To Wordsworth, people appear hopelessly shorn of their proper identities. He shrinks from a prostitute he sees in the street. Inhabiting a Godless world of blasphemy and 'public vice' (7. 420), she is both literally and figuratively a fallen woman. Wordsworth is shocked, but feels little pity:

> . . . the pain was almost lost,
> Absorb'd and buried, in the immensity
> Of the effect: a barrier seem'd at once
> Thrown in, that from humanity divorced
> The human Form, splitting the race of Man
> In twain, yet leaving the same outward shape (7. 422–7).

The city is so alien that the poet can muster little sympathy for some who suffer there. Like other characters in Book 7, the prostitute is less an individual than a representative of vice. In allegorical mode, Wordsworth fixes on the most marginalized, even freakish, characters: monkeys, buffoons, 'Albinos, painted Indians, Dwarfs, / The Horse of Knowledge, and the learned Pig, / The Stone-eater, the Man that swallows fire, / Giants, Ventriloquists' (7. 681–4) in order to abstract purposeful meaning from what he views.[38] He observes people in bond to work and the commodities they make or trade:[39]

> The slaves unrespited of low pursuits,
> Living amid the same perpetual flow
> Of trivial objects, melted and reduced
> To one identity, by differences
> That have no law, no meaning, and no end (7. 701–5).

From his vantage point, surveying society and its apparent detritus, Wordsworth declares that he can see 'the parts / As parts, but with a feeling of the whole' (7. 712–13) and make sense of pandemonium.[40]

However, it is also the case that Wordsworth frequently sees appearances and cannot make out substance; he is often left with fragments that will not combine into an organic whole. Intent on grasping London in its totality, then, he turns again to thoughts of disciplining intercourse with nature. As in Cambridge, he summons to mind the pure outline of a mountain and calls on the 'spirit of Nature' (7. 736) to help him reach 'Through meagre lines and colours, and the press / Of self-destroying, transitory things, / Composure and ennobling harmony' (7. 739–41). Such behaviour is, of course, quite in accord with Shaftesbury's civic humanist philosophy of self-discovery and composure via retreat into nature's bosom. Yet the unease that has preceded this neat resolution remains.

It is not only the prevalence of allegorical figures and unusual characters that undercuts Wordsworth's supposed preference for nature's organic unity, rather than London's broken pieces, at the end of Book 7. The centrality of the theatre to his vision of London also disrupts any confirmation of a stable identity that is predicated on a disinterested and objective perspective or prospect. He admits to the appeal of theatre, its 'lustres, lights, / The carving and the gilding' (7. 441–2). Instead of praising its generation of affects, though, Wordsworth deplores its power to seduce and unseat the will. When the older poet thinks of the stage, he suggests that his youthful imagination would languish in the dark:

> . . . even then it slept,
> When, wrought upon by tragic sufferings,
> The heart was full; amid my sobs and tears
> It slept, even in the season of my youth:
> For though I was most passionately moved,
> And yielded to the changes of the scene
> With most obsequious feeling, yet all this
> Pass'd not beyond the suburbs of the mind (7. 500–7).

Wordsworth loathes the passivity induced by theatre. Anxious that its luxurious spectacle 'feminises' him, he denies that theatre has any deep impact on his mind. Only Shakespeare, articulating what the young poet has already 'shaped / . . . yet not shaped' (7. 514–15), is permitted the capacity to truly seduce.

For Wordsworth, the theatre is essentially bogus. It reminds him of the stage-managed performances of dishonest lawyers, politicians and effete preachers who 'perform a toilette of two hours' (7. 548); certain dangerously rhetorical orations from the pulpit, by which the 'pretty Shepherd . . . / Leads up and down his captivated Flock' (7. 565–6). It is as bewildering as the crowded market, and spectators are effectively caged by such displays. Later, when wandering around St Bartholomew's Fair, he observes an audience staring at 'chattering monkeys dangling from their poles, / . . . children whirling in their roundabouts' (7. 668–9), and other extraordinary sights. Clearly, the audience is as much a spectacle as the drama on stage. There is no happy (and 'manly') prospect for contemplation:

> Tents and Booths,
> Meanwhile, as if the whole were one vast Mill,
> Are vomiting, receiving, on all sides,
> Men, Women, three years Children, Babes in arms (7. 692–5).

The performers are grotesque commodities, their value exhausted in their talent; but the spectators are similarly processed. Wordsworth is barely able to preserve a distance from this vision of subjects running to objects of equivalence. He is lured into the maelstrom.

V

But does Wordsworth respond to the disintegration of his prospect by abandoning the perceived turmoil of the city for the quiet order and certainty of nature? Book 8 begins with the poet in Grasmere, far from the 'blank confusion' (7. 696) of London. Nature is again the teacher described in Book 5, enabling the poet to discern London from a distance, and thus imbue the city's 'temporal shapes / Of vice and folly' (8. 496–7) with some kind of stability.[41] Through nature, Wordsworth has learned to withhold scorn for the residents of London:

> . . . I already had been taught to love
> My Fellow-beings, to such habits train'd
> Among the woods and mountains, where I found
> In thee a glorious Guide, to lead me forth
> Beyond the bosom of my Family (8. 69–73).

Indeed, it is significant that following this (perhaps Burkean) meditation on the social benefits of habit, Wordsworth addresses nature thus:

> 'Twas thy power
> That rais'd the first complacency in me,
> And noticeable kindliness of heart,
> Love human to the Creature in himself
> As he appear'd, a Stranger in my path,
> Before my eyes a Brother of this world (8. 74–9).

This statement echoes Shaftesbury's (and Akenside's) advocacy of the spiritual balm that is retirement into nature. But whereas Shaftesbury praises a solitude and social intercourse confined to class peers, Wordsworth emphasises a more capacious kind of sociability. There is an important ambivalence in Wordsworth's sentiments towards London and nature. London is certainly cavalier with distinctions, and frequently denies the individual his proper affections. However, while restful contemplation in nature is at times acclaimed as an end in itself, it is often also presented as preparation for the kind of unrestricted social interaction that is available only in the metropolis.

Wordsworth's poetry does not piously maintain a 'deep devotion' (8. 62) to nature, the basic regularity of rural life and solitude. In fact, disquiet creeps beneath the pastoral of Book 8:

> Call ye these appearances
> Which I beheld of Shepherds in my youth,
> This sanctity of nature given to man,
> A shadow, a delusion, ye who are fed
> By the dead letter, not the spirit of things,
> Whose truth is not a motion or a shape
> Instinct with vital functions, but a Block
> Or waxen Image which yourselves have made,
> And ye adore (8. 428–36).

He fears that he cannot save those already captive to the turmoil of city life and the market, and suspects that his vision will only appear a desperate contrivance, implausible or even nostalgic. He resorts, then, to the paradox of denying his authority on utterance, purging writing with writing. At this moment, Wordsworth relinquishes his aspiration to a disinterested perspective. Presenting *The Prelude* as the incarnation of natural wisdom, he considers himself a channel rather than a disembodied purveyor of the dead letter of false spiritualisation.

The Cave of Yordas episode in Book 8 suggests that it is impossible to intuit, and then communicate, the vitality of nature from a standpoint that abjures matter for the sake of disinterest: the world is frozen under such a cool gaze. Wordsworth compares the poet's situation with that of a traveller entering a vast cavern that, like London, initially bedazzles comprehension:

> He sees, erelong, the roof above his head,
> Which instantly unsettles and recedes

> Substance and shadow, light and darkness, all
> Commingled, making up a Canopy
> Of Shapes and Forms, and Tendencies to Shape,
> That shift and vanish, change and interchange
> Like Spectres . . . (8. 717–23).

There is only shape and form, no substance, and the unsettled mind cannot command anything it sees. Until, that is, the traveller's spirit steadies, finds a perspective and unifies the disparate. The penalty, though, is that at once 'the scene before him lies in perfect view, / Exposed and lifeless as a written book' (8. 726–7). Ailing imagination then intervenes again to produce a 'new quickening' (8. 729) and choreographs the cavern once more into scenes of splendour: 'forests and lakes, / Ships, rivers, towers, the Warrior clad in Mail, / The prancing Steed, the Pilgrim with his Staff, / The mitred Bishop and the thronèd King' (8. 737–40).

Jacobus holds that in this passage Wordsworth trumps the power of the eye – the organ that threatens to make him hostage to the fearful masses he sees in London and at the fair.[42] He subsumes 'spectacle into spectrality, animating the show in the visionary cinema of the imagination'.[43] The collapse, or suppression, of the visual engenders the visionary poetic mind.[44] However, although Wordsworth claims that, situated among the masses but without abdicating selfhood, he is 'moved with such a swell of feeling' and thus able to sense 'the unity of man, / One spirit over ignorance and vice' (8. 743; 8. 827–8), his vision in the Cave of Yordas episode remains uninspiring. The pageant he describes reads like a parody of the Burkean chivalric tradition.[45] It is a parade of clichéd literary subjects – kings, churchmen, knights, etc. – and fails to make good the conservative insistence on Imagination's triumph over reality. There is an understanding in the poetry that the attempt to divorce spirit from matter, the fleeting stuff of the city from the eternal forms of nature, will result in an empty and derelict poetry – aesthetic failure.

VI

Books 7 and 8 of *The Prelude* attend carefully to form. Although the intense scrutiny Wordsworth directs at London and the Cave of Yordas suggests the close proximity of his art to reality, the ability of Imagination to adequately penetrate ordinary experience is based on the distance it keeps from life's everyday objects and pursuits. What may resemble at times a conservative hauteur towards the labours and pleasures of city-dwellers is, in the event, a function of his effort to know the affective possibilities of the city. For Wordsworth, poetry – or simply, the aesthetic – transforms raw stimulation into experience by revealing the dialectical relationship between feeling and thinking, immediacy and distance.

But how can an art that frequently resorts to allegory – by definition, a mode that negates the material in preference for the abstract – accomplish such a task? According to Wordsworth (and, indeed, de Man) allegory is a figure that is not only abstract but also arbitrary and mechanistic. In Books 7 and 8 of *The Prelude*, these aspects of allegory become both a mimesis of London life *and* the categories used to analyse the 'vulgar forms / Of houses, pavement, streets, of men and things, / Mean shapes on every side' (8. 695–7). The figure retains a degree of objectivity through its commitment to the abstract and general, yet is marked by the society it represents. On the one hand, allegory resembles the objects it reflects; on the other, deriving its significance from poetic tradition (Romantic theories of the difference between symbol and allegory, for example) rather than a particular extra-aesthetic historical moment, it is relatively autonomous. Thus, refracting spirit through matter – or to put it another way, fastening the mental clarity of the prospect, or perspective, to the bodily confusion of affect – Wordsworthian allegory simultaneously discloses the social dimension of the aesthetic and utilises the cognitive force of its relative autonomy. Unable to fully distinguish between people and things, these allegorical books of *The Prelude* reveal the social and material variety of affect in London – the fact that the city is infinite, impossible to master, 'It cannot be seen at once; it never ends'[46] – whilst at the same time drawing back from the tendency of the commercial capital to devour and dehumanise its inhabitants.

Wordsworthian allegory both criticises and celebrates the city. Finding absolute escape undesirable (and impossible), the poem mimics the spell reification casts over London's predominantly commercial society. Yet Wordsworth's love of allegorical abstraction also casts a spell on that spell.[47] According to Adorno, art is only ever 'as abstract as social relations have in fact become'.[48] Abstraction stands as a negative – but determinate – reminder that real sociability is still possible: it maintains that society might one day be liberated from the blind law of competition and that people can be freed from function. In *The Prelude*, the dry bones of such abstract hope are also given flesh by the poet's fond recollection of the exuberance and vigour of London's population. Through allegorical mimesis, Wordsworth attempts to render experiential the reservoirs of affect in London that also threaten to destroy experience for its inhabitants. In short, then, Wordsworthian allegory is not servant to a broadly conservative critique of capitalism. Instead, it is part of Wordsworth's attempt to think capitalism dialectically – as containing fecundity within disaster, elation within misery.

But a problem remains. At the end of Book 7 and the beginning of Book 8, Wordsworth vacates the city and returns to Grasmere and nature. How might one account for this act while still maintaining that the poet is not the conservative that so many critics describe? In Book 7, Wordsworth states that he arrived in London 'wholly free / From dangerous passions' (7. 71–2). He is no green youth, vulnerable to the size and pace of the city. His residence in Cambridge, after all, has taught him how to negotiate life in densely populated environments. There, Wordsworth realised the value of nature – its calming influence enabling him to enter more fully into the novelty of Cambridge life. Thus, he is already prepared for London: he carries nature's 'shapes sublime / Wherewith I had been conversant' (3. 102–3) in his breast. Wordsworth recalls his younger self's imaginative, and highly poetical, expectation of an urban pastoral:

> Vauxhall and Ranelagh! I then had heard
> Of your green groves, and wilderness of lamps,
> Your gorgeous Ladies, fairy cataracts,
> And pageant fire-works (7. 123–6).

> The calmness, beauty of the spectacle;
> Sky, stillness, moonshine, empty streets, and sounds
> Unfrequent as in desarts . . . (7. 634–6).

In these passages, he refuses to choose between the natural and the man-made, real people and fictional beings. A little later, moreover, he describes the 'natural' refuges close to the most boisterous commercial areas:

> Meanwhile the roar continues, till, at length,
> Escaped as from an enemy, we turn
> Abruptly into some sequester'd nook
> Still as shelter'd place when winds blow loud (7. 184–7).

London is likened to a mountainside blasted by storms, scattered with rocky havens.[49] Gladly conflating nature and the city in this way,

Wordsworth admires 'the Spectacles / Within doors, troops of wild Beasts, birds and beasts / Of every nature' (7. 245–7). His delight and pleasure is only heightened by the dissonance of seeing animals in a startling context.

Even the crowd has a double character. At times an alienating throng, it can also attain a curious beauty:

> The face of every one
> That passes by me is a mystery!
> Thus have I look'd, nor ceas'd to look, oppress'd
> By thoughts of what, and whither, when and how,
> Until the shapes before my eyes became
> A second-sight procession, such as glides
> Over still mountains, or appears in dreams;
> And all the ballast of familiar life,
> . . .
> Went from me (7. 597–607).

There is little doubt that St Bartholomew's Fair is a scene of 'anarchy and din / Barbarian and infernal' (7. 660–61); but, equally, Wordsworth finds in it 'A work that's finish'd to our hands, that lays, / If any spectacle on earth can do, / The whole creative powers of man asleep!' (7. 653–5). This 'unmanageable sight' (7. 709) drains and evades Imagination. Yet, the passivity induced by this display of complete power contains a joy for one also devoted to the 'under-sense', who 'sees the parts / As parts, but with a feeling for the whole' (7. 712–13). Difficult complexity fascinates. Of course, such passages could still be recruited for a reading of Wordsworth as reactionary – and it is certainly true that he has something like a civic humanist's desire to command all he sees. Habitual intercourse with nature,

> The mountain's outline and its steady form
> Gives a pure grandeur, and its presence shapes
> The measure and the prospect of the soul
> To majesty (7. 723–6).

It would be over-literal, though, to claim that the above passage represents an escape from the city. Only through exposure to the city's accelerated, and sometimes gruelling, culture does Wordsworth learn that his early and habitual fellowship with nature enables him to dwell among 'transitory things' (7. 740). One could argue that here Wordsworth is quite in accord with Shaftesbury's demand that through the friendly, or otherwise, collisions of social intercourse 'We polish one another, and rub off our Corners and rough Sides' (*C* 1. 39). However, the kind of sociability Shaftesbury advocates occurs among polite gentlemen whose manners have already been cultivated through a liberal education. Shaftesbury's civic humanism adheres to a top-down model: the sociable gentleman achieves an even greater refinement, and distinction from the masses, by way of further society with his distinguished equals. In Wordsworth, the opposite is the case: it is the disorder and social blend of the city that expresses the soothing 'refinement' of nature. This, in turn, encourages additional, unbound, social activity. The permanent forms of nature are mediated by the ephemeral; the ephemeral is mediated by nature. As a result, this dialectic produces an affirmatory critique of many aspects of the city. His poetic thinking refracted through the beneficial, and more 'natural', social relations he observes and experiences there, Wordsworth criticises those aspects of London found damaging. He does not promote a reactionary critique of capitalism, but instead reads the condition of man in the capital dialectically – as at once deadening and creative, mindlessly competitive and affectionate, atomising and communal.

The beginning of Book 8 finds Wordsworth once more in the Lakes:

> What sounds are those, Helvellyn, which are heard
> Up to thy summit? Through the depth of air
> Ascending, as if distance had the power
> To make the sounds more audible: what Crowd
> Is yon, assembled in the gay green Field?
> Crowd seems it, solitary Hill! to thee (8. 1–6).

He envisions Helvellyn looking down upon a small, summer festival. Again, although the rustic setting is obviously very different from that of the preceding book, nature does not negate the human activities it oversees. Rather, the poem reflects the sociable liveliness of the festival by mediating it through the still image of the solitary mountain. Indeed, the solitary and distant qualities of Helvellyn, which observes the activity below 'in the silence of his rest' (8. 13), could itself be an allegory of the role of allegory in the London books. The self-division of allegory – the contradiction between its rejection of, and mimesis of, the world – introduces the element of distance necessary for it to become a form that both extols and criticises society. The relative autonomy of Wordsworth's art ensures that while *The Prelude* sometimes denounces London's 'trivial' objects, it also embraces the intellect's (spirit's) dependence on affective contact with them. Affirming the possibility of human happiness, Wordsworth propels his work out of melancholy isolation and into the pleasurable passions of the social and material world.

Conclusion

At the end of *The Recluse. Home at Grasmere* (published as 'The Prospectus to *The Excursion*' in 1814, but probably written in 1806), Wordsworth calls on Urania to help him pass by, 'unalarmed',[1]

> . . . – all terror, single or in bands,
> That ever was put forth in personal form –
> Jehovah – with his thunder, and the choir
> Of shouting Angels, and the empyreal thrones – (784–7).

Just as the 'dialectical allegory' of Book 7 of *The Prelude* enables Wordsworth to encounter the turbulent affects of the metropolis, the Muse will allow him fearlessly to 'sink / Deep – and aloft' (781–2) into feeling. Through their tumultuous collision, he will experience fear, awe, beauty and joy. Yet when he writes that he will 'chant . . . the spousal verse / Of this great consummation' (810–11) – that is, sing of the marriage of the mind of Man and the universe – one could be forgiven for thinking that this exhilarating affective range and turbulence is not an end in itself but the preamble to a retreat into the quiet and comforting illusions of a totalising aesthetics. Such a disheartening conclusion, though, is soon troubled by perhaps the most troublingly conciliatory passage in the poem:

> . . . my voice proclaims
> How exquisitely the individual Mind
> (And the progressive powers perhaps no less
> Of the whole species) to the external World
> Is fitted: – and how exquisitely, too –
> Theme this but little heard among men –
> The external World is fitted to the Mind (815–21).

The word 'Fitted' is twice secreted inside the verse, and never end-stopped as would formally suit its principal meaning. There are good reasons for this. 'Fit' has two strongly conflicting senses: the dominant one in the passage is 'to accord with', 'to match'; but 'fit' also means 'convulsion', 'paroxysm', or in eighteenth-century terminology a 'transport of enthusiasm'. Moreover, 'both uncontrolled overflow and formal constraint . . . "fytt" is also a term for a medieval stanza form'.[2] The passage, then, does not simply assert the unity of spirit and matter, but that *in poetry* mind and world agree. That is, in a poem – defined as a place where, through concentrated mimesis, feeling switches between the agreeable and the excessive – mind and world can find understanding by shaping themselves to one another.

Numerous poems in Wordsworth would support this surmise. The pun alone in the title of 'Strange fits of passion have I known' implies that the strange passions the poet has known occurred specifically in verse. The emotional drama of the poem, the 'fond and wayward thoughts' (25) that slide into the poet's head, occurs immediately after the almost comically pedantic insistence on the metronome clop of the horse's hooves.[3] The fanciful alarm develops from a soft beat. Similarly, although with much more emphasis on the real-world event lying behind the poetic inspiration, in 'The Solitary Reaper' Wordsworth listens to the woman's song and observes her labour ('Reaping and singing by herself; / Stop here, or gently pass! / Alone she cuts, and binds the grain, / And sings a melancholy strain' [3–6]), its rhythmic qualities stressed by a metre that, already stable, is further disciplined by the punctuation. Once the poem has calmly embodied the pulse of the woman's activity, it works its mild pleasure into something closer to enthusiasm. Like the vale that contains the woman's song, effectively pressurising the music so that it spills over the hilltops (8), the poem elaborates the feeling initially inspired by the sonic patterning 'till I had my fill' (29). The poem attends to an affect until it matures into something that penetrates the heart.[4]

If Whig feeling is the origin of Wordsworth's poetry, feeling in and of itself is its end. In a long epigram, Wordsworth provides an anecdotal background to 'Stepping Westward', the poem that immediately follows 'The Solitary Reaper' in 1807's *Poems, in Two Volumes*: 'two well-dressed Women, one of whom said to us, by way of greeting, "What you are stepping westward?"'[5] Wordsworth repeats this scene in the first line, leaving no doubt about the importance of the event for the verse: '*"What you are stepping westward?"* – *"Yea."*' Having noted that the women are 'well-dressed' – and, presumably, fairly well-to-do – he states that 'I liked the greeting' (13) and that 'The voice was soft . . . / The salutation had to me / The very sound of courtesy' (18–20). The gentle kindness of the women's greeting puts Wordsworth at ease 'In a strange Land, and far from home' (4), and a polite affection gently leads him on to other feelings:

> The dewy ground was dark and cold;
> Behind, all gloomy, to behold;
> And stepping westward seem'd to be
> A kind of *heavenly* destiny (9–12).

The italicised '*heavenly*' – signifying 'of heaven' and 'delightful' – is an expression of enthusiasm that, tonally, is also quite in keeping with the gentlemanly origin of Wordsworth's art. The woman's polite and sociable words give him the 'spiritual right' (15) to imagine daring to travel into the endless unknown. Indeed, the warmth of her voice gives Wordsworth the idea of stepping westward because it (critically, and quite simply) discloses his surroundings as cold and wet.

Wordsworth's art gives a measure of passion and intellect's scope. Nursing feeling, the poetry is a mimesis of what is possible when human being is released from abstract constraint. Wordsworth does not, however, finally reject the earthly for unbounded enthusiasm. On the contrary, with its focus on 'lowly matter' (call it feeling, ordinary language, the common round, regulation, habit or metre) he locates an idea of truth and freedom in 'the transitory Being that beheld / This Vision; when and where, and how he lived' (*The Recluse. Home at Grasmere*, 847; 850–1). His poetry rooted in his affections, Wordsworth finds transcendence in the collapse of the anonymous machineries of transcendence.

Notes

Introduction: Poetry, Feeling and Criticism

1. Fourteen years after the publication of *Lyrical Ballads*, 'poetic feeling' still defined the Poet and his art for Wordsworth: 'the range of poetic feeling is far wider than is ordinarily supposed, and the furnishing new proofs of this fact is the only incontestable demonstration of genuine poetic genius' (William Wordsworth, *The Letters of William and Dorothy Wordsworth*, III, *The Middle Years Part II 1812–1820*, ed. Earnest De Selincourt, revd Mary Moorman and Alan G. Hill [Oxford: Clarendon Press 1970], p.178).
2. Both Peter de Bolla, *Art Matters* (Cambridge: Harvard University Press 2001) and Elaine Scarry, *On Beauty and Being Just* (Princeton: Princeton University Press 1999) state that art in general proposes a 'philosophical' ethics; drawing on Kant and phenomenology, Charles Altieri suggests that because its 'syntax becomes its own most physical force of cadenced conjunctions' (Charles Altieri, *The Particulars of Rapture: An Aesthetics of the Affects* [New York: Cornell University Press 2003], p. 204) poetry is the precondition for new ways of thinking and feeling. Susan Wolfson's *Formal Charges* was one of the first books to explore the critical agency of Romantic poetry's forms. In numerous articles, Robert Kaufman has read Romanticism with Adorno to show how poetry contains 'quasi-conceptual experience whose wealth of thought-feeling cannot be reduced to any determinate concept and from which, therefore, may be constructed new concepts and social arrangements' ('Negatively Capable Dialectics', *Critical Inquiry* 27 [Winter 2001]: 384). With specific reference to Wordsworth, Noel B. Jackson constructs the poet as a phenomenologist of 'embodied aesthetic experience' ('Rethinking the Cultural Divide', *Modern Philology* 102 [2004]: 223). In articles such as 'Wordsworth's Gifts of Feeling', *Romanticism* 4 (1998) and 'Wordsworth and Idolatry', *Studies in Romanticism* 38 (1999), and in his 2006 book on Wordsworth, Simon Jarvis has brilliantly worried at the 'truth-content', as opposed to ideological content, of Wordsworth and poetry in general. See also: essays by Rei Terada and Jonathan Culler in the special section on 'The New Lyric Studies' in *PMLA* 123 (2008); Paul Fry, *Wordsworth and the Poetry of What We Are* (New Haven and London: Yale University Press 2008).
3. For the relationship between Lukács and Adorno, see Timothy Hall, 'Adorno's *Aesthetic Theory* and Lukács's *Theory of the Novel*' in David Cunningham and Nigel Mapp, eds, *Adorno and Literature* (London: Continuum 2006), pp. 145–58.
4. See Adorno's contention that Heidegger's reading of Hölderlin introduces a 'crude textbook separation of content and form' (Theodor Adorno, 'Parataxis' in ed. Rolf Tiedemann, trans. Shierry Weber Nicholson, *Notes to Literature*, vol. 2 [New York: Columbia University Press 1992], p. 128).
5. The most influential account of this kind is Marjorie Levinson's 'The New Historicism: Back to the Future', in Marjorie Levinson *et al.* eds, *Rethinking Historicism* (Oxford: Basil Blackwell 1989). Levinson argues that Wordsworth

idolises his own version of nature while insisting, in the full grip of false consciousness, that he waits 'for his meanings – glimpses and symbols – upon Nature's uncertain generosity' (ibid., p. 37).

6. William Wordsworth, *Poems, in Two Volumes, and Other Poems, 1800–1807*, ed. Jared Curtis (Ithaca: Cornell University Press 1983), p. 150, lines 2–4.

7. Adorno argues that artistic 'domination' of nature is qualitatively different from instrumental domination: '. . . if art really desires to revoke the domination of nature, and if it is concerned with a situation in which men abandon their efforts to exercise control through their intellect, it can only achieve this through the domination of nature. Only music which is in control of itself would be in control of its own freedom from every compulsion, even its own' (Theodor Adorno, 'Vers une musique informelle' in *Quasi una Fantasia*, trans. Rodney Livingstone [London: Verso 2002], p. 318).

8. For a discussion of Wordsworth's 'lingering in feeling', see Richard Eldridge, 'Wordsworth and the Life of a Subject' in *The Meaning of 'Life' in Romantic Poetry and Poetics*, ed. Ross Wilson (London: Routledge 2009), p. 63.

9. Jon Mee, Mopping Up Spilt Religion: The Problem of Enthusiasm' *Romanticism on the Net* 25 (February 2002): §16.

10. Georg Lukács, *Theory of the Novel*, trans. Anna Bostock (London: Merlin Press 1971), p. 63.

11. Ibid.

12. See Theodor Adorno's 'Punctuation Marks' for his discussion of how mimesis in literature has (and has not) migrated into punctuation marks: 'An exclamation point looks like a finger raised in warning; a question mark looks like a flashing light or the blink of an eye. A colon . . . opens its mouth wide' (*Notes to Literature*, p. 91). Adorno writes, with great relevance to this discussion of Wordsworth, that 'in the dash, thought becomes aware of its fragmentary character' (*Notes to Literature*, p. 93).

13. J.H. Prynne, 'English Poetry and Emphatical Language', *Proceedings of the British Academy*, 74 (1998): 168.

14. Ibid.: 163.

15. John O. Hayden identifies 'echoes of Milton (*Paradise Lost*, III, lines 603–4): "And call up unbound / In various shapes old *Proteus* from the Sea") and . . . Spenser (*Colin Clouts Come Home Againe*: "pleasant lea", line 283, and "Triton blowing loud his wreathèd horn", line 245)' (William Wordsworth, *Selected Poems*, ed. John O. Hayden [London: Penguin 1994], p. 543).

16. Jarvis describes the 'speculative' moment of Wordsworth's verse 'as a "spontaneous overflow of powerful feelings" in which poetry blurts out its wish to have back everything which has been taken away by (what is now) sheer common sense. It is an echo of poetry as efficacious magic, but an echo which knows that there is no such thing as magic' (Jarvis, *Wordsworth's Philosophic Song* [Cambridge: Cambridge University Press 2006], p. 21). See also de Man's discussion of suspension and the word 'hangs' in Wordsworth, in 'Time and History in Wordsworth', *Diacritics* 7 (1987): 7.

17. In a rewriting of Benjamin's 'Theses on the Philosophy of History', Adorno remarks that those who denounce kitsch are possibly more guilty of false consciousness than the kitsch object itself: 'Even the highly cultivated aesthetic allergy to kitsch, ornament, the superfluous, and everything reminiscent of luxury has an aspect of barbarism, an aspect – according to

Freud – of the destructive discontent with culture . . . The literal is barbaric'
(Theodor Adorno, *Aesthetic Theory*, trans. Robert Hullot-Kentor [London: The
Athlone Press 1997], p. 61).
18. Ibid., p. 43.
19. Adorno notes that any 'phenomena that are not preoccupied with the
    maintenance of life take on a ridiculous aspect' (ibid., p. 244). Leela Ghandi
    proposes that, if Enlightenment thinking defines itself as adult, anyone
    wishing to escape 'the prison house of Enlightenment rationality' must
    embrace 'An Immature Politics' (Leela Ghandi, *Affective Communities:
    Anticolonial Thought, Fin-De-Siècle Radicalism, and the Politics of Friendship*
    [Durham: Duke University Press 2006], p. 181).
20. Theodor Adorno and Max Horkheimer, *Dialectic of Enlightenment*, trans. John
    Cumming (London: Verso 1997), p. 149.
21. Adorno, *Aesthetic Theory*, p. 54.
22. See Nigel Mapp, 'History and the Sacred in de Man and Benjamin', in
    Michael Rossington and Anne Whitehead, eds, *Between the Psyche and the
    Polis: Refiguring History in Literature and Theory* (Aldershot: Ashgate 2001),
    p. 41.
23. Robert Kaufman argues that because of its constitutive refusal to be 'beholden
    to extant, status-quo concepts and their contents', lyric poetry will always
    orientate, or 'stretch', its language towards the future (Robert Kaufman,
    'Lyric's Constellation, Poetry's Radical Privilege', *Modernist Cultures* 1. 2
    [2005]: 212).
24. Chris Jones, *Radical Sensibility: Literature and Ideas in the 1790s* (London:
    Routledge 1993), p. vii.
25. See Claudia L. Johnson, *Equivocal Beings: Politics, Gender, and Sentimentality in
    the 1790s – Wollstonecraft, Radcliffe, Burney, Austen* (Chicago: The University
    of Chicago Press 1995), p. 5.
26. Jones, *Radical Sensibility*, p. 208.
27. In a similar vein, John Mullan presents the novel of Sensibility as an append-
    age to eighteenth-century philosophy and its efforts to discipline unruly
    emotions through the discourse of taste. Allowing readers to exercise their
    taste, the novel would 'inoculate them against the more excessive passions
    generated by commercial economy' (John Mullan, *Sentiment and Sociability:
    The Language of Feeling in the Eighteenth Century* [Oxford: The Clarendon Press
    1991], p. 12).
28. From *Wordsworth's Second Nature* (1984), through *England in 1819* (1998),
    to 2008, Chandler has maintained his thesis that Wordsworth was 'already
    Burkean' by 1798 (James Chandler, 'The "Power of Sound" and the Great
    Scheme of Things: Wordsworth Listens to Wordsworth', *Romantic Praxis*
    [April 2008]: §12.
29. James Chandler, *Wordsworth's Second Nature: A Study of the Poetry and Politics*
    (Chicago: The University of Chicago Press 1984), p. 199.
30. Ibid., pp. 209–10; my italics.
31. Kurt Fosso borrows this same temporal pattern to argue that Wordsworth
    builds a 'model of community organized around the [Burkean] dead' (Kurt
    Fosso, *Buried Communities: Wordsworth and the Bonds of Mourning* [New York:
    SUNY Press 2004], p. 24). Fosso suggests that a Burkean Wordsworth binds
    the living to the dead, predicating community on the 'cohesive force'

(p. 129) of collective mourning and remembrance. In 'Michael', for instance, 'a breach in the past becomes the basis for an interpretative community to come, salvaged by elegiac narrative' (p. 159).

32. Adela Pinch, *Strange Fits of Passion: Epistemologies of Emotion, Hume to Austen* (Stanford: Stanford University Press 1997), p. 11. Emma Mason and Isobel Armstrong would agree with Pinch, blaming the 'lacrymogenically-challenged' state of academia on 'both its own theories and the hegemony of safe professionalisation' (Emma Mason and Isobel Armstrong, 'Introduction: "Feeling: an indefinite dull region of the spirit?"', *Textual Practice* 22. 1 [2008]: 14).

33. For probably the finest discussion to date of how Wordsworth's poetry is philosophical without being subsumed beneath philosophy, see Simon Jarvis' *Wordsworth's Philosophic Song*. Jarvis posits 'not that philosophy gets fitted into a song – where all the thinking is done by philosophy and only the handiwork by verse – but that the song itself, *as song*, is philosophic' (pp. 3–4). An important, and related, statement of the case against recent historicisms follows: 'the "historical" contexts necessary to a consideration of any modern poetry extend back through centuries, and even millennia, rather than decades' (p. 6). See also his excellent discussions of the inadequate conceptualisation of *ideology* in much contemporary criticism that defines itself as historicist or materialist (p. 5; pp. 33–107). Whereas Jarvis reads the poetry with Continental philosophy, I emphasise Wordsworth's British context.

34. While my reading of Wordsworthian affect also foregrounds politics, I attempt to give due respect to Wordsworth's initially 'scientific' interest in feeling – that is, his studying feeling for its own sake. In the note to 'The Thorn', Wordsworth writes that 'Poetry is passion: it is the history or science of feelings' (William Wordsworth, *Lyrical Ballads, and Other Poems, 1797–1800*, James Butler and Karen Green eds [Ithaca: Cornell University Press 1992], p. 288). See Anya Taylor, 'Coleridge and the Pleasures of Verse', *Studies in Romanticism* 40 (Winter 2001): 559 for an excellent analysis of the differences between Coleridge and Wordsworth's 'scientific' approaches to poetic pleasure.

35. Pinch, *Strange Fits*, p. 9. Claudia L. Johnson avers that 'Classic texts of sentimentalism by Samuel Richardson, Henry Mackenzie, Hugh Kelly, Henry Brooke, and Oliver Goldsmith similarly recur to the spectacle of suffering womanhood to elicit the melting humanity of male onlookers, and to make possible their *lacrimo, ergo sum*' (Johnson, *Equivocal Beings*, p. 5).

36. Pinch, *Strange Fits*, p. 81.

37. G. Gabrielle Starr also analyses lyric in terms of power. She regards Wordsworth's declarations of opposition to prose as part of the musculature of 'Romantic self-fashioning' (G. Gabrielle Starr, *Lyric Generations: Poetry and the Novel in the Long Eighteenth Century* [Baltimore: The Johns Hopkins University Press 2004], p. 14). In a fascinating discussion of the 'novelistic' (p. 187) strategies of 'When to the attractions of the busy world', Starr claims that Wordsworth's description of his brother as 'A silent poet [. . .] elevates the lyric to the mystical status of an indelible inscription' (p. 187). She concludes that the novel is thus 'brought under the rubric of the poetic; it is rendered as a mode ultimately under poetic control' (p. 187).

38. Pinch, *Strange Fits*, p. 80; p. 88; p. 92. Pinch is clearly shaping Wordsworth to agree with Johnson's observations about the sentimental novel: 'the spectacle of immanent and outrageous female suffering may not be the unthinkable crime which chivalric sentimentality forestalls, but rather the one-thing-needful to solicit male tears and the virtues that supposedly flow with them, and the preposterousness of the work emerges from and engages this horrifying realization' (Johnson, *Equivocal Beings*, p. 15). Regardless of whether Johnson and Pinch correctly identify the sexual politics of the texts by the male writers they discuss, the fact remains that, for all the debate about genre, fiction and poetry are treated as equivalent in their readings. Johnson's discovery in women's fiction of the period a 'grotesqueness, . . . flaunted strain, incoherence, and excess' (p. 18) that resists and subverts the appropriation of female suffering in poetry by men leaves untouched the implicit gender essentialism of an argument that might be complicated by greater attention to 'the literary'.

39. Emotion-as-movement is discussed in James Chandler, 'The languages of sentiment', *Textual Practice* 22. 1 (2008): 21–39.

40. Timothy Hall puts it neatly when he writes that 'The deletion of the illusion of the modern work of art's autonomy by any criticism that identifies art and ideology thus amounts to throwing out the baby with the bathwater. The relentless demystification of the work in recent literary criticism (whether Marxist, feminist, post-colonial or queer-theoretical) inadvertently liquidates what in the artwork testifies to the possibility of relating to nature and others otherwise than we do' (Timothy Hall, 'Adorno's *Aesthetic Theory* and Lukács's *Theory of the Novel*', p. 153).

 From a very different methodological position, Alan Bewell makes a similar point. Defending Wordsworth against accusations that he gags marginal figures in his poetry, Bewell observes: 'this silence represents Wordsworth's resistance to the textual marginalization that these individuals underwent during the previous century – in short, his attempt to write the Enlightenment discourse of marginality out of existence by seeking to undo its pleasure in producing marginals and in taking rhetorical advantage of those who cannot speak or who suffer from physical or mental hardships. Their silence disrupts the moral, anthropological, and political framework that brought the Enlightenment into contact with marginals and the lower classes, allowing philosophers to speak through them by ventriloquism' (Alan Bewell, *Wordsworth and the Enlightenment: Nature, Man, and Society in the Experimental Poetry* [New Haven: Yale University Press 1989], p. 40).

41. For G. Gabrielle Starr, genre criticism becomes materialist when it attends, for example, 'to the marks the novel left on its generic successors' (Starr, *Lyric Generations*, p. 199). She reads 'The Solitary Reaper' as an instance in which 'The novelistic narrative is replaced by a poetic one; the novel, represented synecdochally by its conventions, disappears at the point where the professional poet solidifies his position in the world' (p. 191). For Starr, novels 'open up a range of emotions to serious literary treatment' (p. 7), which innovations are 'stolen' by a (Wordsworthian) poetry that then denies its debt. Sarah Zimmerman, by contrast, points out that Wordsworth's use of novelistic conventions is not quite so simple. Sometimes narrative is emotionally capacious, at other times (in 'Simon Lee', for example) it signifies

exploitative entertainment, and at still other moments 'lyricism demands engagement' (Sarah Zimmerman, *Romanticism, Lyricism, and History* [Albany: SUNY Press 1999], p. 92).

42. G. Gabrielle Starr, 'Ethics, Meaning, and the Work of Beauty', *Eighteenth-Century Studies* 35. 3 (2002): 304. Ronald Paulson argues that the influence of the Neo-Platonic Shaftesbury on British aesthetics has been overemphasised. Taking issue with John Barrell, Paulson offers Hogarth as a well-known alternative to Shaftesburean thinking in the period, 'a counterdiscourse that is *not* covert, hesitant or "relative only"' (*The Beautiful, Novel, and Strange: Aesthetics and Heterodoxy* [Baltimore: The Johns Hopkins University Press 1996], p. 321 n. 15).

43. G. Gabrielle Starr, 'Ethics, Meaning': 363.

44. Ibid.: 366.

45. Ibid.: 369.

46. 'There are *no* objects which are sheerly indifferent in and of themselves. The idea of sheer matter . . . is itself a chimera, an idol' (Jarvis, *Wordsworth's Philosophic Song*, p. 50).

47. Starr pits the 'materialism' of the novel against the abstraction of 'the British tradition of moral philosophy' (Starr, *Lyric Generations*, p. 270 n. 66). Writing about a later period, Allison Pease contrasts 'the tradition of Shaftesbury and Kant, which privileged cognitive response, to a modernist, twentieth-century aesthetic, which incorporated and demanded . . . an embodied response' (Allison Pease, *Modernism, Mass Culture, and the Aesthetics of Obscenity* [Cambridge: Cambridge University Press 2000], p. xv). I argue that, rather than uncritically privileging abstraction, Whig philosophy constantly explores, or at the very least notices, its dependence upon the material.

48. Bewell, *Wordsworth and the Enlightenment*, p. 5. Bewell puts his attempt to distinguish between the philosophical and poetic in Wordsworth thus: 'On one hand, we will see the poems in a different light: as poetic "essays" on specific moral subjects, not only on the faculties of the mind (as in the 1815 classification of *Poems*), but also on the origin and progress of social institutions such as the family, property, religion, myth, poetry, and language. On the other hand, it will allow us to discern how the poems achieved their modernity in their departures from and displacement of this textual paradigm' (p. 17).

49. My view that Wordsworth's poetry is 'increasingly autonomous' does not disavow the important work critics like Pinch, Johnson and Starr have done to show the presence of the novel and eighteenth-century women's writing in his art. In a parallel argument, I make a case for his use of 'figures' (for example, enthusiasm, habit, tradition) taken from Whig philosophy. The term 'increasingly autonomous' suggests, not the absence of heterogeneous elements in Wordsworth, but that the verse is more interested its own formal procedures than in 'instrumental' communication.

50. Paul Hamilton, 'Post-Secular Conviviality', *Romantic Praxis* (August 2008): §7.

51. Some work on Shaftesbury's *Second Characters* (published posthumously in 1914) has begun to disclose this 'other' Shaftesbury. See, for example: Richard Checketts, 'Pleasure's Objects: Commodity, Manufacture, and the Art Theories of Shaftesbury and Hogarth', *Anglia* 120 (2002); James A. Steintrager, 'Perfectly Inhuman: Moral Monstrosity in Eighteenth-Century

Discourse', *Eighteenth-Century Life* 21.2 (1997). For a broader perspective on the 'others' of Whig aesthetics, see Maureen Harkin, 'Theorizing Popular Practice in Eighteenth-Century Aesthetics' in *Aesthetic Subjects*, Pamela R. Matthews and David McWhirter eds (Minneapolis: University of Minnesota Press 2003).
52. Like Bewell, I am wary of imposing a narrative of development or decline on a poet whose finest work is marked by internal conflict, even if a vocabulary that includes *conflict* and *struggle* inevitably evokes drama. I maintain that across Wordsworth's *oeuvre* there are more cases of, as Kurt Fosso puts it, 'recurrence than lock-stop evolutionary progress' (Fosso, *Buried Communities*, p. 23).

1   Shaftesbury, Wordsworth and Affective Critique

1. Jon Mee, *Romanticism, Enthusiasm, and Regulation: Poetics and the Policing of Culture in the Romantic Period* (Oxford: Oxford UP 2003), p. 256.
2. See Paul Fry's comment 'that Wordsworth was never radically politicized (although at least in 1793 he was without a doubt politically radical)' (Paul Fry, *Wordsworth and the Poetry of What We Are* [New Haven and London: Yale University Press 2008], p. 4).
3. Andrew Ashfield and Peter de Bolla, eds, *The Sublime: A Reader in British Eighteenth-Century Aesthetic Theory* (Cambridge: Cambridge University Press 1996), p. 1.
4. Ibid., p. 2.
5. Duncan Wu claims that Wordsworth had read Shaftesbury 'whilst still a schoolboy, by 1785' (Duncan Wu, *Wordsworth's Reading 1770–1799* [Cambridge: Cambridge University Press 1993], p. 36). In 'Essay Supplementary to the Preface', Wordsworth refers to Shaftesbury as 'an author at present unjustly depreciated' (*PrW* 3, 72).
6. Wu, *Wordsworth's Reading 1770–1799*, p. 36.
7. Michael Meehan, *Liberty and Poetics in Eighteenth Century England*, p. 59; Wu, *Wordsworth's Reading 1770–1799*, p. 137. See also R. L. Brett, *The Third Earl of Shaftesbury: A Study in Eighteenth-Century Literary Theory*, pp. 160–1 and Michael Meehan, *Liberty and Poetics*, pp. 52–63 for the influence of Shaftesbury on Thomson and Akenside, respectively. Jacobus discusses the presence of the same poets in Wordsworth (Mary Jacobus, *Tradition and Experiment in Wordsworth's Lyrical Ballads (1798)* [Oxford: The Clarendon Press 1976], pp. 38–58) and Rader finds allusions to Shaftesbury in Wordsworth's mature work (Melvin Rader, *Wordsworth: A Philosophical Approach* [Oxford: The Clarendon Press 1967], pp. 54–5.)
8. See Jacobus, *Tradition and Experiment*, p. 52.
9. S. T. C. Coleridge, *Collected Letters of Samuel Taylor Coleridge*, ed. Earl Leslie Griggs, 6 vols [Oxford: The Clarendon Press 1956–71], 1. 279.
10. Kelvin Everest, *Coleridge's Secret Ministry: The Context of the Conversation Poems* 1795–1798 (Brighton: Harvester Press 1979), pp. 191–2.
11. Julie Ellison, *Cato's Tears and the Making of Anglo-American Emotion* (Chicago: The University of Chicago Press 1999), p. 47.
12. Discussing Shaftesbury's advice to authors that they 'retire to solitary places, "Woods and Riverbanks," to test their work against themselves so that the "fancy" may evaporate and the "vehemence" of the "Spirit and Voice" may

be reduced (*C* 1: 107–08)', Jon Mee suggests that 'Already . . . we can see the outlines of a Wordsworthian definition of poetry as "emotion, recollected in tranquillity"' (Jon Mee, 'Mopping Up Spilt Religion: The Problem of Enthusiasm', *Romanticism on the Net* 25 (2002): §5.

13. *The Prelude*'s 'spots of time' are, of course, Wordsworth's most ambitious expression of this view. See Jon Mee, *Romanticism, Enthusiasm, and Regulation: Poetics and the Policing of Culture in the Romantic Period* (Oxford: Oxford UP 2003), p. 239.

14. Anne Janowitz, *England's Ruins: Poetic Purpose and the National Landscape* (Oxford: Basil Blackwell 1990), p. 32.

15. Lawrence Klein, *Shaftesbury and the Culture of Politeness* (Cambridge: Cambridge University Press 1994), p. 126.

16. John Barrell, *English Literature in History, 1730–80: An Equal, Wide Survey* (London: Hutchinson 1983), p. 22. My italics.

17. Barrell, *The Birth of Pandora and the Division of Knowledge* (London: Macmillan 1992), p. 64.

18. Donald Paulson, *The Beautiful, Novel, and Strange: Aesthetics and Heterodoxy* (Baltimore: The Johns Hopkins University Press 1996), pp. 4–5.

19. Shaun Irlam, *Elations: The Poetics of Enthusiasm in Eighteenth-Century Britain* (Stanford: Stanford University Press 1999), p. 19.

20. J. G. A. Pocock, *Virtue, Commerce and History: Essays on Political Thought and History, Chiefly in the Eighteenth Century* (Cambridge: University of Cambridge Press 1985), p. 210.

21. Michael Meehan, *Liberty and Poetics in Eighteenth Century England* (New Hampshire: Croom Helm 1986), pp. 10, 22. See Anne Janowitz's discussion of how in the *Monthly Magazine* of the early 1800s 'Literature shifts from being the vehicle of principles to being the principle of liberality itself' (Anne Janowitz, 'Memoirs of a dutiful niece: Lucy Aikin and literary reputation' in Heather Glen and Paul Hamilton, eds., *Repossessing the Romantic Past* [Cambridge: Cambridge University Press 2006], p. 89).

22. John Barrell makes the link between Wordsworth's 'language of conversation in the middle and lower classes of society' (*PrW* 1. 116) and civic humanist disinterest: 'by virtue of his lack of occupation, the gentleman . . . was believed to be the only member of society who spoke a language universally intelligible: his usage was "common", in the sense of being neither a local dialect nor infected by the terms of any particular art' (Barrell, *English Literature in History*, pp. 33–4).

23. Terry Eagleton, *The Ideology of the Aesthetic* (Oxford: Basil Blackwell 1994), p. 32.

24. Ibid., p. 34.

25. G. J Barker-Benfield, *The Culture of Sensibility: Sex and Society in Eighteenth-Century Britain* (Chicago: The University of Chicago Press 1992), p. 119.

26. Klein, *Shaftesbury and the Culture of Politeness*, p. 8.

27. Ibid.

28. See William Wordsworth, *The Thirteen-Book Prelude*, Vol. 1, ed. Mark L. Reed (Ithaca: Cornell University Press 1991), 10. 848. All references are to this edition, unless stated otherwise.

29. See Chapter 2 for a discussion of Burke's use of this Shaftesburean move, and Chapter 3 for Wordsworth's similar position in his claim that a poem's

'feeling . . . gives importance to the action and the situation and not the action and situation to the feeling' (*PrW* 1. 128).
30. Klein, *Shaftesbury and the Culture of Politeness*, p. 158.
31. Ibid., p. 56.
32. Chris Jones, *Radical Sensibility: Literature and Ideas in the 1790s* (London: Routledge 1993), p. 197.
33. William Wordsworth, *An Evening Walk by William Wordsworth*, ed. James Averill (Cornell: Cornell University Press 1984), 119–32.
34. Jones, *Radical Sensibility*, p. 195. Jones reminds readers that if 'love of nature is linked as firmly as it is in Shaftesbury with a virtue which implies universal benevolence, [Wordsworth] expanded beyond Shaftesbury's limited formulations into the egalitarian sympathy of radical sensibility' (p. 199). See also *C* 2: 110–11.
35. Basil Willey, *The Eighteenth-Century Background* (London: Routledge 1986), p. 70.
36. R. L. Brett, *The Third Earl of Shaftesbury: A Study in Eighteenth-Century Literary Theory* (New York: Hutchinson's University Library 1951), p. 74.
37. Chris Jones argues that 'Shaftesbury, in championing freedom and criticising social and religious traditions, argued only for the equality and naturalness of his cultured milieu, but his formulations were taken out of context to become the basis of a radical, even revolutionary ideology' (Chris Jones, *Radical Sensibility*, p. 8).
38. John Brown, *An Estimate of the Manners and Principles of the Times* (London: 1757), p. 154.
39. Pocock, *Virtue, Commerce and History*, p. 114.
40. Barrell, *English Literature in History*, p. 49.
41. For a fine reading of the relationship between money, speculation and fantasy in the period, see Thomas Laqueur, 'Sexual Desire and the Market Economy during the Industrial Revolution' in *Discourses of Sexuality: From Aristotle to AIDS*, ed. Domna C. Stanton (Michigan: University of Michigan Press 1992). See also Laqueur's 'Masturbation, Credit and the Novel during the Long Eighteenth Century', *Qui Parle*, 8 (1995): 1–19.
42. See also Coleridge's letter of 1820 in which he remarks that 'The age seems *sore* from excess of stimulation' (S.T.C. Coleridge, *Collected Letters*, 1. 228).
43. Jerome J. McGann, *The Poetics of Sensibility: A Revolution in Literary Style* (Oxford: The Clarendon Press 1996), p. 79.
44. Ibid., p. 121.
45. Mark Akenside, *The Pleasures of the Imagination. To which is prefixed a critical essay on the poem, by Mrs. Barbauld* (London 1794), p. 124. All references are to Mrs Barbauld's 1794 edition of The Pleasures of the Imagination, which Dorothy Wordsworth received in 1795 (Duncan Wu, *Wordsworth's Reading*, p. 2).
46. Akenside, *The Pleasures of the Imagination*, 1. 116–32.
47. Meehan, *Liberty and Poetics*, p. 42; William Wordsworth, *The Fourteen-Book Prelude*, ed. W. J. B. Owen (Ithaca: Cornell University Press 1985), 8. 729.
48. In the twentieth century, the idea that energy must, of necessity, be released in order to maintain good health was developed by Georges Bataille: '. . . solar energy is the source of life's exuberant development. The origin and essence of our wealth are given in the radiation of the sun, which dispenses

energy – wealth – without any return. The sun gives without ever receiving' (Georges Bataille, *The Bataille Reader*, eds Fred Botting and Scott Wilson [Oxford: Blackwell 1997], p. 189).

49. Jason Frank writes that 'Shaftesbury believed in the necessary persistence of enthusiasm as a crucial part of the sociability he pursued . . . Enthusiasm marked a space of persistent enchantment in a world that seemed to Shaftesbury bent on ridding itself of its enchantments' (Jason Frank, '"Besides Our Selves": An Essay on Enthusiastic Politics and Civil Subjectivity', *Public Culture* 17. 3 (2005): 389.

50. In Shaftesbury, 'citizenship is envisioned as an ongoing practice of encounter and negotiation rather than a primarily juridical category' (ibid. 372).

51. William Wordsworth, *The Salisbury Plain Poems of William Wordsworth*, ed. Stephen Gill (Cornell: Cornell University Press 1975), 102–3.

52. On the poem's anti-Whig aspect, Tom Duggett writes: '*Salisbury Plain*'s nightmare of relapse into Druidical sacrifice is apparently a deliberate challenge to the Whig model of English history whereby, in the words of James Thomson's *Liberty* (1735–6), the successive invasions of the "Gothic nations" of Saxons, Danes and Normans had woken Britain "from Celtic night / To present grandeur" (IV, 624–5)' (Tom Dugget, 'Celtic Night and Gothic Grandeur: Politics and Antiquarianism in Wordsworth's *Salisbury Plain*', *Romanticism* 13. 2 [2007]: 168.

53. For Neil Saccamano, 'Shaftesbury's understanding of moral self-regulation . . . is premised on a natural economy of affections in which individual happiness is coordinated with "the strictest society and rule of common good", and "the most unnatural of all affections are those which separate from this community"' (Neil Saccamano, 'Inheriting Enlightenment, or Keeping Faith with Reason in Derrida', *Eighteenth-Century Studies* 40. 3 [2007]: 414.

54. With its numerous lines to Coleridge, *The Prelude* often draws upon the regulatory influence of an internalised form of conversation. Wordsworth's description of how he responded ecstatically to 'the sweet breath of Heaven / . . . blowing on my body' with a 'corresponding mild creative breeze' (1. 41–2; 1. 43) is quickly followed by an address to Coleridge that secures such vivid 'present joy' (1. 56) in the past.

55. William Wordsworth, *Lyrical Ballads, and Other Poems, 1797–1800*, ed. James Butler and Karen Green, (Ithaca: Cornell University Press 1992), 15–16.

56. Martha Ray is so alone in her sorrow that, the narrator says, 'I never heard of such as dare / Approach the spot when she is there' ('The Thorn', 98–9). The depth of her emotion completely cuts her off from any possibly restorative society.

57. Richard Gravil notes that Wordsworth here constructs Hazlitt as a Burkean: 'Five years earlier Wordsworth had rebuked Burke's piety to the dead as "a refinement in cruelty superior to that which in the East yokes the living to the dead" [*PrW*, 1: 48]'. In doing so, Wordsworth signals that he is 'of Paine's party' (Richard Gravil, *Wordsworth's Bardic Vocation, 1787–1842* [Basingstoke: Palgrave Macmillan 2003], p. 100).

58. Frank, '"Besides Our Selves"': 379.

59. See Richard Gravil's excellent chapter, 'The Pathos of Humanity', on Wordsworthian irony in *Wordsworth's Bardic Vocation*, pp. 92–114.

60. Pierre Bourdieu, *Distinction: A Social Critique of the Judgement of Taste*, trans. Richard Nice (Cambridge, Mass.: Harvard University Press 1984), p. 6.

61. Shaftesbury argues that one of the ways taste regulates enthusiasm is by directing it towards the neatly circumscribed domain of the arts, such as 'Architecture, Painting, Musick' (*C* 2. 104). Although still concerned with the totality of affective experience, Shaftesbury here anticipates the future focus of aesthetics on artworks.
62. McGann, *The Poetics of Sensibility*, p. 121.
63. Ibid.
64. Pierre Bourdieu, *The Field of Cultural Production*, trans. Randal Johnson (Cambridge: Polity Press 1993), p. 112.
65. Clifford Siskin notes that 'the expansion of print in general leads to the formation of a mass market and the emergent behaviour of "culture", including commodification into "high" and "low" forms' (Clifford Siskin, 'More is different: literary change in the mid and late eighteenth century' in *The Cambridge History of English Literature, 1610–1780* 810, ed. John Richetti [Cambridge: Cambridge University Press 2005], p. 822). From this follows 'the notion of a "national tradition", the apotheosis of key genres and the professional and academic enterprise of "criticism"' (p. 822).
66. Bourdieu contends that

    > Those 'inventions' of Romanticism – the representation of culture as a kind of superior reality, irreducible to the vulgar demands of economics, and the ideology of free, disinterested 'creation' founded on the spontaneity of innate inspiration – appear to be just so many reactions to the pressures of an anonymous market (*The Field of Cultural Production*, p. 114).

    See Siskin's similar argument that in the later eighteenth century 'More of "literature" became "Literature", a difference that marks the advent of what we now call Romanticism' (Clifford Siskin, 'More is different, p. 822). Jon Mee remarks that from 1775 Coleridge 'is concerned to respect a distinction between poetry and prophecy' (Jon Mee, 'Anxieties of Enthusiasm: Coleridge, Prophecy, and Popular Politics in the 1790s', *Huntington Library Quarterly: Studies in English and American History and Literature* 60 [1998]: 195). Coleridge fears the democratic possibilities of enthusiastic inspiration: the passion it arouses robs individuals of their autonomy and sense, and thus threatens the social order. The civic humanist Coleridge, therefore, distances himself from 'the enthusiasm of the crowd' and aligns himself with the discipline of poetry and poets – 'the disinterested band of the elect' (200). According to Mee, Coleridge came to believe that Wordsworth had flouted the distinction between poetry and prophecy, or enthusiasm.

2 Burke, Wordsworth and the Poet

1. Ian Haywood, *Bloody Romanticism: Spectacular Violence and the Politics of Representation, 1776–1832* (Basingstoke: Palgrave Macmillan 2006), p. 60. Haywood cites Luke Gibbon's remark that Burke's aesthetics of '"violence, pain and sympathy"' gave him a '"set of diagnostic tools to probe the dark side of enlightenment"' (p. 60).

2. Ernest Tuveson, 'Shaftesbury and the Age of Sensibility', *Studies in Criticism and Aesthetics 1600–1800*, eds H. Anderson and J. Shea (Minneapolis: University of Minneapolis Press 1967), p. 74.

3. Shaun Irlam, *Elations: The Poetics of Enthusiasm in Eighteenth-Century Britain* (Stanford: Stanford University Press 1999), p. 86.

4. John Barrell, *English Literature in History, 1730–80: An Equal, Wide Survey* (London: Hutchinson 1983), p. 64.

5. See Robert Jones' discussion of fears that 'while commerce polished and improved, it also assaulted and softened the basis of republican personality' (Robert Jones, *Gender and the Formation of Taste in Eighteenth-Century Britain* (Cambridge: Cambridge University Press 1998), p. 21.

6. John Hume, *Essays, Moral, Political and Literary* (Oxford: Oxford University Press 1963), p. 234.

7. Ibid., p. 242.

8. Ibid.

9. Ibid., p. 245.

10. Ibid.

11. Michael Meehan, *Liberty and Poetics in Eighteenth Century England* (New Hampshire: Croom Helm 1986), p. 42. On the first page of his *An Essay on Taste*, Gerard admits his debt to another prominent Shaftesburean: 'Mr Hutcheson was the first who considered the powers of imagination as so many senses. In his *Inquiry concerning beauty and virtue*, and his *Essay on the passions*, he calls them *internal* senses' (*ET* 1). All references to Gerard's *Essay* are to this – the greatly expanded third edition.

12. Peter de Bolla, *The Discourse of the Sublime: Readings in History, Aesthetics and the Subject* (Oxford: Blackwell 1989), p. 81.

13. See Chapter 3 for Wordsworth's related claim about poetry, that the 'feeling therein developed gives importance to the action and the situation and not the action and situation to the feeling' (*PrW* 1. 128).

14. On the subject of taste in architecture, Smith writes: 'Can any reason, for example, be assigned why the Doric capital should be appropriated to a pillar, whose height is equal to eight diameters; the Ionic volute to one of nine; and the Corinthian foliage to one of ten? The propriety of each of those appropriations can be founded upon nothing but habit and custom' (Adam Smith, *The Theory of Moral Sentiments* [Edinburgh 1759], p. 264).

15. Duncan Wu does not include Gerard's *Essay* among Wordsworth's reading between 1770 and 1799; but W. J. B. Owen and J. W. Smyser find evidence of at least a second-hand awareness of Gerard in the Preface to *Lyrical Ballads*, as well as evidence of a familiarity with the intellectual concerns of Shaftesbury, Dennis, Hutcheson, Kames and Blair. See, particularly, the detailed notes and commentary in *PrW* 1. 174–5. Also see Chapter 3 for further discussion of the claims Wordsworth makes for the Poet and poetry.

16. On the word 'literature', Siskin writes: 'The word that referred through most of the eighteenth century to all kinds of writing – *Britannica* still defined "literature" in the 1770s as simply "learning or skill in letters" – came, in the space of a few decades, to refer more narrowly to only certain texts in within certain genres. It came to define, that is, the specialised subject matter of a discipline' (Clifford Siskin, 'More is different: literary change in the mid and late

eighteenth century' in *The Cambridge History of English Literature, 1610–1780* 810, ed. John Richetti [Cambridge: Cambridge University Press 2005], p. 810).
17. Clifford Siskin, *The Work of Writing: Literature and Social Change in Britain, 1700–1830* (Baltimore: The Johns Hopkins University Press 1998), p. 6.
18. Ibid., p. 95.
19. See Siskin's well-known argument that *The Prelude* is Wordsworth's 'résumé' for the job of National Poet (ibid., p. 114).
20. Brian Goldberg, '"Ministry More Palpable": Wordsworth and the Making of Romantic Professionalism', *Studies in Romanticism* 36 (1997): 336.
21. John Barrell suggests that Wordsworth's solution is to develop a 'personal, ironic mode of authority' in his poetry (Barrell, *English Literature in History*, p. 49).
22. This is not to say, of course, that a *de-politicisation* of aesthetics does actually occur in Gerard. The separation of taste from virtue, and the promotion of the role of the critic, is itself an act of political reorientation. By wrestling taste from the aristocracy and delivering it into the care of the bourgeoisie, in the guise of an enquiry into the *truth* of taste, Gerard himself contributes to the mystification of the relationship between politics and aesthetics.
23. H. A. Wichelns argues that the additions Burke made to the second edition of the *Enquiry* in 1759 – the most notable being the new 'Introduction on Taste' – were almost all 'called forth by the opinions expressed in the three reviews' that greeted the first edition (H. A. Wichelns, 'Burke's Essay on the Sublime and its Reviewers', *Journal of English and Germanic Philology*, XXI [1922]: 649). Burke's *Enquiry*, then, was noticed on publication: its impact on debate, however, was not necessarily immediate.
24. Edmund Burke, *The Correspondence of Edmund Burke*, vol. 1, *1 April 1744–June 1768*, ed. Thomas Wordsworth (Cambridge: Cambridge University Press 1958a), p. 18. See also F. P. Lock: 'Hutcheson, *An Inquiry into the Original of Our Ideas of Beauty and Virtue* . . . is the probable source of E. B.'s remarks. The idea of beauty as 'variety in uniformity' is a leitmotiv in Hutcheson's *Inquiry*. E. B.' s letter continues in a rhapsodic style that may be intended as a parody of Shaftesbury. Whether meant seriously or not, the letter shows E. B.'s familiarity with current modes of aesthetic discourse' (F. P. Lock, *Edmund Burke Vol. I, 1730–84* [The Clarendon Press: Oxford 1998], p. 94 n. 11.
25. Jean-Francois Lyotard, *The Lyotard Reader*, ed. Andrew Benjamin (Oxford: Basil Blackwell 1993), p. 202.
26. Ibid., p. 203.
27. Pierre Bourdieu, *The Field of Cultural Production*, trans. Randal Johnson (Cambridge: Polity Press 1993), p. 114.
28. Jean-Francois Lyotard, *The Lyotard Reader*, ed. Andrew Benjamin (Oxford: Basil Blackwell 1993), p. 202. The number of texts on the sublime produced in eighteenth-century England testifies to the heightened interest in the relationship between art and sensation in the period. Lyotard, however, working out of a primarily Germanic tradition, considers the work of Kant to be the major text in the development of the aesthetic into what Lacoue-Labarthe calls '"sensuous knowledge" (*cognito sensitiva)*' (Philippe Lacoue-Labarthe, *The Subject of Philosophy*, ed. Thomas Trezise, trans. Thomas Trezise, Hugh J. Silverman, Gary M. Cole, Timothy D. Bent, Karen McPherson, and Claudette Sartiliot [Minneapolis: University of Minnesota Press 1993], p. 151). In the *Critique of Judgement*, Kant even incorporates the sublime into the heart of

philosophy. The Kantian sublime is 'the giddy feeling of unboundedness which then yields us a negative presentation of the infinity of moral Reason' (Terry Eagleton, *The Ideology of the Aesthetic* [Oxford: Basil Blackwell 1994], p. 91): this newly sensuous version of the aesthetic is taken as one of the main conditions for reason. Indeed, for Lacoue-Labarthe the privileging of sensation in aesthetics occurs in 1735 with Baumgarten's *Meditaiones philosophicae de nonnullis ad poema pertinentibus*, a work which, like Kant's, signals a 'revalorization of the sensuous (of the *aïstheta*) [that] is all the stronger and more powerful as it is not accompanied by any correlative devalorization of the intelligible' (Philippe Lacoue-Labarthe, *The Subject of Philosophy*, p. 152). There are distinct differences between the structures of the Kantian and British sublime, but both adhere to an idea of the aesthetic as typified by sensation and ethical force.

29. Bourdieu, *The Field of Cultural Production*, p. 114.
30. See Chapter 6 for a discussion of the social abstraction contained in Wordsworthian allegory.
31. William H. Galperin, *The Return of the Visible in British Romanticism* (Baltimore: The Johns Hopkins University Press 1993), p. 123.
32. Two years after publication of the *Enquiry*, Adam Smith's *The Theory of the Moral Sentiments* – the book which 'opened the floodgate to a rising tide of interest in the sympathetic imagination' (James Engell, *The Creative Imagination: Enlightenment to Romanticism* [Cambridge, Mass.: Harvard University Press 1981], p. 149) – predicated the bonds of social affection on pleasure. He argued that 'nothing pleases us more than to observe in other men a fellow-feeling with all the emotions of our own breast' (Adam Smith, *Moral Sentiments*, p. 9). The sentiments do not arise from self-love, but more often from shared delight: 'A man is mortified when, after having endeavoured to divert the company, he looks around and sees that nobody laughs at his jests but himself. On the contrary, the mirth of the company is highly agreeable to him, and he regards this correspondence of their sentiments with his own as the greatest applause' (p. 10). An individual's pleasure is hardly a pleasure at all, it seems, without a social component.
33. Frances Ferguson, *Solitude and the Sublime: Romanticism and the Aesthetics of Individuation* (London: Routledge 1992), p. 1; italics mine.
34. Tom Furniss, *Edmund Burke's Aesthetic Ideology: Language, Gender and Political Economy in Revolution* (Cambridge: Cambridge University Press 1993).
35. Smith, *Moral Sentiments*, p. 37.
36. For Smith, imitation works both ways, and becomes a form of regulating social spectatorship. An individual experiencing an emotion is affected by the sympathy of others: 'As they are continually placing themselves in his situation, and thence conceiving emotions similar to what he feels, so he is as constantly placing himself in theirs, and hence conceiving some degree of coolness about his own fortune' (ibid., p. 25). Imagining how he appears to others, the individual adjusts his behaviour appropriately.
37. Ferguson, *Solitude and the Sublime*, p. 59.
38. Ibid., p. 61.
39. Robert Mitchell argues that in *The Theory of the Moral Sentiments* Adam Smith makes a similarly surprising link between sympathy, violence and death: 'Through the action of sympathy, criminal actions generate

contagious resentment, which threatens to undo the social bond. However, the execution of the condemned allows justice to prevail, while at the same time attending to the need for sympathy on the part of *both* the condemned and the execution spectators' (Robert Mitchell, 'The Violence of Sympathy; Adam Smith on Resentment and Executions', *1650–1850; ideas, aesthetics, and inquiries in the early modern era* 8 [January 2003]: 322).

40. By contrast, Elizabeth Samet argues that theatre, for Burke, 'trains us how to react, especially during historical crises in which excessive suffering is generally regarded with indifference' (Elizabeth D. Samet, 'Spectacular History and the Politics of Theatre: Sympathetic Arts in the Shadow of the Bastille', *PMLA* 118.5 [2003]: 1311).

41. Fergusson, *Solitude and the Sublime*, p. 60.

42. Ibid.

43. See the discussion of Burke's 'linguistic sublime' in Chapter 3, and Chapter 5 for a detailed comparison of the Burkean sublime of self-preservation with Kantian and Wordsworthian versions.

44. Susan Manly writes that 'We might draw an analogy between Wordsworth's fear of the "rapid communication" of "men in cities" and the "rashness of decision" of those who do not recognize his poetry as such, and Burke's anxiety about "innovation" and the loss of "wise prejudice" in the depredations of the French revolutionaries' (Susan Manly, *Language, Custom and Nation in the 1790s; Locke, Tooke, Wordsworth, Edgeworth* [Aldershot: Ashgate 2007], p. 116).

45. Wordsworth had probably read the *Reflections* by 1793 (Wu, *Wordsworth's Reading 1770–1799* [Cambridge: Cambridge University Press 1993], p. 22).

46. Steven Blakemore, *Burke and the Fall of Language: The French Revolution as Linguistic Event* (Hanover, N. H.: University Press of New England 1988), p. 7.

47. J. G. A. Pocock, *Virtue, Commerce and History: Essays on Political Thought and History, Chiefly in the Eighteenth Century* (Cambridge: University of Cambridge Press 1985), p. 20. See the discussion in Chapter 4 of Wordsworth's letter about *Michael* and *The Brothers* for his counterview.

48. Pocock argues that Burke's antipathy to the Revolution was a resistance to 'the freedom of discourse to create the world unilaterally' (J. G. A. Pocock, 'Edmund Burke and the Redefinition of Enthusiasm: the Context as Counter-Revolution' in *The French Revolution and the Creation of Modern Political Culture. Vol. 3: The Transformation of Political Culture 1789–1848*, eds Francois Furet and Mona Ozouf [Oxford: Pergamon 1989], p. 20). However, Pocock does not conclude that Burke's objections to the Revolution were a dispute over linguistic theory. Burke was defending the 'ideology of manners, which English and Scottish moralists had constructed to explain how ethics and culture could flourish in a society based on an economy of moveable goods' (p. 31). The linguistic enthusiasm of the Revolutionaries – an enthusiasm in which 'All must be *transparence*; the world must incarnate itself immediately' (p. 20) in identity with the self-sufficient word – fatally undermined, so Burke believed, the delicate pattern of social interrelations necessary for commerce.

49. For a useful discussion of Burke's conception of 'experience', see Martin Jay, *Songs of Experience: Modern American and European Variations on a Universal Theme* (Berkley: University of California Press 2005), p. 177–83.

50. Ibid., p. 101.

51. Wordsworth read the *Letter to a Member of the National Assembly* by Spring 1793 (Duncan Wu, *Wordsworth's Reading*, p. 22).
52. Edmund Burke, *The Writings and Speeches of Edmund Burke*, IX, *I: The Revolutionary War 1794–1997, II: Ireland*, eds R. B. McDowell and William B. Todd (Oxford: The Clarendon Press 1991), p. 198.
53. Steven Goldsmith, *Unbuilding Jerusalem: Apocalypse and Romantic Representation* (Ithaca: Cornell University Press 1993), p. 4.
54. William Wordsworth, *The Borderers by William Wordsworth*, ed. Robert Osbourne (Ithaca: Cornell University Press 1982), p. 64.
55. Lucy Newlyn, *'Paradise Lost' and the Romantic Reader* (Oxford: The Clarendon Press 1993), p. 110; p. 111.
56. Ibid., p. 110.
57. William Wordsworth, *The Fourteen-Book Prelude*, ed. W. J. B. Owen (Ithaca: Cornell University Press 1985), 7. 512.
58. William Wordsworth, *The Letters of William and Dorothy Wordsworth*, V, *The Later Years, Part II, 1829–34*, ed. Alan G. Hill (Oxford: The Clarendon Press 1979), pp. 407–8.
59. H. T. Dickinson, *Liberty and Property: Political Ideology in Eighteenth-Century Britain* (London: Weidenfeld and Nicholson 1977), p. 248.
60. Maik Philp, 'English Republicanism in the 1790s', *The Journal of Political Philosophy* 6 (1998): 240. Philp continues: 'The claim was intelligible because they contrast republics with despotisms or tyrannies, not with monarchies. Republican government was a government of laws directed towards the common good of the people; despotism was arbitrary government, with the capricious will of the tyrant subordinating the political realm to his or her interests' (240).
61. William Wordsworth, *Poems, in Two Volumes, and Other Poems, 1800–1807*, ed. Jared Curtis (Ithaca, New York: Cornell University Press, 1983), p. 275.
62. James Chandler, *Wordsworth's Second Nature: A Study of the Poetry and Politics* (Chicago: The University of Chicago Press 1984), p. 80.
63. Paul Hamilton, 'Coleridge's Stamina' in *Repossessing the Romantic Past*, eds Heather Glen and Paul Hamilton (Cambridge: Cambridge University Press 2006), p. 174.
64. For a discussion of poetry as a life-animating force in Wordsworth, see Richard Eldridge, 'Wordsworth and the Life of a Subject' in *The Meaning of 'Life' in Romantic Poetry and Poetics*, ed. Ross Wilson (London: Routledge 2009), pp. 61–5.
65. Timothy Fulford, 'Wordsworth's "The Haunted Tree" and the Sexual Politics of Landscape', *Romantic Circles Praxis Series: Romanticism and Ecology* (November 2001): §8.
66. Ibid.
67. On the tension between individual and national freedom in *Cintra*, Benjamin Kim observes that although the essay 'stresses the importance of personal liberty, . . . whenever the two come into conflict, Wordsworth chooses national liberty' (Benjamin Kim, 'Generating a National Sublime: Wordsworth's *The River Duddon* and *The Guide to the Lakes*', *Studies in Romanticism* 45 [Spring 2006]: 54).
68. Richard Gravil argues that while 'Certain phrases and arguments in *The Convention of Cintra* seem Burkean . . . it requires considerable sophistry to interpret the work as Burkean in the common acceptance of the term. Such

common acceptance tends ... to forget that Burke came to prominence as an advocate of cultural diversity (India's for example) and of national independence and liberty (America's most notably)' (Richard Gravil, *Wordsworth's Bardic Vocation, 1787–1842* [Basingstoke: Palgrave Macmillan 2003], p. 230).
69. David Simpson, *Romanticism, Nationalism and the Revolt against Theory* (Chicago: The University of Chicago Press 1993), p. 48.

3 Poetry and the Liberty of Feeling

1. On the difficulty of pigeon-holing Burke either politically or philosophically, see Kevin Gilmartin, *Writing Against Revolution: Literary Conservatism in Britain, 1790–1832* (Cambridge: Cambridge University Press 2007), pp. 8–9.
2. See, once again, Burke's insistence that 'We are not the converts of Rousseau; ... we think that no discoveries are to be made, in morality; nor many in the great principles of government, nor in the ideas of liberty, which were understood long before we were born' (*R* 137).
3. Steven Goldsmith, *Unbuilding Jerusalem: Apocalypse and Romantic Representation* (Ithaca: Cornell University Press 1993), p. 168.
4. Thomas Paine, *The Complete Writings of Thomas Paine*, Vol. I, ed. Philip S. Foner (New York: The Citadel Press 1945), p. 295.
5. Wordsworth had read *The Rights of Man* by Spring 1793 (Duncan Wu, *Wordsworth's Reading 1770–1799* [Cambridge: Cambridge University Press 1993], pp. 109–10).
6. Paine, *Complete Writings*, p. 331.
7. Ibid., p. 300.
8. As Tom Furniss notes, conservatives were highly conflicted about print culture: 'While Counterrevolutionary print culture and organization were felt to be necessary responses to revolutionary print culture and organization, they risked aping and even reinforcing the ways that radicalism had mobilized extra-parliamentary opinion and thereby extended both the public sphere and the political nation' (Tom Furniss, 'Re-reading the Politics of Romanticism', *Eighteenth-Century Culture* 42.1 [2008]: 164.
9. Thomas Pfau, *Romantic Moods: Paranoia, Trauma, and Melancholy, 1790–1840* [Baltimore: The Johns Hopkins University Press 2005], p. 87.
10. Dionysius Longinus, *Dionysius Longinus on the Sublime: Translated from the Greek, with Notes and Observations, and Some Accounts of the Life, Writings, and Character of the Author. By William Smith*, ... (London 1739), p. 3.
11. Ibid., p. 16.
12. Ibid.
13. Ibid.
14. Barbara Maria Stafford, *Body Criticism: Imaging the Unseen in Enlightenment Art and Medicine* (Cambridge, Mass.: The MIT Press 1991), p. 136.
15. Lucy Newlyn, '"Questionable Shape": The Aesthetics of Indeterminacy' in *Questioning Romanticism*, ed. John Beer [Baltimore and London: The Johns Hopkins University Press 1995], p. 215.
16. According to Duncan Wu, Wordsworth read the *Enquiry* in September 1790 (Wu, *Wordsworth's Reading*, p. 21).

17. Marilyn Butler, *Romantics, Rebels, and Reactionaries: English Literature and its Background, 1760–1830* (Oxford: Oxford University Press 1981), p. 84.

18. Philip Cardinal, 'Coleridge's "Nightingale": A Note on the Sublime', *Notes and Queries* 49. 1 (2002): 35. Cardinal adds that 'Burke's characterizations of the sublime enter the poem in exactly the same order as Burke lists them in Part II of his *Enquiry*' (35).

19. Stafford, *Body Criticism*, p. 245.

20. Paul de Man, *The Rhetoric of Romanticism* (New York: Columbia University Press 1984), p. 107.

21. See Paul Fry's view – formulated almost in opposition to de Man's – that poetry's monotony represents (mimics) reality by sounding 'the unity of disarticulated being before the Mirror Stage' (Paul Fry, *Wordsworth and the Poetry of What We Are* [New Haven and London: Yale University Press 2008], p. 102).

22. de Man, p. 113.

23. Ibid., p. 113.

24. Ibid., p. 116.

25. See de Man's point that 'Language posits and language means (since it articulates) but language cannot posit meaning' (ibid., p. 117).

26. Ibid., p. 118.

27. Ibid., p. 120.

28. Paine, *Complete Writings*, p. 259.

29. Elizabeth D. Samet, 'Spectacular History and the Politics of Theatre: Sympathetic Arts in the Shadow of the Bastille', *PMLA* 118. 5 (2003): 1308. Samet adds: 'Burke touted artificial representation as a means for retraining the social passions' in the aftermath of revolutionary change (1312).

30. Steven Blakemore and Fred Hembree point out that 'Burke's account of the invasion of the queen's bedroom was neither an invention nor a falsification: it was historically grounded and closer to the actual primary sources than many critics have realized' (Steven Blakemore and Fred Hembree, 'Edmund Burke, Marie Antoinette, and the Procédure Criminelle', *The Historian* 63. 3 [2001]: 520.

31. Tom Furniss, *Edmund Burke's Aesthetic Ideology: Language, Gender and Political Economy in Revolution* (Cambridge: Cambridge University Press 1993), p. 155.

32. Iain McCalman, 'Mad Lord George and Madame La Motte: Riot and Sexuality in the Genesis of Burke's *Reflections on the Revolution in France*', *Journal of British Studies* 35 (1996): 357.

33. Ibid.: 364.

34. David Simpson, *Romanticism, Nationalism and the Revolt against Theory* (Chicago: The University of Chicago Press 1993), p. 127.

35. Cardinal, 'Coleridge's "Nightingale"': 36.

36. S. T. C. Coleridge, *Biographia Literaria*, eds J. Engell and Jackson Bate, 2 vols, *The Collected Works of S. T. Coleridge*, VII, gen. ed. Kathleen Coburn, Bollingen Series LXVV (London: Routledge 1983), 2. 51.

37. Ibid., 2. 54.

38. Coleridge was an admirer of Shaftesbury. See S. T. C. Coleridge, *Collected Letters of Samuel Taylor Coleridge*, ed. Earl Leslie Griggs, 6 vols (Oxford: The Clarendon Press 1956–71), 1. 214. See also his praise for the Shaftesburean

Akenside in the same letter: 'But why so violent against *metaphysics* in poetry? Is not Akenside's a metaphysical poem? Perhaps, you do not like Akenside – well – *but I do* – & so do a great many others' (1. 215).

39. Adam Smith, *The Theory of Moral Sentiments* (Edinburgh 1759), p. 21.
40. Coleridge, *Biographia Literaria*, 2. 52.
41. Ibid., 2. 54.
42. Jon Mee, *Dangerous Enthusiasm: William Blake and the Culture of Radicalism in the 1790s* (Oxford: The Clarendon Press 1992), p. 113.
43. Ibid., p. 114.
44. It is important to be clear about what 'relatively autonomous' means. According to Theodor Adorno, in order to have an identity at all, art defines itself in opposition to society. Poetry establishes its distinctiveness by defying society's insistence that human practices be, for example, useful, serious or productive. Nevertheless, because it founds its identity upon what it is not, art remains constitutively entwined with the very thing it rejects. As 'the social antithesis of society', then, art is only *relatively* autonomous (Theodor Adorno, *Aesthetic Theory*, trans. Robert Hullot-Kentor [London: The Athlone Press 1997], p. 8).
45. Coleridge, *Biographia Literaria*, 2. 52.
46. Ibid., 2. 55.
47. Ibid.
48. Ibid., 2. 56.
49. For a discussion of Coleridge's embrace of poetry's 'animating' anti-mimeticism in 'Dejection: An Ode', see Susan Stewart, 'What Praise Poems Are For', *PMLA* 120. 1 (January 2005): 242–3. Similarly, in 'This Lime-Tree Bower My Prison', Coleridge poetically dwells with his sense of loss until 'A delight / Comes sudden on my heart' (44–5) and both he and his relation to the world are transformed (*Coleridge's Poetry and Prose*, eds. Nicholas Halmi, Paul Magnuson and Raimonda Modiano [New York: W. W. Norton & Co. 2004], p. 138.
50. Paul Fry implies something similar, I think, when he remarks that Wordsworth is 'the most imposing figure on the border between vision and enlightenment, "fiction and reason", in the history of thought over the last two hundred years' (Paul Fry, 'Progresses of Poetry', *The Wordsworth Circle* 37. 1 [2006]: 23).
51. On Ernst Bloch's idea that 'Art is . . . fundamentally concerned not with the imitation but the revelation of the world', see Ruth Levitas, *The Concept of Utopia* [London: Philip Allan 1990], p. xxxii. See also Regina Hewitt, 'Utopianism and Joanna Baillie: A Preface to Converging Revolutions', *Romantic Circles Praxis Series: Utopianism and Joanna Baillie* (July 2008): §1; §5–7.
52. Coleridge, *Biographia Literaria*, 2. 132.
53. Ibid., 2. 45–6.
54. John Barrell, *The Birth of Pandora and the Division of Knowledge* (London: Macmillan 1992), p. 41.
55. Ibid.
56. Ibid., p. 215. Furniss argues that 'For Coleridge especially, the root of all evil was the very existence of a reading public . . . Coleridge came to believe that the attempt to use the press to address the public in support of a conservative

model of society was to give sustenance to phenomena that ought to be eliminated' (Furniss, 'Re-reading the Politics of Romanticism': 165).
57. See Chapter 6 for discussion of how Wordsworth uses what he calls distorted language (in this case, allegory) to critical effect.
58. Barbara Johnson, *A World of Difference* (Baltimore: The Johns Hopkins University Press 1987), p. 94.
59. See the discussion of 'Michael' in the next chapter.
60. Johnson, *A World of Difference*, p. 95.
61. Ibid., p. 94.
62. Edmund Burke, *The Writings and Speeches of Edmund Burke*, IX, I: *The Revolutionary War 1794–1997, II: Ireland*, eds R. B. McDowell and William B. Todd (Oxford: The Clarendon Press 1991), p. 247; my italics. Thomas Pfau hears in Wordsworth's use of the word 'habit' a reference to 'Burke's paean to the "cold sluggishness of our national temper"' (Pfau, *Romantic Moods*, p. 64).
63. See De Quincey's essays 'Letters to a Young Man Whose Education has been Neglected' and 'The Poetry of Pope' for his discussion of Wordsworth's idea of the inexhaustibility of poetry (Thomas De Quincey, 'Letters to a Young Man Whose Education has been Neglected', in *De Quincey as Critic*, ed. John E. Jordan [London: Routledge 1973], p. 269).

4   Wordworth's Ear and the Place of Aesthetic Autonomy

1. For a consideration of 'the singularity, the individuation of, a life in verse', see Stefan Uhlig, 'Gray, Wordsworth, and the Poetry of Ordinary Life' in *The Meaning of 'Life' in Romantic Poetry and Poetics*, ed. Ross Wilson (London: Routledge 2009), pp. 49–50.
2. See Chapter 1 for a discussion of landownership as the basis of civic humanism. In the *Enquiry*, Burke argues that 'Taste does not depend upon a superior principle in men, but upon superior knowledge' (*PE* 19). It is those with time and disinterest enough – in other words, landed gentlemen – who 'have cultivated that species of knowledge which makes the object of Taste, by degrees and habitually attain not only a soundness, but a readiness of judgement' (*PE* 26).
3. Mary Wollstonecraft, *The Works of Mary Wollstonecraft*, Vol. 5, eds Janet Todd and Marilyn Butler (London: William Pickering 1989), p. 13.
4. Ibid.
5. Ibid., p. 17.
6. Ibid., p. 48.
7. All poems are taken from William Wordsworth, *Lyrical Ballads, and Other Poems, 1797–1800*, eds James Butler and Karen Green (Ithaca: Cornell University Press 1992), unless stated otherwise.
8. David Collings, *Wordsworthian Errancies: The Poetics of Cultural Dismemberment* (London: The Johns Hopkins UP, 1994), p. 177.
9. Ibid., p. 178.
10. In the *Reflections*, Burke proposes the British monarchy as exemplary of the transmission of British tradition. Tradition is bequeathed through the *institution* of the monarchy (the crown), rather than through the person of

an individual monarch (*R* 72). This 'symbolic' reading of the relationship between monarchy and tradition is at the heart of Burke's thought: 'We wished at the period of the [English] Revolution, and do now wish, to derive all we possess as *an inheritance from our forefathers*. Upon that body and stock of inheritance we have taken care not to inoculate any cyon alien to the nature of the original plant. All the reformations we have hitherto made have proceeded upon the principle of reference to antiquity' (*R* 81).

11. See Burke's famous passage on the link between place, affection and nation in the *Reflections* (*R* 97–8).
12. This poem was published at the same time as 'Michael'. For a virtuoso reading of 'The Old Cumberland Beggar', see David Bromwich, *Disowned by Memory* (Chicago: The University of Chicago Press 1998), pp. 30–43.
13. Recall Mark Philp's argument that in the eighteenth century republican-ism and Whiggism drew from a common vocabulary (Mark Philp, 'English Republicanism in the 1790s', *The Journal of Political Philosophy* 6 [1998]: 244).
14. It is important to stress here that there is no suggestion that feeling is, at some level, unmediated. As Simon Jarvis argues: 'When thinking comes to a halt with an *abstract* appeal to history, or society, or "socio-historical mate-rial specificity," or any other form of non-interrogable givenness, it might as well stop with God. Absolute sheer givenness, whether it is invoked by meta-physicians, "materialists," historicists, or anyone else, is a chimera. It is the demarcated nothing, the "empty space" of Hegel's *The Spirit of Christianity and its Fate*, a nothing which is supposed to permit the most undeluded thinking, yet which itself becomes a fetish – the fetish of nihilism' (Simon Jarvis, 'Wordsworth and Idolatry', *Studies in Romanticism* 38. 1 [1999]: 24).
15. Theodor Adorno, 'Music and Language: A Fragment' in *Quasi una Fantasia: Essays on Modern Music*, trans. Rodney Livingstone (London: Verso 1992), p. 4.
16. See Adam Smith, *The Theory of Moral Sentiments* (Edinburgh 1759), p. 10 on the intimacy between sympathy and pleasure.
17. Michael's changing relationship to the wind signals a similar, if more subtle, deterioration. Prior to Luke's birth, Michael understood 'the meaning of all winds, / Of blasts of every tone' and would remark that '"The winds are now devising work for me!"' (48–9; 55). While Michael still 'Listened to the wind; and, as before / Performed all kinds of labour' (457–8) after his son's fall, any sense that the farmer's relationship with nature communicates with a living future is absent.
18. James K. Chandler, *Wordsworth's Second Nature: A Study of the Poetry and Politics* (Chicago: The University of Chicago Press 1984), p. 75.
19. Ibid., p. 140. Chandler argues that 'second nature' does not 'mean being in an original, naked, or habitless condition, or even an approximation of such a condition. It means being in the condition of one's authentic habits and of their attendant feelings. And this is not a Rousseauist state of nature but a Burkean state of second nature' (p. 75). In other words, second nature consists of a subject's adherence to the demands of personal and familial customs, local and national traditions.
20. This poem is cited from William Wordsworth, *The Ruined Cottage and The Pedlar*, ed. James Butler (Ithaca: Cornell University Press 1979), p. 49.
21. Burke's notion of tradition as that which links the 'little platoon' to 'our country and to mankind' (*R* 97–8) is, after all, in large part conceived in spatial terms.

22. Chandler, *Wordsworth's Second Nature*, p. 140.

23. Ibid., p. 141.

24. Paul Hamilton observes that Romantic internalisation has been equated with conservative politics from Thomas Love Peacock to Jerome McGann ('A Shadow of Magnitude: The Dialectics of Romantic Aesthetics" in *Beyond Romanticism: New Approaches to Texts and Contexts 1780–1832*, eds Stephen Copley and John Whale [London: Routledge 1992], p. 15).

25. Marjorie Levinson, *Wordsworth's Great Period Poems* (Cambridge: Cambridge UP 1986), p. 39.

26. For a fascinating critique of this reading of Wordsworthian vision, see J.H. Prynne, *Field Notes: 'The Solitary Reaper' And Others* (Cambridge: Barque Press 2007), pp. 69–71.

27. Geoffrey Hartman, *The Unremarkable Wordsworth* (London: Methuen 1987), p. 29.

28. For Hartman, Wordsworth's poetry is orientated towards the past rather than a dream of the future: 'the object of Wordsworth's nature poems is not nature but the "one dear Presence" lost yet perhaps recoverable – like Eurydice' (Hartman, *Unremarkable Wordsworth*, p. 27).

29. Theodor Adorno, 'Lyric Poetry and Society', trans. Bruce Mayo, in *The Adorno Reader*, ed. Brian O'Connor (Oxford: Blackwell Publishers 2000), p. 215.

30. This idea that Wordsworth is a poet orientated towards the future not only departs from Levinson and Hartman, but also from Hugh Sykes-Davies, a critic without theoretical allegiance. Speculating that Wordsworth would disapprove of science fiction, Davies writes: 'It must have followed from his deepest convictions, that wherever men may travel, to whatever distance, they will find themselves still at home, still in a world which watches their own minds' (Hugh Sykes-Davies, *Wordsworth and the Worth of Words*, eds John Kerrigan and Jonathan Wordsworth [Cambridge: Cambridge UP 1986], p. 183).

31. Adorno, 'Lyric Poetry', p. 214.

32. Ibid., p. 214.

33. See Bolingbrook's lines in *Richard III*: 'How long a time lies in one little word! / Four lagging winters and four wanton springs / End in a word: such is the breath of Kings' (*The Complete Works of Shakespeare*, ed. Peter Alexander [London and Glasgow: Collins 1990], I. iii. 213–15).

34. William Wordsworth, *The Thirteen Book Prelude*, ed. Mark Reed, 2 vols. (Ithaca: Cornell University Press 1991), 5. 10–13. All references are to volume 1 of this edition.

35. Paul Fry argues that the episode dramatises a failure to communicate with nature. The boy's subsequent 'death at ten is the death of the poet's trust in the anthropocentric community of things, and today the adult poet stands "mute" (V, 422) joining the somatic unity of the things that are silent and inert in the Hawkshead churchyard, possessed of a negative knowledge that is literally superior to – "hangs / . . . above" in an emblem of its own suspense of knowing (V, 417–18) – the semantic knowledge taught to children like the Winander boy at "the village school" (V, 418)' (Paul Fry, *Wordsworth and the Poetry of What We Are* [New Haven and London: Yale University Press 2008], p. 129.

36. For the relationship between Being, language and listening, see Martin Heidegger, 'The Way to Language' in *Martin Heidegger: Basic Writings*, ed. David Farrell-Krell (London: Routledge 1993), pp. 397–426.

37. See David Haney, 'Rents and Openings in the Ideal World: Eye and Ear in Wordsworth', *Studies in Romanticism* 36 (1997): 195.
38. S. T. Coleridge, *Biographia Literaria*, eds J. Engell and W. Jackson Bate, 2 vols, *The Collected Works of S. T. Coleridge*, VII, gen. ed. Kathleen Coburn, Bollingen Series LXVV (London: Routledge 1983), 2. 19.
39. Ibid., 2. 65.
40. William Wordsworth, *Last Poems. 1821–150*, eds Jared Curtis, Apryl Lea Denny-Ferris and Jillian Heydt-Stevenson (Ithaca: Cornell University Press 1999), p. 116.
41. Paul de Man, 'Time and History in Wordsworth', *Diacritics* 7 (1987): 7.
42. William Wordsworth, *Poems, in Two Volumes, and Other Poems, 1800–1807*, ed. Jared Curtis (Ithaca, New York: Cornell University Press 1983), p. 277.
43. Stephen Bygrave notes that Hegel's *Lectures on the Philosophy of World History* (1822–31) 'structure their account of world history on a biographical model – the Orient, childhood; Greece, adolescence; Rome, manhood; culminating in German culture as an old age which, unlike the diminutions of old age in nature, is an epoch of maturity and strength' (Stephen Bygrave, 'Land of the Giants: Gaps, Limits and Audiences in Coleridge's *Biographia Literaria*' in *Beyond Romanticism*, p. 37).
44. Thomas De Quincey, *Confessions of an English Opium Eater*, ed. Grevel Lindop (Oxford: Oxford University Press 1985), p. 73.
45. Arguing that *The Prelude* opposes 'the poverty of signs', Paul Fry suggests that Wordsworth's claim that he experienced "no vulgar fear" (5. 473) on seeing the corpse is an 'instance of familiarization with things by means of signs . . . which can only serve further to alienate consciousness from actuality (V, 479)' (Fry, *Wordsworth*, p. 130; p. 135).
46. Adorno, 'Lyric Poetry', p. 215.
47. Adorno remarks: 'Ideas that are treated, depicted, or deliberately advanced by a work of art are not its ideas but "materials"' (Theodor Adorno, *Mahler: A Musical Physiognomy*, trans. Edmund Jephcott [Chicago: The University of Chicago Press 1996], p. 3).
48. Wordsworth, *Poems, in Two Volumes*, pp. 184–5.
49. Against Romantic-internalisation readings of this poem, Prynne writes that in *giving himself* to the woman's 'singing music without culmination', Wordsworth will 'learn the melody's shape and thus will inwardly hear its small changes of inflection at each return, the woman's voice guiding its contour' (Prynne, *Field Notes*, p. 15).

5   Poetry and Embodiment

1. Richard Gravil argues that Wordsworth 'comes to refuse the choice' between conservative and radical abstractions (Richard Gravil, *Wordsworth's Bardic Vocation, 1787–1842* [Basingstoke: Palgrave Macmillan 2003], p. 234).
2. Withdrawing from the world in attention to its own forms, relatively autonomous art achieves what Robert Kaufman describes as 'freedom from determination by extant governing (or, for that matter, extant *oppositional*) concepts of the sociohistorical or political' (Robert Kaufman, 'Poetry's Ethics? Theodor W. Adorno and Robert Duncan on Aesthetic Illusion and Sociopolitical Delusion', *New German Critique* 97. 1 [Winter 2006]: 105).

Such art, as a result, is 'inherently experimental' (105): it 'plays around with, is free to recombine, stretch, or extend the conceptual materials, in ways not usually sanctioned where an already determined conceptual content necessarily delimits the acceptable range of results' (105).

3. Frances Ferguson, *Solitude and the Sublime* (London: Routledge 1992), p. 52.
4. Mary Wollstonecraft, *The Works of Mary Wollstonecraft*, Vol. 5, eds Janet Todd and Marilyn Butler (London: William Pickering 1989), p. 47. Wordsworth had read *A Vindication of the Rights of Men* by 1791 (Duncan Wu, *Wordsworth's Reading* [Cambridge: Cambridge University press 1993], p. 152).
5. Linda M. G. Zerilli, 'Text/Woman as Spectacle: Edmund Burke's "French Revolution"', *The Eighteenth Century* 33 (1991): 55.
6. Tom Furniss, *Edmund Burke's Aesthetic Ideology: Language, Gender and Political Economy in Revolution* (Cambridge: Cambridge University Press 1993), p. 38.
7. Lucy Newlyn, '"Questionable Shape": The Aesthetics of Indeterminacy', in *Questioning Romanticism*, ed. John Beer (Baltimore and London: The Johns Hopkins University Press 1995), p. 211.
8. Ibid., p. 214. According to Newlyn, the sublime 'succeeds in closing off, or "finishing", the expansiveness of subjectivity' (p. 216). In her reading of the sublime, then, the subject is preserved, rather than undermined. She emphasises completion and wholeness over process and destruction.
9. R. Bourke, *Romantic Discourse and Political Modernity* (London: Harvester Press 1993), p. 241.
10. For Benjamin Kim, the absence of discussion about 'art and the human figure' in 'The Sublime and the Beautiful' suggests that Wordsworth's aesthetics owe very little to Kant (Benjamin Kim, 'Wordsworth's *The River Duddon* and *The Guide to the Lakes*', *Studies in Romanticism* 45 [Spring 2006]: 57 n. 22).
11. For a classic statement of the argument that Book 13 contains 'Wordsworth's moment of Absolute Knowledge', see Alan Liu, *Wordsworth: The Sense of History* (Stanford: Stanford University Press 1989), p. 447. More recently, Anne Janovitz has asserted the poet's Kantianism: 'The austerity of the Wordsworthian sublime co-exists with and compensates for its superfluity, its immateriality, its transcendence, its positing of an experience which is counter to the material' (Anne Janovitz, 'The artifactual sublime: making London poetry' in, *Romantic Metropolis: The Urban Scene of British Culture, 1780–1840*, eds James Chandler and Kevin Gilmartin [Cambridge: Cambridge University Press 2005], p. 250). She adds: 'the sublime offers a severe mental regime of anxiety. If the sublime experience were to be actual, you would be falling down the pit, vomiting from vertigo, and *be in* rather than *looking at* the sublime object' (ibid.). See Chapter 6 for my argument that Wordsworthian allegory makes simultaneously 'being in' and 'looking at' possible.
12. The definitions of the sublime given by both Burke and Kant can be considered ideological. For Burke, the sublime is a mechanism that disciplines the subject and motivates permitted activity. The sublime, in effect, trains the subject to acquiesce to the demands of second nature. For Kant, however, the mind's inability to encompass nature teaches Reason that it is superior to the senses. Freed from the bondage of sensory experience, it is possible for reason to *create* 'a second nature out of the material supplied to it by actual nature. It affords us entertainment where experience proves commonplace;

and we even use it to remodel experience' (Immanuel Kant, *The Critique of Judgement*, trans. James Creed Meredith [Oxford: Oxford University Press 1952], p. 176). Whereas Burke's sublime *subjects* the individual to the power of an already existing second nature, Kant's sublime allows the subject to help *produce* second nature. The former demands habitual and passive obedience, whereas the latter encourages active collaboration.

13. See Chapter 3.
14. E. W. Stoddard, '"Flashes of the Invisible World": Reading *The Prelude* in the context of the Kantian sublime', *The Wordsworth Circle* 16 (1985): 33.
15. For the difficulties involved in dating 'The Sublime and the Beautiful' see Mark L. Reed, *Wordsworth: The Chronology of the Middle Years, 1800–15* (Harvard University Press: Cambridge, Massachusetts 1975), p. 670.
16. T. M. Kelley, 'Wordsworth and the Rhinefall', *Studies in Romanticism* 23 (1984): 77.
17. For a powerful and influential feminist reading of this part of *The Prelude*, see Mary Jacobus, *Romanticism, Writing and Sexual Difference* (Oxford: The Clarendon Press 1989), p. 194. I disagree with Jacobus' view that Wordsworth's 'use' of le Brun's painting is basically conservative and heterosexist.
18. Although Burke uses the aesthetic categories of the *Enquiry* to read the Revolution in the *Reflections*, he gradually plays down the importance of his terms, which he can no longer adequately govern, and relocates the habitat of the sublime and beautiful away from the sensual, individual body to the historical body – the institutions and customs – of Britain. The beautiful rituals and sublime purpose of the Church, for example, embody his desired aesthetic order. Indeed, the unruly sublime and beautiful are controlled by being securely anchored to the Church's ancient foundations.
19. See Elizabeth Samet, 'Spectacular History and the Politics of Theatre: Sympathetic Arts in the Shadow of the Bastille', *PMLA* 118. 5 (2003): 1305–19. Samet notes that 'Danton himself . . . complained during the trial of Louis XVI that the audience had forgotten they were involved in a tragedy rather than a comedy' (1308).
20. See Chapter 2.
21. Jon Mee, *Romanticism, Enthusiasm, and Regulation: Poetics and the Policing of Culture in the Romantic Period* (Oxford: Oxford University Press 2003), p. 247.
22. Ibid.
23. Ibid.
24. Ibid., p. 249.
25. James K. Chandler, *Wordsworth's Second Nature: A Study of the Poetry and Politics* (Chicago: The University of Chicago Press 1984), p. 75.
26. Ibid., p. 198.
27. Ibid., p. 199.
28. See Chapter 4.
29. Chandler, *Wordsworth's Second Nature*, pp. 209–10.
30. See the introduction.
31. J. H. Prynne, 'English Poetry and Emphatical Language', *Proceedings of the British Academy* 74 (1988): 63.
32. With reference to Jonathan Culler, Robert Kaufmann calls apostrophe 'lyric's perhaps constitutive gesture' (Kaufmann, 'Poetry's Ethics?': 108).
33. Geraldine Friedman, *The Insistence of History* (Stanford: Stanford University Press 1996), p. 82.

34. See Adorno's comment that 'Neutralization is the social price of aesthetic autonomy' (Theodor Adorno, *Aesthetic Theory*, trans. Robert Hullot-Kentor [London: The Athlone Press 1997], p. 228).

6 Melancholy and Affirmation

1. See Bataille's description of the problem that confronts art: 'Art constitutes a minor free zone outside action, paying for its freedom by giving up the real world. A heavy price! Rare is the writer who doesn't yearn for the rediscovery of a vanished reality; but the payment required is relinquishing his or her freedom and serving propaganda' (Georges Bataille, *On Nietzsche*, trans. Bruce Boone [St. Paul, Minnesota: Paragon House 1994], p. xxxii).
2. For a tantalisingly brief discussion of the relationship between 'lyric's self-cancelling gestures' and reality in Wordsworth, see Karen Weisman, 'The Bounds of Lyric: Romantic Grasps Upon the Actual', *European Romantic Review* 15. 2 (June 2004): 346.
3. See, for example, Paul de Man, *Blindness and Insight* (London: Routledge 1989), pp. 187–228, and Geoffrey Hartman, *The Unremarkable Wordsworth* (London: Methuen 1987), pp. 18–30.
4. de Man, *Blindness and Insight*, p. 244.
5. Ibid.
6. David Bromwich, *Disowned by Memory: Wordsworth's Poetry of the 1790s* (Chicago: The University of Chicago Press 1998), p. 127.
7. Ibid., p. 129.
8. Ibid., p. 132.
9. Ibid., p. 131.
10. Paul Fry finds in much of Wordsworth's verse 'the emitted half-life blips of poetry's ever more protracted decay' (Paul Fry, 'Progresses of Poetry', *The Wordsworth Circle* 37. 1 [2006]: 23.
11. Ibid., p. 129.
12. Andrew Bennett reads this poem in terms of incompatible vocabularies, the 'breakdown of communication, [and] the dysfunctional nature of the language supposedly used by men' (Andrew Bennett, *Wordsworth Writing* [Cambridge: Cambridge University Press 2007], p. 117).
13. See the discussion of 'Expostulation and Reply' and 'The Tables Turned' in Chapter 1.
14. Bromwich, *Disowned by Memory*, p. 119.
15. Ibid.
16. Emphasising the Preface's description of poetry as carrying 'everywhere relationship and love' (*PrW* 1. 141), Charles Altieri makes a similar point. 'Nutting' suggests, he argues, that 'poetry must become self-reflexive enough to provoke errors, then test the capacities of the composing voice to spell out new lines of relation between a mind in excess of nature and a force of nature that reveals its powers only through the collapse of kindliness' (Charles Altieri, 'Wordsworth's Poetics of Eloquence', in *Romantic Revolutions: Criticism and Theory*, eds Kenneth Johnston *et al.* [Indianapolis: Indiana University Press 1990], p. 393).
17. The conclusion of the 'Discharged Soldier' episode in *The Prelude* is comparable to that of 'Nutting'. The boy's fairly condescending advice to the

soldier to not 'linger in the public ways / But ask for timely furtherance and help / Such as his state requir'd' (4. 490–2) puts the brakes on any temptation to subsume the suffering of an individual beneath the sanitised (and 'state-sponsored'?) rhetoric of care and community. (Much the same could be said for the conclusion to "Resolution and Independence') Even so, the pity the boy clearly feels has, perhaps, already further diminished the broken soldier:

> . . . solemn and sublime
> He might have seem'd, but that in all he said
> There was a strange half-absence, and a tone
> Of weakness and indifference, as of one
> Remembering the importance of his theme
> But feeling it no longer (4. 473–8).

18. In 'Michael', for example, Luke leaves the family home and travels to 'the dissolute city', where he is lost forever 'To evil courses' (443–4).
19. John Barrell, *English Literature in History, 1730–80: An Equal, Wide Survey* (London: Hutchinson 1983), p. 22.
20. Jon Mee, *Romanticism, Enthusiasm, and Regulation: Poetics and the Policing of Culture in the Romantic Period* (Oxford: Oxford University Press 2003), p. 246.
21. Ibid.
22. Mary Jacobus, 'Wordsworth and the Language of the Dream', *ELH* 46 (1979): 56 n. 58.
23. See Neil Hertz, *The End of the Line: Essays on Psychoanalysis and the Sublime* (New York: Columbia University Press 1985), p. 56.
24. Ross King, 'Wordsworth, Panoramas, and the Prospect of London'. *Studies in Romanticism* 32 (Spring 1993): 70.
25. Ibid.: 72.
26. Lucy Newlyn, 'Lamb, Lloyd and London: A Perspective on Book Seven of *The Prelude*', *Charles Lamb Bulletin* 47–8 (July–October 1984): 181.
27. Ibid.: 183.
28. Ibid.: 182–3.
29. It might be argued that the relatively autonomous artwork is no different from the 'escapist' products of the culture industry, and thus more than likely a variety of false consciousness. However, Adorno remarks, crucially, that 'No authentic work of art . . . has ever exhausted itself in itself alone, in its being-in-itself. They have always stood in relation to the actual life-process of society from which they distinguish themselves' (Theodor Adorno, 'Culture Criticism and Society', trans. Bruce Mayo, in *The Adorno Reader*, ed. Brian O'Connor [Oxford: Blackwell Publishers 2000], p. 200). Poetic language is simultaneously a product of social reality and of 'a created art-language' (Theodor Adorno, 'Lyric Poetry and Society', trans. Bruce Mayo, in *The Adorno Reader*, ed. Brian O'Connor [Oxford: Blackwell Publishers 2000], p. 219) – that is, a language some meanings of which are specifically determined by literary tradition. In the case of Wordsworth, as will become apparent, allegory is used because of both its mimetic suitability for the treatment of urban life *and* because of the place it occupies in eighteenth-century poetic theory and

practice. Wordsworthian allegory – and his relatively autonomous art, in general – is, then, far from socially disengaged.

30. Chester Chaplin, *Personification in Eighteenth-Century English Poetry* (New York: King's Crown Press 1955), pp. 81–97.

31. It is important to note that, for all his misgivings, Wordsworth often describes his happiness in Cambridge:

> But delight,
> That, in an easy temper lull'd asleep,
> Is still with innocence its own reward,
> This surely was not wanting. Carelessly
> I gaz'd, roving as through a Cabinet
> Or wide Museum (thronged with fishes, gems,
> Birds, crocodiles, shells) where little can be seen
> Well understood, or naturally endear'd,
> Yet still does every step bring something forth
> That quickens, pleases, stings; and here and there
> A casual rarity is singled out,
> And has its brief perusal (3. 649–59).

In this odd passage, Wordsworth expresses an enjoyment of the town that is actually enhanced by the 'detachment' he achieves when he find a prospect from which he can observe.

32. de Man, *Blindness and Insight*, p. 207. De Man contrasts allegory to symbol, which is characterised by the 'organic' unity of signifier and signified. It is the mechanistic repetition inherent in allegory that renders it a figure of division.

33. Ibid., p. 207.

34. Ibid., p. 214.

35. Theresa Kelley, *Reinventing Allegory* (Cambridge: Cambridge University Press 1997), p.129.

36. Kelley notes that front means 'face or forehead' (ibid., p.129).

37. For the view that Wordsworth's approach to London is fundamentally conservative, that he 'used the discourse of the sublime as a way poetically to master and make an aesthetic shape of the city in its brutality and its luxury', see Anne Janovitz, 'The artifactual sublime: making London poetry', in *Romantic Metropolis: The Urban Scene of British Culture, 1780–1840*, eds James Chandler and Kevin Gilmartin (Cambridge: Cambridge University Press 2005), p. 250.

38. Kelley remarks that 'Exaggerated figures like catachresis, prosopopeia, and synecdoche are what allegory requires to make border raids on what is real, or what mimesis represents as real, even as allegorical figures are something "other" to reality' (Kelley, *Reinventing Allegory*, p. 131). She continues that many of the sights described in Book 7 are not necessarily allegorical, but are object fragments suitable for allegorical transformation.

39. David Simpson writes: 'It can seem at times as if Wordsworth's poems amount collectively to one long spirit show . . . an encounter with what Derrida calls "the ghosts that are commodities", the commodities that "transform human producers into ghosts" (*Specters* 156)' (David Simpson, 'Derrida's Ghosts: The State of our Debt', *Studies in Romanticism* 46 [Summer/Fall 2007]: 190–1.

40. Saree Makdisi argues that the representation of the London crowd in Book 7 betrays the more 'conservative' tendency of Wordsworth's politics: 'There is, indeed, a very fine line in *The Prelude* between the London crowd and its politically charged Janus-face, the mob of the revolutionary panic of 1790s London. Part of Wordsworth's ongoing effort to distinguish individual faces in the crowd is an attempt to keep the crowd from working any sudden (and not quite understood) transformation into a mob' (Saree Makdisi, *Romantic Imperialism: Universal Empire and the Culture of Modernity* [Cambridge: Cambridge University Press 1998], p. 29). However, it is also reasonable to claim that the Revolutionary mob is, in fact, modelled on the London hordes:

> I stared and listen'd with a stranger's ears
> To Hawkers and Haranguers, hubbub wild!
> And hissing Factionists with ardent eyes,
> In knots, or pairs, or single, ant-like swarms
> Of Builders and Subverters, every face
> That hope or apprehension could put on,
> Joy, anger, and vexation, in the midst
> Of gaiety and dissolute idleness (9. 55–62).

The peculiar intermingling of fear and fascination, abstraction and particularity, with which this chapter is concerned, can be seen even here. Burke's comments on the Gordon riots in the *Reflections* had already made possible the comparison between the London and Parisian 'rabble' (*R* 135).
41. See 5. 10–17.
42. See 11. 176.
43. Mary Jacobus, *Romanticism, Writing and Sexual Difference* (Oxford: The Clarendon Press 1989), p. 110.
44. See 6. 525–48 for the paean to Imagination that follows the anti-climactic crossing of the Alps.
45. *R* 129.
46. According to Simon Jarvis, the city in Wordsworth 'perhaps remains in itself an ideality, retains also the shape of a norm rather than becoming a bare fact, even after successive fantasies of it have been chastened. It cannot be seen at once; it never ends. "There is always something more to see"' (Simon Jarvis, *Wordsworth's Philosophic Song* [Cambridge: Cambridge University Press 2006], p. 139).
47. Part of the importance of Wordsworthian allegory is its imagination of an alternative to reified social relations. Although captured by the enchantment of the commodity, his allegory is able to 'transcend' the world-as-it-is – without, however, resorting to a nihilistic renunciation of the same world.
48. Theodor Adorno, *Aesthetic Theory*, trans. Robert Hullot-Kentor (London: The Athlone Press 1997), p. 31.
49. James Chandler and Kevin Gilmartin observe that 'Wordsworth represents the metropolis in the terms of landscape' (James Chandler and Kevin Gilmartin [eds], *Romantic Metropolis: The Urban Scene of British Culture, 1780–1840* [Cambridge: Cambridge University Press 2005], p. 12).

Conclusion

1.   William Wordsworth, *Selected Poems*, ed. John O. Hayden (London: Penguin 1994), p. 262, 788.
2. Barbara Johnson, *A World of Difference* (Baltimore: The Johns Hopkins University Press 1987), pp. 91–2.
3. 'My horse moved on; hoof after hoof / He raised, and never stopped' (21–2).
4. 'The music in my heart I bore' (31).
5. William Wordsworth, *Poems, in Two Volumes, and Other Poems, 1800–1807*, ed. Jared Curtis (Ithaca: Cornell University Press 1983), p. 185.

Bibliography

Adorno, T. W. (1992) *Notes to Literature*, vol. 2, trans. Shierry Weber Nicholson, New York: Columbia University Press.

—— (1996) *Mahler: A Musical Physiognomy*, trans. Edmund Jephcott, Chicago: The Chicago University Press.

—— (1997) *Aesthetic Theory*, trans. Robert Hullot-Kentor, London: The Athlone Press.

—— (2000) 'Lyric Poetry and Society', trans. Bruce Mayo, in Brian O'Connor (ed.) *The Adorno Reader*, Oxford: Blackwell Publishers.

—— (2002) *Quasi una Fantasia: Essays on Modern Music.*, London: Verso.

Adorno, Theodor and Horkheimer, Max (1997) *Dialectic of Enlightenment*, trans. John Cumming, London: Verso.

Akenside, Mark (1794) *The Pleasures of the Imagination. To which is prefixed a critical essay on the poem, by Mrs. Barbauld*, London; first published in 1744.

Altieri, Charles (1990) 'Wordsworth's Poetics of Eloquence', in Kenneth R. Johnston *et al.* (eds) *Romantic Revolutions: Criticism and Theory*, Indianapolis: Indiana University Press, 371–407.

—— (2003) *The Particulars of Rapture: An Aesthetics of the Affects*, New York: Cornell University Press.

Ashfield, Andrew and de Bolla, Peter (eds) (1996) *The Sublime: A Reader in British Eighteenth-Century Aesthetic Theory*, Cambridge: Cambridge University Press.

Baillie, John (1747) *An Essay on the Sublime*, London.

Barker-Benfield, G. J. (1992) *The Culture of Sensibility: Sex and Society in Eighteenth-Century Britain*, Chicago: The University of Chicago Press.

Barrell, John (1983) *English Literature in History, 1730–80: An Equal, Wide Survey*, London: Hutchinson.

—— (1992) *The Birth of Pandora and the Division of Knowledge*, London: Macmillan.

Bataille, Georges (1994) *On Nietzsche*, trans. Bruce Boone, St. Paul, Minnesota: Paragon House.

—— (1997) *The Bataille Reader*, eds Fred Botting and Scott Wilson, Oxford: Blackwell.

Bennett, Andrew (2007) *Wordsworth Writing*, Cambridge: Cambridge University Press.

Bewell, Alan (1989) *Wordsworth and the Enlightenment: Nature, Man, and Society in the Experimental Poetry*, New Haven: Yale University Press.

Blackwell, Thomas (1735) *An Enquiry into the Life and Writings of Homer*, London.

Blakemore, Steven (1988) *Burke and the Fall of Language: The French Revolution as Linguistic Event*, Hanover, N. H.: University Press of New England.

Blakemore, Steven and Hembree, Fred (2001) 'Edmund Burke, Marie Antoinette, and the Procédure Criminelle', *The Historian* 63. 3: 505–20.

Bourdieu, Pierre (1984) *Distinction: A Social Critique of the Judgement of Taste*, trans. Richard Nice, Cambridge, Mass.: Harvard University Press.

—— (1993) *The Field of Cultural Production*, trans. Randal Johnson, Cambridge: Polity Press.

Bourke, R. (1993) *Romantic Discourse and Political Modernity*, London: Harvester Press.

Brett, R. L. (1951) *The Third Earl of Shaftesbury: A Study in Eighteenth-Century Literary Theory*, New York: Hutchinson's University Library.

Bromwich, David (1998) *Disowned by Memory: Wordsworth's Poetry of the 1790s*, Chicago: The University of Chicago Press.

Brown, John (1757) *An Estimate of the Manners and Principles of the Times*, London.

Burke, Edmund (1791) *An Appeal from the New to the Old Whigs*, London.

—— (1958) *A Philosophical Enquiry into the Origin of our Ideas of the Sublime and Beautiful*, ed. J. T. Boulton, London: Routledge.

—— (1958a) *The Correspondence of Edmund Burke*, vol. 1, *1 April 1744–June 1768*, ed. Thomas Wordsworth. Copeland, Cambridge: Cambridge University Press.

—— (1967), *The Correspondence of Edmund Burke*, vol. 6, *July 1789–December 1791*, eds A. Cobbin and R. A. Smith, Cambridge: Cambridge University Press.

—— (1989) *The Writings and Speeches of Edmund Burke*, VIII: *The French Revolution*, eds L. G. Mitchell and William B. Todd, Oxford: The Clarendon Press.

—— (1991) *The Writings and Speeches of Edmund Burke*, IX, I: *The Revolutionary War 1794–1997*, II: *Ireland*, eds R. B. McDowell and William B. Todd, Oxford: The Clarendon Press.

Butler, Marilyn (1981) *Romantics, Rebels, and Reactionaries: English Literature and its Background, 1760–1830*, Oxford: Oxford University Press.

Bygrave, Stephen (1992) 'Land of the Giants: Gaps, Limits and Audiences in Coleridge's *Biographia Literaria*', in Stephen Copley and John Whale (eds) *Beyond Romanticism: New Approaches to Texts and Contexts 1780–1832*, London: Routledge, 32–52.

Cardinal, Philip (2002) 'Coleridge's 'Nightingale': A Note on the Sublime', *Notes and Queries* 49. 1: 35–6.

Chandler, James K. (1984) *Wordsworth's Second Nature: A Study of the Poetry and Politics*, Chicago: The University of Chicago Press.

—— (1998) *England in 1819: The Politics of Literary Culture and the Case of Romantic Historicism*, Chicago: The University of Chicago Press.

—— (2008) 'The Languages of Sentiment', *Textual Practice* 22. 1: 21–39.

—— (2008) 'The "Power of Sound" and the Great Scheme of Things: Wordsworth Listens to Wordsworth', *Romantic Praxis: 'Soundings of Things Done': The Poetry and Poetics of Sound in the Romantic Ear and Era:* 20 pars. <http://www.rc.umd.edu/praxis/soundings/chandler/chandler.html> [April 2008]: §12.

Chandler, James and Gilmartin, Kevin (eds) (2005) *Romantic Metropolis: The Urban Scene of British Culture, 1780–1840*, Cambridge: Cambridge University Press 2005].

Chaplin, Chester (1955) *Personification in Eighteenth-Century English Poetry*, New York: King's Crown Press.

Checketts, Richard (2002) 'Pleasure's Objects: Commodity, Manufacture, and the Art Theories of Shaftesbury and Hogarth', *Anglia* 120. 3: 339–71.

Coleridge, S. T. C. (1956–71) *Collected Letters of Samuel Taylor Coleridge*, ed. Earl Leslie Griggs, 6 vols, Oxford: The Clarendon Press.

—— (1983) *Biographia Literaria*, eds J. Engell and W. Jackson Bate, 2 vols, *The Collected Works of S. T. Coleridge*, VII, gen. ed. Kathleen Coburn, Bollingen Series LXVV, London: Routledge.

—— *Coleridge's Poetry and Prose* (2004), eds Nicholas Halmi, Paul Magnuson and Raimonda Modiano, New York: W. W. Norton & Co.
Collings, David (1994) *Wordsworthian Errancies: The Poetics of Cultural Dismemberment*, London: The Johns Hopkins University Press.
Copely, Stephen and Whale, John (eds) (1992) *Beyond Romanticism: New Approaches to Texts and Contexts 1780–1832*, London: Routledge.
de Bolla, Peter (1989) *The Discourse of the Sublime: Readings in History, Aesthetics and the Subject*, Oxford: Blackwell.
—— (2001) *Art Matters*, Cambridge, Mass. Harvard University Press.
—— (2002) 'Toward the Materiality of Aesthetic Experience', *Diacritics* 32: 1: 19–37.
de Man, Paul (1979) *Allegories of Reading: Figural Language in Rousseau, Nietzsche, Rilke, and Proust*, New Haven: Yale University Press.
—— (1984) *The Rhetoric of Romanticism*, New York: Columbia University Press.
—— (1987) 'Time and History in Wordsworth', *Diacritics* 7. 4 (Winter): 4–17.
—— (1989) *Blindness and Insight*, London: Routledge.
De Quincey, Thomas (1973) 'Letters to a Young Man whose Education Has Been neglected', in John E. Jordan (ed.) *De Quincey as Critic*, London: Routledge, 266–305.
—— (1985) *Confessions of an English Opium Eater*, ed. Grevel Lindop, Oxford: Oxford University Press.
Dickinson, H. T. (1977) *Liberty and Property: Political Ideology in Eighteenth-Century Britain*, London: Weidenfeld and Nicholson.
Dugget, Tom (2007) 'Celtic Night and Gothic Grandeur: Politics and Antiquarianism in Wordsworth's *Salisbury Plain*', *Romanticism* 13. 2: 164–76.
Eagleton, Terry (1994) *The Ideology of the Aesthetic*, Oxford: Basil Blackwell.
Eldridge, Richard (2009) 'Wordsworth and the Life of a Subject' in Ross Wilson (ed.) *The Meaning of 'Life' in Romantic Poetry and Poetics*, London: Routledge, 57–80.
Ellison, Julie (1999) *Cato's Tears and the Making of Anglo-American Emotion*, Chicago: The University of Chicago Press.
Engell, James (1981) *The Creative Imagination: Enlightenment to Romanticism*, Cambridge, Mass.: Harvard University Press.
Everest, Kelvin (1979) *Coleridge's Secret Ministry: The Context of the Conversation Poems 1795–1798*, Brighton: Harvester Press.
Ferguson, Frances (1977) *Wordsworth: Language as Counter-Spirit*, New Haven: Yale University Press.
—— (1992) *Solitude and the Sublime: Romanticism and the Aesthetics of Individuation*, London: Routledge.
Fosso, Kurt (2004) *Buried Communities: Wordsworth and the Bonds of Mourning*, New York: SUNY Press.
Frank, Jason (2005) '"Besides Our Selves": An Essay on Enthusiastic Politics and Civil Subjectivity', *Public Culture* 17. 3: 371–92.
Friedman, Geraldine (1996) *The Insistence of History*, Stanford: Stanford University Press.
Fulford, Timothy (2001) 'Wordsworth's "The Haunted Tree" and the Sexual Politics of Landscape', *Romantic Praxis: Romanticism and Ecology*: 26 pars. <http://www.rc.umd.edu/praxis/ecology/fulford/fulford.html>.
Fry, Paul (2006) 'Progresses of Poetry', *The Wordsworth Circle* 37. 1: 22–7.
—— (2008) *Wordsworth and the Poetry of What We Are*, New Haven and London: Yale University Press.

Furniss, Tom (1993) *Edmund Burke's Aesthetic Ideology: Language, Gender and Political Economy in Revolution*, Cambridge: Cambridge University Press.

—— (2008) 'Re-reading the Politics of Romanticism', *Eighteenth-Century Culture* 42.1: 161–6.

Galperin, William H. (1993) *The Return of the Visible in British Romanticism*, Baltimore: The Johns Hopkins University Press.

Gandhi, Leela (2006) *Affective Communities: Anticolonial Thought, Fin-De-Siècle Radicalism, and the Politics of Friendship*, Durham: Duke University Press.

Gerard, Alexander (1774) *An Essay on Genius*, London.

—— (1780) *An Essay on Taste. To which is now added Part Fourth, Of the Standard of Taste; With Observations Concerning the Imitative Nature of Poetry*, London: Cadell; Edinburgh; first published 1759.

Gilmartin, Kevin (2007) *Writing Against Revolution: Literary Conservatism in Britain, 1790–1832*, Cambridge: Cambridge University Press.

Goldberg, Brian (1997) '"Ministry More Palpable": Wordsworth and the Making of Romantic Professionalism', *Studies in Romanticism* 36: 327–47.

Goldsmith, Steven (1993) *Unbuilding Jerusalem: Apocalypse and Romantic Representation*, Ithaca: Cornell University Press.

Gravil, Richard (2003) *Wordsworth's Bardic Vocation, 1787–42*, Basingstoke: Palgrave Macmillan.

Hall, Timothy (2006) 'Adorno's *Aesthetic Theory* and Lukács's *Theory of the Novel*', in David Cunningham and Nigel Mapp (eds) *Adorno and Literature*, London: Continuum, 145–58.

Hamilton, Paul (1992) '"A Shadow of Magnitude": The Dialectic of Romantic Aesthetics', in Stephen Copley and John Whale (eds) *Beyond Romanticism: New Approaches to Texts and Contexts 1780–1832* , London: Routledge, 11-31.

—— (2006) 'Coleridge's Stamina', in Heather Glen and Paul Hamilton (eds) *Repossessing the Romantic Past*, Cambridge: Cambridge University Press, 163–82.

—— (2008) 'Post-Secular Conviviality', *Romantic Praxis: Secularism, Cosmopolitanism, and Romanticism*: 31 pars. <http://www.rc.umd.edu/praxis/secularism/hamilton/hamilton.html>.

Haney, David (1997) 'Rents and Openings in the Ideal World: Eye and Ear in Wordsworth', *Studies in Romanticism* 36: 173–99.

Harkin, Maureen (2003) 'Theorizing Popular Practice in Eighteenth-Century Aesthetics', in Pamela R. Matthews and David McWhirter (eds) *Aesthetic Subjects*, Minneapolis: University of Minnesota Press, 171–89.

Hartman, Geoffrey (1987) *The Unremarkable Wordsworth*, London: Methuen.

Haywood, Ian (2006) *Bloody Romanticism: Spectacular Violence and the Politics of Representation, 1776–1832*, Basingstoke: Palgrave Macmillan.

Heidegger, Martin (1993) *Basic Writings*, ed. David Farrell-Krell, London: Routledge.

Hertz, Neil (1985) *The End of the Line: Essays on Psychoanalysis and the Sublime*, New York: Columbia University Press.

Hewitt, Regina (2008) 'Utopianism and Joanna Baillie: A Preface to Converging Revolutions', *Romantic Circles Praxis Series: Utopianism and Joanna Baillie*: 33 pars. <http://www.rc.umd.edu/praxis/utopia/hewitt_preface/hewitt_preface.html>.

Hume, John (1963) *Essays, Moral, Political and Literary*, Oxford: Oxford University Press.

Irlam, Shaun (1999) *Elations: The Poetics of Enthusiasm in Eighteenth-Century Britain*, Stanford: Stanford University Press.

Jackson, Noel (2004) 'Rethinking the Cultural Divide: Walter Pater, Wilkie Collins, and the Legacy of Wordsworthian Aesthetics', *Modern Philology* 102: 207–34.

Jacobus, Mary (1976) *Tradition and Experiment in Wordsworth's Lyrical Ballads (1798)*, Oxford: The Clarendon Press.

—— (1979) 'Wordsworth and the Language of the Dream', *ELH* 46: 618–44.

—— (1989) *Romanticism, Writing and Sexual Difference*, Oxford: The Clarendon Press.

Janowitz, Anne (1990) *England's Ruins: Poetic Purpose and the National Landscape*, Oxford, Basil Blackwell.

—— (2005) 'The artifactual sublime: making London poetry', in James Chandler and Kevin Gilmartin (eds) *Romantic Metropolis: The Urban Scene of British Culture, 1780–1840*, Cambridge: Cambridge University Press, 246–60.

—— (2006) 'Memoirs of a dutiful niece: Lucy Aikin and literary reputation', in Heather Glen and Paul Hamilton (eds) *Repossessing the Romantic Past*, Cambridge: Cambridge University Press, 80–94.

Jarvis, Simon (1998) 'Wordsworth's Gifts of Feeling', *Romanticism* 4: 90–103.

—— (1999) 'Wordsworth and Idolatry', *Studies in Romanticism* 38 (Spring): 3–27.

—— (2006) *Wordsworth's Philosophic Song*, Cambridge: Cambridge University Press.

Jay, Martin (2005) *Songs of Experience: Modern American and European Variations on a Universal Theme*, Berkley: University of California Press.

Johnson, Barbara (1987) *A World of Difference*, Baltimore: The Johns Hopkins University Press.

Johnson, Claudia L. (1995) *Equivocal Beings: Politics, Gender, and Sentimentality in the 1790s – Wollstonecraft, Radcliffe, Burney, Austen*, Chicago: The University of Chicago Press.

Johnston, Kenneth R. (1998) *The Hidden Wordsworth: Poet, Lover, Rebel, Spy*, New York: W. W. Norton & Company.

Jones, Chris (1993) *Radical Sensibility: Literature and Ideas in the 1790s*, London: Routledge.

Jones, Robert (1998) *Gender and the Formation of Taste in Eighteenth-Century Britain*, Cambridge: Cambridge University Press.

Kant, Immanuel (1952) *The Critique of Judgement*, trans. James Creed Meredith, Oxford: Oxford University Press.

Kaufman, Robert (2001) 'Negatively Capable Dialectics: Keats, Vendler, Adorno, and the Theory of the Avant-Garde', *Critical Inquiry* 27: 354–84.

—— (2005) 'Lyric's Constellation, Poetry's Radical Privilege', *Modernist Cultures* 1. 2: 209–34.

—— (2006) 'Poetry's Ethics? Theodor W. Adorno and Robert Duncan on Aesthetic Illusion and Sociopolitical Delusion', *New German Critique* 97. 1: 73–118.

Keen, Paul (1999) *The Crisis of Literature in the 1790s: Print Culture and the Public Sphere*, Cambridge: Cambridge University Press.

Kelley, Theresa (1984) 'Wordsworth and the Rhinefall', *Studies in Romanticism* 23: 61–79.

—— (1997) *Reinventing Allegory*, Cambridge: Cambridge University Press.

Kim, Benjamin (2006) 'Generating a National Sublime: Wordsworth's *The River* and *The Guide to the Lakes*', *Studies in Romanticism* 45: 49–75.

King, Ross (1993) 'Wordsworth, Panoramas, and the Prospect of London', *Studies in Romanticism* 32 (Spring): 57–73.

Klein, Lawrence (1994) *Shaftesbury and the Culture of Politeness*, Cambridge: Cambridge University Press.

Lacoue-Labarthe, Philippe (1993) *The Subject of Philosophy*, ed. Thomas Trezise, trans. Thomas Trezise, Hugh J. Silverman, Gary M. Cole, Timothy D. Bent, Karen McPherson, and Claudette Sartiliot, Minneapolis: University of Minnesota Press.

Laqueur, Thomas Wordsworth (1992) 'Sexual Desire and the Market Economy during the Industrial Revolution' in *Discourses of Sexuality: From Aristotle to AIDS*, ed. Domna C. Stanton (Michigan: University of Michigan Press).

—— (1995) 'Masturbation, Credit and the Novel during the Long Eighteenth Century', *Qui Parle* 8: 1–19.

Levinson, Marjorie (1986) *Wordsworth's Great Period Poems*, Cambridge: Cambridge University Press.

—— (1989) 'The New Historicism: Back to the Future', in Marjorie Levinson *et al.* (eds) *Rethinking Historicism*, Oxford: Basil Blackwell.

Levitas, Ruth (1990) *The Concept of Utopia* London: Philip Allan, p. xxxii.

Liu, Alan (1989) *Wordsworth: The Sense of History*, Stanford: Stanford University Press.

Longinus, Dionysius (1739) *Dionysius Longinus on the Sublime: Translated from the Greek, with Notes and Observations, and Some Accounts of the Life, Writings, and Character of the Author. By William Smith, . . .* , London.

Lukács, Georg (1971) *Theory of the Novel*, trans. Anna Bostock, London: Merlin Press.

Lyotard, Jean-Francois (1993) *The Lyotard Reader*, ed. Andrew Benjamin, Oxford: Basil Blackwell.

McCalman, Iain (1996) 'Mad Lord George and Madame La Motte: Riot and Sexuality in the Genesis of Burke's *Reflections on the Revolution in France*', *Journal of British Studies* 35: 343–67.

McGann, Jerome J. (1996) *The Poetics of Sensibility: A Revolution in Literary Style*, Oxford: The Clarendon Press

Makdisi, Saree (1998) *Romantic Imperialism: Universal Empire and the Culture of Modernity*, Cambridge: Cambridge University Press.

Manly, Susan (2007) *Language, Custom and Nation in the 1790s; Locke, Tooke, Wordsworth, Edgeworth*, Aldershot: Ashgate.

Mapp, Nigel (2001) 'History and the Sacred in de Man and Benjamin', in Michael Rossington and Anne Whitehead (eds) *Between the Psyche and the Polis: Refiguring History in Literature and Theory*, Aldershot: Ashgate.

Mason, Emma and Armstrong, Isobel (2008) 'Introduction: "Feeling: an indefinite dull region of the spirit?"', *Textual Practice* 22. 1: 1–19.

Mee, Jon (1992) *Dangerous Enthusiasm: William Blake and the Culture of Radicalism in the 1790s*, Oxford: The Clarendon Press.

—— (1998) 'Anxieties of Enthusiasm: Coleridge, Prophecy, and Popular Politics in the 1790s', *Huntington Library Quarterly: Studies in English and American History and Literature* 60: 179–203.

—— (2002) 'Mopping up Spilt Religion: The Problem of Enthusiasm'. *Romanticism on the Net* 25: 21 pars. <http://www.erudit.org/revue/ron/2002/v/n25/006009ar. html>.

—— (2003) *Romanticism, Enthusiasm, and Regulation: Poetics and the Policing of Culture in the Romantic Period*. Oxford: Oxford University Press.

Meehan, Michael (1986) *Liberty and Poetics in Eighteenth Century England*, New Hampshire: Croom Helm.

Mitchell, Robert (January 2003) 'The Violence of Sympathy; Adam Smith on Resentment and Executions', *1650–1850; ideas, aesthetics, and inquiries in the early modern era* 8: 321–41.

Mullan, John (1991) *Sentiment and Sociability: The Language of Feeling in the Eighteenth Century*, Oxford: The Clarendon Press.

Newlyn, Lucy (1984) 'Lamb, Lloyd and London: A Perspective on Book Seven of *The Prelude*', *Charles Lamb Bulletin* 47–8 (July–October): 169–85.

—— (1993) *'Paradise Lost' and the Romantic Reader*, Oxford: The Clarendon Press.

—— (1995) '"Questionable Shape": The Aesthetics of Indeterminacy', in John Beer (ed.) *Questioning Romanticism*, Baltimore and London: John Hopkins University Press, 209–33.

Owen, W. J. Burke (1969) *Wordsworth as Critic*, Oxford University Press, London.

Pease, Allison (2000) *Modernism, Mass Culture, and the Aesthetics of Obscenity*, Cambridge: Cambridge University Press.

Paine, Thomas (1945) *The Complete Writings of Thomas Paine*, Vol. I, ed. Philip S. Foner, New York: The Citadel Press.

Paulson, Donald (1996) *The Beautiful, Novel, and Strange: Aesthetics and Heterodoxy*, Baltimore: The Johns Hopkins University Press.

Pfau, Thomas (2005) *Romantic Moods: Paranoia, Trauma, and Melancholy, 1790–1840*, Baltimore: The Johns Hopkins University Press.

Philp, Mark (1998) 'English Republicanism in the 1790s', *The Journal of Political Philosophy* 6: 235–62.

Pinch, Adela (1997) *Strange Fits of Passion: Epistemologies of Emotion, Hume to Austen*, Stanford: Stanford University Press.

Pocock, J. G. A. (1985) *Virtue, Commerce and History: Essays on Political Thought and History, Chiefly in the Eighteenth Century*, Cambridge: Cambridge University Press.

—— (1989) 'Edmund Burke and the Redefinition of Enthusiasm: the Context as Counter-Revolution' in Francois Furet and Mona Ozouf (eds) *The French Revolution and the Creation of Modern Political Culture. Vol. 3: The Transformation of Political Culture 1789–1848*, Oxford: Pergamon, 19–43.

Price, Richard (1789) *A Discourse on the Love of our Country*, London.

Prynne, J.H. (1988) 'English Poetry and Emphatical Language', *Proceedings of the British Academy* 74: 135–69.

—— (2007) *Field Notes: 'The Solitary Reaper' And Others*, Cambridge: Barque Press.

Rader, Melvin (1967) *Wordsworth: A Philosophical Approach*, Oxford: The Clarendon Press.

Reed, Mark L. (1975) *Wordsworth: The Chronology of the Middle Years, 1800–15*, Cambridge, Mass.: Harvard University Press.

Reresby, Tamworth (1721) *A Miscellany of Ingenious Thoughts and Reflections*, London.

Saccamano, Neil (2007), 'Inheriting Enlightenment, or Keeping Faith with Reason in Derrida', *Eighteenth-Century Studies* 40. 3: 405–24.

Samet, Elizabeth D. (2003) 'Spectacular History and the Politics of Theatre: Sympathetic Arts in the Shadow of the Bastille', *PMLA* 118. 5 (2003): 1305–19.

Scarry, Elaine (1999) *On Beauty and Being Just*, New Jersey: Princeton University Press.

Shakespeare, William (1990) *The Complete Works of Shakespeare*, ed. Peter Alexander, London and Glasgow: Collins.

Shaftesbury, Anthony Ashley Cooper, Third Earl of (1999): *Characteristicks of Men, Manners, Opinions, Times*, 2 vols, ed. Philip Ayres, Oxford: The Clarendon Press.

Simpson, David (1993) *Romanticism, Nationalism and the Revolt against Theory*, Chicago: The University of Chicago Press.

—— (Summer/Fall 2007) 'Derrida's Ghosts: The State of our Debt', *Studies in Romanticism* 46: 183–201.

Siskin, Clifford (1998) *The Work of Writing: Literature and Social Change in Britain, 1700–1830*, Baltimore: The Johns Hopkins University Press.

—— (2005) 'More is Different: Literary Change in the Mid and Late Eighteenth Century', in John Richetti (ed.) *The Cambridge History of English Literature, 1610–1780* 810, Cambridge: Cambridge University Press, pp. 797–823.

Smith, Adam (1759) *The Theory of Moral Sentiments*, Edinburgh.

—— (1776) *An Enquiry into the Nature and Causes of the Wealth of Nations*, London.

Starr, G. Gabrielle (2002) 'Ethics, Meaning, and the Work of Beauty', *Eighteenth-Century Studies* 35. 3: 361–78.

—— (2004) *Lyric Generations: Poetry and the Novel in the Long Eighteenth Century*, Baltimore: The Johns Hopkins University Press.

Stafford, Barbara Maria (1991) *Body Criticism: Imaging the Unseen in Enlightenment Art and Medicine*, Cambridge, Mass.: The MIT Press.

Steintrager, James A. (1997) 'Perfectly Inhuman: Moral Monstrosity in Eighteenth-Century Discourse', *Eighteenth-Century Life* 21. 2: 114–32.

Stewart, Susan (2005), 'What Praise Poems Are For', *PMLA* 120.1: 235–45.

Stoddard, E. W. (1985) '"Flashes of the Invisible World": Reading *The Prelude* in the context of the Kantian sublime', *The Wordsworth Circle* 16 : 33.

Sykes-Davies, Hugh (1986), *Wordsworth and the Worth of Words*, eds Jonathan Kerrigan and Jonathan Wordsworth, Cambridge: Cambridge University Press.

Taylor, Anya (2001) 'Coleridge and the Pleasures of Verse', *Studies in Romanticism* 40: 547–69.

Terada, Rei and Culler, Jonathan (2008) 'The New Lyric Studies', *PMLA* 123.

Tuveson, Ernest (1967) 'Shaftesbury and the Age of Sensibility' in H. Anderson and J. Shea (eds) *Studies in Criticism and Aesthetics 1600–1800*, Minneapolis: University of Minneapolis Press, 73–93.

Uhlig, Stefan (2009) 'Gray, Wordsworth, and the Poetry of Ordinary Life' in Ross Wilson (ed.) *The Meaning of 'Life' in Romantic Poetry and Poetics*, London: Routledge, 33–56.

Weisman, Karen (2004) 'The Bounds of Lyric: Romantic Grasps Upon the Actual', *European Romantic Review* 15. 2: 343–9.

Wichelns, H. A. (1922) 'Burke's Essay on the Sublime and its Reviewers', *Journal of English and Germanic Philology* XXI: 645–61.

Willey, Basil (1986) *The Eighteenth-Century Background*, London: Routledge.

Wolfson, Susan (1997) *Formal Charges: The Shaping of Poetry in British Romanticism*, Stanford: Stanford University Press.

Wollstonecraft, Mary (1989) *The Works of Mary Wollstonecraft*, Vol. 5, ed. Janet Todd and Marilyn Butler, London: William Pickering.

Wordsworth, (1970) *The Letters of William and Dorothy Wordsworth*, III, *The Middle Years Part II, 1812–20*, ed. Ernest de Selincourt, revd Mary Moorman and Alan G. Hill, Oxford: The Clarendon Press.

—— (1974) *Prose Works of William Wordsworth*, eds W. J. B. Owen and J. W. Smyser, 3 vols, Oxford: The Clarendon Press.

—— (1975) *The Salisbury Plain Poems of William Wordsworth*, ed. Stephen Gill, Cornell: Cornell University Press.

—— (1977) *The Prelude, 1798–1799*, ed. Stephen Parrish. Ithaca: Cornell University Press.

—— (1977–88). *The Letters of William and Dorothy Wordsworth*, ed. Ernest De Selincourt, I, *The Early Years 1787–1805*, ed. Ernest de Selincourt, revd Chester L. Shaver, Oxford: The Clarendon Press.

—— (1979) *The Ruined Cottage and The Pedlar*, ed. James Butler, Ithaca: Cornell University Press.

—— (1979a) *The Letters of William and Dorothy Wordsworth*, V, *The Later Years, Part II, 1829–34*, ed. Ernest de Selincourt, revd Alan G. Hill, Oxford: The Clarendon Press.

—— (1982) *The Borderers by William Wordsworth*, ed. Robert Osbourne, Ithaca: Cornell University Press.

—— (1983) *Poems, in Two Volumes, and Other Poems, 1800–1807*, ed. Jared Curtis, Ithaca: Cornell University Press.

—— (1984) *Wordsworth's Poetical Works*, ed. Ernest de Selincourt, revised by Thomas Hutchinson, Oxford: Oxford University Press.

—— (1984) *An Evening Walk by William Wordsworth*, ed. James Averill, Cornell: Cornell University Press.

—— (1985) *The Fourteen-Book Prelude*, ed. W. J. B. Owen, Ithaca: Cornell University Press.

—— (1991) *The Thirteen-Book Prelude*, Vol. 1, ed. Mark L. Reed, Ithaca: Cornell University Press.

—— (1992) *Lyrical Ballads, and Other Poems, 1797–1800*, eds James Butler and Karen Green, Ithaca: Cornell University Press.

—— (1994) *Selected Poems*, ed. John O. Hayden, London: Penguin.

—— (1999) *Last Poems. 1821–1850*, eds Jared Curtis, Apryl Lea Denny-Ferris, Jillian Heydt-Stevenson, Ithaca: Cornell University Press.

Wu, Duncan (1993) *Wordsworth's Reading 1770–1799*, Cambridge: Cambridge University Press.

Zerilli, Linda M. G. (1991) 'Text/Woman as Spectacle: Edmund Burke's "French Revolution"', *The Eighteenth Century* 33: 55.

Zimmerman, Sarah (1999) *Romanticism, Lyricism, and History*, Albany: SUNY Press.

Index